SUPER CORE!

TURBOCHARGING YOUR BASAL READING PROGRAM WITH MORE READING, WRITING, AND WORD WORK

MARK WEAKLAND

INTERNATIONAL
Reading Association
800 BARKSDALE ROAD, PO BOX 8139
Newark, DE 19714-8139, USA
www.reading.org

The International Reading Association attempts, through its publications, to provide a forum for a wide spectrum of opinions on reading. This policy permits divergent viewpoints without implying the endorsement of the Association.

Executive Editor, Publications   Shannon Fortner
Acquisitions Manager   Tori Mello Bachman
Managing Editors   Susanne Viscarra and Christina M. Lambert
Editorial Associate   Wendy Logan
Creative Services/Production Manager   Anette Schuetz
Design and Composition Associate   Lisa Kochel

Cover   Lise Holliker Dykes and © Danomyte/Shutterstock

The publisher would appreciate notification where errors occur so that they may be corrected in subsequent printings and/or editions.

Library of Congress Cataloging-in-Publication Data
Weakland, Mark.
    Super core : supercharging your basal reading program with more reading, writing, and word work / Mark Weakland.
        pages   cm
    Includes bibliographical references and index.
    ISBN 978-0-87207-083-7 (alk. paper)
    1. Basal reading instruction. 2. Reading comprehension—United States. 3. English language—Composition and exercises. 4. Language arts—Standards—United States. 5. English language—Study and teaching—Standards—United States. I. Title.
    LB1050.36.W43   2014
    372.4—dc23

                                    2013040952

Suggested APA Reference
Weakland, M. (2014). *Super core! Turbocharging your basal reading program with more reading, writing, and word work*. Newark, DE: International Reading Association.

To my mother

Inner Space (a poem for two voices)*
by Mark Weakland

Attention.
This is Mission Control.
Please prepare for departure.

                                        (khhht) ROGER.

Unplug the Internet,
Log off the Log In,
Reset the Attitude,
Pressurize the Noggin.

                                        (khhht) ROGER.

Take off the Kid Gloves,
Unfold the Mental Map,
Pull on the Go-Go Boots,
Strap tight the
Thinking Cap.

                                        (khhht) ROGER.

Shut down the Game Boy,
Rotate the Thrusters,
Raise the Expectations,
Turn off the Distrusters.

                                        (khhht) ROGER.

Orient the Listening Lobes.
Maximize the Hemispheres.
Initiate the Intellect.
Ignite the Thing
between your ears.

10...9...8...7...6...   10...9...8...7...6...
5...4...3...2...1   5...4...3...2...1

Blast off!   *Blast off!*

---

*You can listen to audio clips of Mark's poems on his website at springwatercreative.com/kidsMusic.php#.
The poem is from *The Delicious Chocolate Donut: And Other Off-Kilter Poems* (pp. 16–17), by M.
Weakland, 2011, Hollsopple, PA: Happy Hummer. Copyright © 2011 by Mark Weakland.

CONTENTS

CHAPTER 6: **New Heights of Extended Writing**   138

ABOUT THE AUTHOR

 **Mark Weakland** is an author, educator, and musician. His more than two dozen children's books include *Zombies and Electricity* (Capstone, 2013); *Football ABC* (Capstone, 2013); *How Tall? Wacky Ways to Compare Height* (Picture Window, 2014); *The Delicious Chocolate Donut: And Other Off-Kilter Poems* (Happy Hummer, 2011); and *Onion Juice, Poop, and Other Surprising Sources of Alternative Energy* (Capstone, 2011), winner of the 2012 Santa Monica Public Library Green Prize for Sustainable Literature.

Mark holds a master's of education degree from the University of Pittsburgh. His teaching certifications include general science, special education, elementary education, and reading. A learning support teacher for nine years, he spent 10 years as an educational consultant, providing professional development in the areas of reading and instructional practices. His workshops and presentations at the local, regional, and state levels address topics ranging from metacognition to using music and movement in the classroom. He studied in Japan under the auspices of the Japanese Fulbright Memorial Fund and coauthored the book *The Dramatically Different Classroom: Multiple Intelligences Activities Across the Curriculum* (Kagan, 2002) with Christine Laitta. He's in his fourth year as an elementary school Title I reading specialist.

A musician at heart, Mark still performs occasionally as a singer, drummer, and guitarist. His original songs have finished as finalists in the John Lennon and USA Songwriting contests, and his collections of kids' songs have won numerous Parents' Choice awards.

Mark's many interests are tied together in his business, Springwater Creative. He lives at Springwater Farm in the hills of western Pennsylvania with his wife, Beth Good, and flies to Seattle to visit his parents and sisters.

Feel free to contact Mark with questions about this book via springwatermg@earthlink.net, Facebook, or links found at www.markweakland.com and www.springwatercreative.com.

Acknowledgments

My educational career has not been linear, to say the least. As I've meandered down the path, friends and strangers alike have given me a nudge, a push, a choice, and a chance. I am grateful for all I've been given, and I believe that if I accept life with an open heart, I will always have much to learn, new directions to explore, and a lot to be thankful for.

With that in mind, I would like to acknowledge my gratitude for everything the following people have given to me:

- Lynne Weakland, who has taught me a great deal about reading, writing, and education over the years and whose willingness to discuss educational issues of the day and carefully critique the rough draft of each chapter made the final book so much better. Many, many thanks, Mom.

- Tori Bachman, who encouraged me to rewrite and resubmit my original manuscript, who provided the structure for much of this book, and who expertly and enthusiastically guided me through the process of writing and revising. I couldn't have asked for a better editor. Thank you, Tori!

- Susanne Viscarra, whose editing and suggestions polished and perfected this book. Many thanks, Susanne.

- Toni Draksler, a person of great energy and heart, who graciously gave me the opportunity to introduce many new reading and writing routines into her communications class. Thank you, Toni!

- Rachael Weakland and Melissa Weakland, who, except for my first three years, have been sources of inspiration, encouragement, and friendship throughout my entire life. Thank you, sisters.

- Beth Good, who provided words of confidence, gave me space to operate, and broke up my long hours of writing with cat antics, lovely evening walks, and random (but fascinating) interjections about flowers and frogs. Thank you, B.

- Carol Boone, my friend, book buddy, and presentation partner who taught me much about reading, speech, and language and who graciously listened to my many educational schemes and dreams. Sincere thanks, Carol.

- Gil Weakland, my father, and my friends Merrily Swoboda, Jeff Lesak, Doug Wilkin, and Chris Laitta, who gave encouragement.

- Donna Smith and Irene Mergen, my IU supervisors who pointed me in the direction of reading, gave me great latitude to learn about curriculum and instruction, and allowed me to explore educational issues and grow as a professional. Thank you, Donna and Irene.

- Dan Henning, Patricia Berezansky, and Lewis Kindja, United School District administrators who allowed me to implement some of the ideas in this book. Thank you.

- Fellow educators, who have taught me so much over the years: PaTTAN and Western Region consultants, Mimi Kontoulis, Lauri Shoup, the ARIN TAC team and Curriculum Council members, Jodi Orr, Michelle Dunn, the teachers at United Elementary School, and the teachers at Blairsville Elementary School. Thank you, all!

A core reading program shouldn't be your complete reading program. Publisher-created core reading programs aren't flexible enough, powerful enough, or motivating enough to enable all students to reach important reading goals. What's more, core reading programs can create an environment in which reading teachers become less effective over time instead of more effective.

By subtracting a few core reading program components, adding a few research-based instructional practices, and becoming mindful of a few basic content and instructional values, teachers can create a more effective and engaging reading program in which most students will make great progress in reading.

To make it more effective, infuse these four time-tested values into your core reading program:

1. *Extended reading:* Use independent reading routines, guided reading groups, and a large variety of books to increase the amount of time that students spend on practicing reading in independent- and instructional-level texts.

2. *Extended writing:* Use guided writing time, independent writing routines, and real-world/authentic topics to increase the amount of time that students spend on practicing writing (and spelling and grammar).

3. *The big ideas of reading and writing:* Know each big idea deeply. Bring awareness of the big ideas to your reading and writing lessons.
   • Phonemic awareness
   • Phonics (decoding) and spelling (encoding)
   • Fluency (including rate, accuracy, and prosody)
   • Vocabulary
   • Comprehension (fix-it-up, clarify, and metacognition strategies)
   • Writing (including grammar, spelling, and reading)

4. *Teaching chops (instructional expertise):* Become fluent in each practice and use the practices in your day-to-day instruction.
   • Direct and explicit instruction
   • Social and cooperative learning
   • Whole-group physical response
   • Modeling and practice

- Task analysis and mastery learning
- Formative assessment

Core Program Areas and Ways to Improve Them

Grammar

- Focus your core program's scope and sequence on what is most essential.
- Use writing, not worksheets, to teach grammar.
- Teach directly and explicitly; model and practice.
- Practice skill work with brainstorming and whole-group physical response activities (e.g., response cards, sentence writing).
- Formatively assess progress toward the most essential goals.

Vocabulary

- Focus your core program's vocabulary word lists.
- Teach directly and explicitly, model and practice, and use social and cooperative-learning activities.
- Increase chances of mastery by using the vocabulary card method.
- Formatively assess progress toward vocabulary mastery.

Comprehension

- Focus your core program's comprehension strategies on 12 specific strategies.
- Teach directly and explicitly; model and practice.
- Teach comprehension during anthology time and again during guided reading.
- Formatively assess the use of essential fix-it-up, clarify, and metacognition strategies.

Extended Reading

- Build students' vocabulary, demonstrate grammar, teach decoding and comprehension, and practice fluency through reading, not worksheets.
- Increase reading practice time by decreasing the emphasis on one specific story, worksheets, and summative testing, among others.

- Use independent reading routines and guided reading groups to create time for students to practice reading in independent- and instructional-level texts.
- Formatively assess progress toward the most essential goals.

Extended Writing

- Teach grammar and spelling skill work with writing activities, not worksheets.
- Increase time to practice writing by decreasing the emphasis on worksheets, summative testing, and handwriting, among others.
- Use independent writing routines and whole-class guided writing to create time for students to practice writing on authentic topics and teacher assignments.
- Formatively assess progress toward the most essential goals.

Spelling and Phonics

- Practice spelling with word work and writing activities, not worksheets.
- Focus the core program's spelling scope and sequence.
- Come up with a logical and organized system of spelling. Use this, and your teaching chops, to teach students how to spell, not what to spell.
- Formatively assess progress toward the most essential goals.

INTRODUCTION

Core reading programs, comprehensive literacy programs, basal programs—call them what you will, but the fact remains that the majority of reading teachers in the United States use publisher-created reading programs to teach their students how to read and write. According to a recent report, almost three out of four U.S. elementary schools use basal readers (Merrow, 2012). These publisher-created reading programs run the gamut from Treasures (Macmillan/McGraw-Hill) and Reading Street (Scott Foresman) to Open Court (McGraw-Hill) and Storytown (Harcourt).

Regardless of the particular product and regardless of whether they are called core reading programs or the basal, these programs permeate the U.S. educational system. We all know what they look like. Teachers who use them typically teach from a manual, use an anthology of stories, and employ practice books and worksheets to drill students in specific reading and writing skills. Students who experience these programs typically work quietly at their desks on identical assignments, take part in whole-group classroom routines, and read from the anthology as a full class or in small groups.

This is not to say that publisher-created reading programs are the only game in town. Many teachers and districts still embrace teacher-constructed or student-centered programs such as readers' workshop, guided reading, balanced literacy, and The Daily Five. While using these programs, teachers engage students with individualized classroom routines, minilessons, small-group activities, and trade books of all genres. Additional components may include literacy centers, classroom libraries, individualized spelling lists, an emphasis on reading strategies, and grammar taught via the writing of stories and essays. These process-driven and student-centered reading classrooms, however, are not the norm in the United States today.

Basal reading programs are deeply rooted in our educational system. Dating all the way back to 1836, when the McGuffey Readers first appeared, and continuing through the iconic Dick and Jane series, basal programs morphed into comprehensive core reading programs and research-based literacy programs during the No Child Left Behind era. As they attempted to leave no child behind, school districts jettisoned curricula based on novels, themes, guided reading groups, and literature circles and adopted publisher-created programs based on anthologies of stories, workbooks and worksheets, and large-group instruction. Although these sprawling programs don't contain the kitchen sink, they do contain almost everything else, including spelling lists, vocabulary lists, teacher manuals, grammar worksheets, specific skill practice books, phonics programs, writing prompts, leveled readers, ideas for instructional groupings, English as a second language programming, and story and unit assessments. Whew!

Now a new era is rolling round, the era of the Common Core State Standards. Much of what No Child Left Behind wrought, including accountability, high-stakes tests, and research-based reading practices, will be here to stay, even as a new set of standards is adopted by much of the nation. I suspect that basal programs will also be here to stay because school boards, administrators, and perhaps even teachers will continue to push for them, and even without an intentional push, historical inertia tends to carry past practices forward.

Why You Need This Book

If you're a 75-percenter—a teacher who will use or is currently using a publisher-created core reading program—*Super Core: Supercharging Your Basal Reading Program With More Reading, Writing, and Word Work* has two important messages for you. First, a simple statement: A core reading program should not be your complete reading program (Dewitz, & Sullivan, 2010). Publisher-created core reading programs simply aren't flexible enough, powerful enough, or motivating enough to enable all students to reach important reading goals. What's more, core reading programs can create an environment in which reading teachers become less effective over time instead of more effective (Baumann & Heubach, 1996).

A published core reading program is not a complete reading program.

The second message is a call to action. By subtracting a few core reading program components, adding a few research-based instructional practices, and becoming mindful of a few basic content and instructional values, you can create a more effective and engaging reading program in which most students will make great progress in reading.

Super Core provides direct and explicit steps for creating this success. These steps can be of a gradual nature. You're free to take a couple of small steps this year, a few next year, and a few more after that. Three or four years into the journey, you will have left much of your manual behind, rid yourself of most "drill and kill" worksheets, and rocketed off to a world where students are engaged in reading and writing because they love to read and write. Yes, it will take some years to accomplish this goal, but if you sit back and enjoy the process, the journey will be a rewarding one. After all, what's better than seeing struggling readers transformed into strong and capable readers?

The Rocket Ship Analogy

I'd like you to think of a reading program as a rocket ship. At the tip of this rocket sits the capsule, and in this capsule sits some very precious cargo: your students! Every teacher wants his or her rocket ship to be powerful enough to overcome gravity (all the reading difficulties that hold students down), reach escape velocity (the point at which students move from learning to read to reading to learn), and gain orbit (the free-floating state of reading independence in which students never fall back to earth).

When it comes to reading rocket ships, districts can choose from any number of vehicles. Some teachers and districts choose to assemble their own ship. First, they choose an excellent how-to teacher reference book, such as *Guided Reading: Good First Teaching for All Children* by Fountas and Pinnell (1996) or *The Daily Five: Fostering Literacy Independence in the Elementary Grades* by Boushey and Moser (2006). They read and read, effectively becoming rocket scientists, and then they begin to build their own rocket. They purchase trade books, leveled readers, and book bins. They build classroom libraries and put together browsing boxes. They create classroom reading routines, teach them to their students, and display the routines on posters in their rooms. And they model, practice, formatively assess, and then do it all again and again. These build-your-own reading programs are effective, and many teachers wouldn't want to teach any other way. Why? The process of teaching these programs is interesting, creative, and challenging. More importantly, by the end of the school year, teachers see most of their students floating serenely in reading orbit.

About 75% of districts, however, choose to go with the ready-made rocket ship (a.k.a. one of the various publisher-created programs). Truth be told, there are positives to this type of ship. First of all, because someone else built it, the ship is ready to launch. All a district has to do is go to "Rockets-R-Us" and buy one very large box! A prebuilt ship saves teachers and administrators a lot of time.

Second, if a teacher is very busy, poorly trained, or new to the field of teaching, the publisher-created ship is easy to launch and fly. Simply follow the directions in the manual. Once the ship is launched, the teacher can turn control over to the manual, and the ship flies along on autopilot.

Third, districts like ready-made reading programs because (a) the teachers become well acquainted with the materials because they are available for use year after year; (b) the program provides consistency across the grade levels and between district buildings; (c) the terms *scientifically based* and *research-based* are stamped all over the materials, which lends an air of validity to the program; and (d) the program often comes with consultants who provide technical assistance and professional development to the teachers implementing it.

Fourth, a publisher-created ship contains many, if not most, of the basic components needed for any effective reading program. This means that if the program is used well, it will lift a lot of the district's students at least partway up the gravity well. It also means that school boards and administrators gain a sense of security because the rocket looks so impressive. Surely, such a large and complex ship is also powerful and effective!

As we know, looks can be deceiving. There are downsides to publisher-produced rocket ships, and the downsides are big. Although the ship looks impressive, it has so many bells and whistles that it's difficult to determine which parts work effectively and which do not. Some components are skipped over because there simply isn't time to teach everything, no matter what publishers and administrators say, and over time other components are minimized until they are no longer used. And in some ships, the engines are of an inferior quality. This means the rocket doesn't have enough thrust to push all the students into orbit. More than a few will fall back to earth. Ouch!

On occasion, teachers and administrators realize their basal rocket isn't working very well, but they don't know how to correct problems because no one bothered to learn the basics of rocket science! They've never been trained to strip down the engines and build them back up to be more efficient or to reboot the onboard computer when it goes down, so educators attempt to patch the problems by adding a bunch of secondary components and programs. What they don't realize is that their attempts to preserve their core program in its entirety and use it with fidelity, while simultaneously minimizing its ineffectiveness, are mutually exclusive activities. I'd go as far as to say it's nonsensical. Nonetheless, teachers and administrators move kids in and out of various homogeneous groupings, add intervention activities and programs, and pile on materials and technology, all the while continuing to stress that teachers should use and teach everything in the core program. The end result is a rocket ship that has grown to be so complex and cumbersome that it's less powerful than before the "fix."

Finally, basal programs say almost nothing about how to pilot the rocket ship. That is, teacher manuals say little about how one should teach content. Some programs are heavily scripted but never explain why certain methodologies are used or why the publisher believes them to be effective. In general, there's little in a manual about the nuances of instructional pedagogy. For example, what's the best way to model a comprehension strategy? How does one explicitly and directly teach vocabulary words? What types of formative assessments are best, and how often should they be given? Teachers who turn over teaching operations to the autopilot (the teacher's manual) may think, The components are there, the engines are firing, and I'm teaching and assessing, so this must mean my students are achieving escape velocity. But about halfway through the year, these same teachers discover that many of their students are not on course to achieve orbit. In fact, some students have never even left the ground!

As for the rocket scientists (a.k.a. masterful reading teachers), well, they tend to hate these publisher-produced ships. They chafe at using someone else's design because (a) they know it doesn't work well enough to get many of their students into orbit, and (b) they really want to build and fly their own ship!

The Aim of Super Core

Super Core aims to identify and then help you correct the basic problems of core reading programs. Specifically, this book does the following:

- Revisits the fundamentals of reading theory
- Calls attention to specific, ineffective components of basal programs
- Describes how the "mile-wide and inch-deep" content of a comprehensive core program can be streamlined and focused to be more efficient and effective
- Provides easy-to-use and more effective vocabulary, fluency, phonic, spelling, writing, and comprehension activities, materials, and routines that take the place of ineffective or missing components
- Reviews basic but highly effective instructional techniques that strengthen the effectiveness of a core reading program by strengthening the power of your teaching

Unlike reading models such as readers' workshop, guided reading, or The Daily Five, Super Core is not dependent on trade books and classroom libraries (although it does advocate for them). As the title implies, Super Core is based on your core reading program. It does not ask you to abandon it. Rather, it asks you to make changes in your instruction, narrow the scope of what you teach, decrease the amount of time your kids spend in workbooks, and increase the amount of time they spend on reading real books and writing authentically and for real purposes.

Each chapter revisits fundamental facts about the reading process and guides you through instructional techniques that can help you gradually rely less on the basal reader and more on your own knowledge and experience as an educator. In these pages, I help you pinpoint the reasons why some students struggle to learn how to read, and I offer strategies and routines that you can use to help those students overcome their struggles. Most importantly, this book provides ways to strengthen your core reading program's components, specifically in the areas of phonemic awareness, phonics, vocabulary, fluency, comprehension, grammar, writing, and spelling. We'll explore these areas together, starting with grammar, vocabulary, and comprehension (subjects that are easily fortified with just a few new activities and strategies), then moving onto extended reading and writing (complex subjects, but my personal favorites), and ending with spelling, phonics, and word work. Each chapter is designed to build your knowledge base and your instructional and assessment skills so your teaching is more effective and engaging. The chapters also address many Common Core State Standards, weaving them into the fabric of reading content and instruction that is described in this book.

To summarize, this book gives you the tools to dismantle your clunky and underpowered basal program and reassemble it into a streamlined and turbocharged rocket. In the end, you'll have a reading program that gets results. The first step toward this end is to identify your educational values. Onward to Chapter 1!

Super Core Values

S uper Core is based on four ideas that are near and dear to my
teaching heart. I call them the four values. It took me a while to
come up with the term *values*. I deliberated over the word and
considered a number of others, but none seemed quite right. "The four
components" sounded too dry, "the four pillars" seemed too grandiose,
and "the Four Tops" was already taken.

Actually, I settled on the term when I remembered a small epiphany
I had a few years ago. In 2008, I was feeling more and more miserable
in my role as a provider of staff development, and I was struggling to
identify my future career options. Should I return to school for a doctoral
degree, strike out on my own as a freelance consultant, or head off in
an entirely different direction: jazz musician, cat care provider, stay-at-
home freeloader? Ultimately, I rejected doctoral degree, freelancer, jazz
musician, and cat care provider. My wife helped me rule out freeloader.

Knowing what I *didn't* want to do was of little help, so I decided
to consult a career counselor. Meeting with her was an illuminating
experience. She helped me see that many, if not most, of my personal
decisions arose from my value system. For example, when I decided in
1988 to work with children rather than take a position as a research
assistant in a biology lab, my decision was value based. I just couldn't
bring myself to harm the lab animals, even when the research might lead
to future medical gains that would benefit others.

Now that I'm aware of my decision-making process, I can see how
I regularly make decisions based on my values. Because I value the
freedom to follow my personal interests (more than climbing a career
ladder), I haven't followed a sequential career track over the last 25
years. Because I value the natural world, I won't work for corporations
or organizations that contribute to its destruction. Even my decision to
leave staff development and return to public school teaching was a value-
based one.

We all hold values. Sometimes we act on them, and sometimes we
don't. Some people make the bulk of their decisions based on values.
Others regularly put their values aside and make decisions based on a
more pragmatic analysis of the situation. It's not a good versus bad thing,
and one way is no more right or wrong than the other.

I believe that educational systems harbor values just like individuals do. Some values, however, are more discernible than others. Consider the Montessori system. Montessori values spring from the idea that learning is an active process that begins with the learner and extends outward into the world. Montessori educators value activities that promote student discovery, exploration of the environment, self-direction, independence, and concentration. These values permeate the Montessori system and are reflected in the way the classrooms are arranged, teachers are trained, and lessons are taught.

Another system, such as Waldorf, harbors a different set of values. The Waldorf system values the arts, developmental psychology, and the spiritual and social components of education. Thus, one teacher moves with a group of students through eight years of their education, guiding them through various stages of educational, developmental, and spiritual growth. Lessons are typically augmented with art, poetry, music, drama, and movement. Valued lessons are ones that create a classroom atmosphere that fills students with wonder, interest, and enthusiasm.

With the release of the National Reading Panel's report in 2000 (National Institute of Child Health and Human Development [NICHD], 2000a), the rise of the Common Core State Standards, and the lessening of conflict among historically warring reading camps, higher education and research communities in the United States are coming to a greater consensus on what they value most in reading instruction. I don't believe, though, that these values have fully found their way into public school systems. Although a consensus on what should be valued in reading is closer than it was 20 years ago, many differences of opinion still exist.

When it comes to teachers and what they value, I can't claim to truly know more than a handful of individuals. I can, however, extrapolate to the general population. Concerning reading and communication skills, I'd bet that most teachers value fluency (up to a point), comprehension and the strategies that enable it, writing that is grammatically and mechanically correct, and critical thinking. Additionally, I believe teachers value a student's ability to pick up a book, read it, and enjoy it. More broadly speaking, teachers value the safety and well-being of their students. They want to see the kids in their classrooms experience academic, social, and personal success.

Although many in education hold broad "success for all" values, I wonder how many have well-defined content and instruction values. To explore this point, quickly answer the following questions, taking a few minutes to jot down the answers before reading further:

- What aspects of reading instruction do you value the most?
- What types of general instruction do you value the most?

- What components of a reading curriculum do you value the most?
- What reading content holds the most value to you?
- What assessments do you value?
- At the end of the year, what do you want your students to value when it comes to reading and writing?

If you had a hard time answering any of these questions quickly, I would argue that your teaching values are not firmly established in your mind. If you did come up with answers quickly, I'd say your educational values are front and center in your mind. I've *Teach what you value; value what you teach.* been mulling over my values for a number of years now, and in the next section, I list them for you. They're important because they form the foundation of this book.

The Evolution of Super Core

Three years ago, when I left my educational consultant job and came back to elementary school teaching, I was brimming with excitement. I couldn't wait to put all of my knowledge into practice. I was a man on a mission, and that mission was to get all the students under my tutelage as close to grade-level reading as possible. How would I do it?

My plan went something like this: Design a reading program that provides students with a wide variety of books, structure the schedule so there's time for extended reading and writing practice, allow students to write about what they know and love while simultaneously teaching them grammar and spelling, and make use of the toolbox of reading and teaching strategies that I'd accumulated and tried to perfect over 19 years. As I prepared to introduce my plan, however, I realized that I'd made a crucial mistake. There can be only one grand design, one master plan, and my school already had one—Treasures, published by Macmillan/McGraw-Hill. My district called it our core reading program. I called it the basal.

When I first realized that I'd have to use a basal program, I was crushed! My heart was set on using all that I had learned to construct my own highly effective reading program. Using someone else's program struck me as uninteresting, uncreative, and downright dictatorial. My district, however, had made it clear that the basal program was the one that was to be used, and teachers were expected to use the program, in the jargon of the day, "with a high degree of fidelity." In other words, don't mess with the manual!

However, I had major qualms about the effectiveness of publisher-produced programs. During my years as a teacher-trainer, I'd read articles about and heard reading authorities speak to the shortcomings of basal programs (Allington, 2011; Brenner & Hiebert, 2010; Dewitz, Jones, & Leahy, 2009; Reutzel & Daines, 1987). As I traveled to local districts, reading teachers complained that their core programs didn't provide enough opportunities for struggling readers to master phonic patterns, read motivating books, or write authentic pieces of writing.

After returning to a district classroom and using a core reading program for one year, I became a complaining teacher, too. In my eyes, our basal program had numerous problems. For starters, the scope of phonics instruction was too broad and the sequence too haphazard. Few decoding skills were taught to mastery. Spelling was not integrated with real writing. There was a dearth of word work activities and an overreliance on worksheets and practice book pages. The end result was that the struggling students weren't mastering the basics of decoding.

Second, students had no choice in the story selection. If the story was mediocre or the majority of kids didn't like it, we went on with the story anyway. Also, struggling readers couldn't read the grade-level texts. I wondered what the students in other classrooms were reading, especially those who were homogeneously grouped in the "advanced group." If the teachers were following the core program, the advanced readers would have few, if any, opportunities to read authentic literature on an advanced level.

In addition, our basal series left little time for independent reading practice or extended and authentic writing activities. This really bothered me because I knew both were crucial if my students (or, rather, students in any classroom) were going to become successful readers and writers. For many reasons, I valued independent reading and extended time for writing, and it troubled me to leave them out of our reading program.

Finally, because I was trying to follow the dictates of the manual, my cooperating teacher and I were assigning dozens of worksheets and practice book pages. I disliked most of these pages, especially when I considered the neediest readers. Not only were the practice book pages divorced from real-world reading and writing, but they were also often above the instructional level of the struggling readers.

In the end, I had no faith that an unmodified core program was an effective way to teach students, especially those who struggle. What was I to do? In the words of special education visionary Marc Gold, it was time to try another way. Knowing I'd go crazy trying to teach reading with just a basal program, and realizing that my district wouldn't allow me, a new employee, to simply cast it aside, I set out to find a way to meld my educational values with the program already in place. I jotted down the four things uppermost in my mind—my four core values, if you will—submitted them to the curriculum director, and petitioned him to allow me to create a third-grade reading program based on them.

Here's what I shared with my curriculum director:

1. Time for extended reading
2. Time for extended writing
3. Attention to the big ideas in reading and writing
4. Use of effective instructional practices and strategies

That list became my four values. In Figure 1.1 you'll see how the four values exist with a basal reading program. The core reading program, or basal, which is the foundation of this book, surrounds the values. For the purposes of this book, we'll never leave that core program behind. We will, however, insert a vital, beating heart into its body—namely, the four values. The arrows that connect the bubble of each value and crisscross in the center show that every value informs and works with the others. When you work on all four values at once, you create synergy, thus producing an effect that is much greater than the sum of the parts.

And what about the two columns at the top? These are the actions that enable you to build your supercharged program. The first step is to simply do something! First, create a schedule that works for you. Carve out blocks of time in which effective practices replace ineffective ones. Then, continue forward by implementing a few of the ideas laid out in this book. Finally, keep track of what you're doing and how the new ideas, strategies, and activities are working. Constant assessment and personal reflection form a critical feedback mechanism: Assess and reflect, take action based on your assessment and reflection, then assess and reflect some more.

The language of these values may sound familiar to you. After all, there's nothing new under the sun. If you're a student of reading instruction and an aficionado of teacher resource books, you'll see that many of my ideas come from the four blocks and balanced literacy models, readers' and writers' workshops, and Pearson and Gallagher's (1983) gradual release of responsibility, and you'll know my values are constructed from the writings of instructional clinicians, researchers, and innovators such as Calkins, Allington, Moats, and Archer. What's new and different in Super Core is that my values are incorporated into the broad structure of a core reading program.

Now that we have an overview, let's look a little deeper into each of the values.

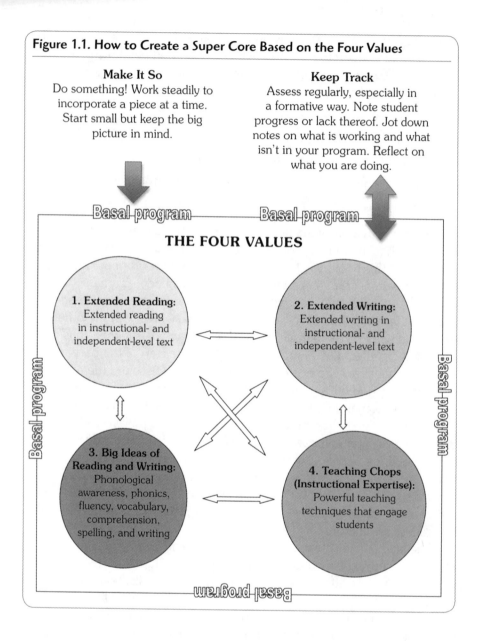

Figure 1.1. How to Create a Super Core Based on the Four Values

Make It So
Do something! Work steadily to incorporate a piece at a time. Start small but keep the big picture in mind.

Keep Track
Assess regularly, especially in a formative way. Note student progress or lack thereof. Jot down notes on what is working and what isn't in your program. Reflect on what you are doing.

Basal program   Basal program

THE FOUR VALUES

1. Extended Reading:
Extended reading in instructional- and independent-level text

2. Extended Writing:
Extended writing in instructional- and independent-level text

3. Big Ideas of Reading and Writing:
Phonological awareness, phonics, fluency, vocabulary, comprehension, spelling, and writing

4. Teaching Chops (Instructional Expertise):
Powerful teaching techniques that engage students

Basal program   Basal program

Basal program

Value 1: Extended Reading

Children love to read. Given personal space and a book that they can independently read, most kids will settle into a story and read for at least 10–15 minutes. Older readers (and some young ones, too) can go longer. When instructed in an enthusiastic manner and with an effective program, kids who don't currently love reading will at least come to appreciate it, and in time, they may even grow to love it. I've seen this happen in my own classroom and in the classrooms of master teachers who have permitted me to work with them.

How do children come to love reading? In a word: success. Success is the best motivator. When children experience success in reading, their confidence and enthusiasm grow. It's a cycle: Enthusiasm leads to more reading, which creates more success, which leads to even more reading.

Success is crucial for struggling readers. Without it, they're discouraged and demoralized by a persistently difficult activity. Think about your own response to a demanding task that's beyond your current ability level. If you've ever tried something and failed over and over again over a long period of time, you'll understand the sense of defeat and frustration experienced by struggling readers. So, it's critical that reading teachers structure their basal program so all students experience success in reading.

One way to begin this structuring is to create opportunities for students to read for extended periods of time on their independent and instructional levels. Reading is a skill that must be practiced for much more than five or 10 minutes a day. Allington (2001) proposed that students spend at least 90 minutes a day reading in school. That's in addition to any instructional time that takes place.

To engage students in reading for extended periods of time, you'll first need extended periods of time. I don't mean to be flippant here, merely lighthearted, because I know teachers never have enough time to accomplish all that is expected of them. I'll talk about time in more detail later. For now, let me just say that one of the basic premises of this book is that you must narrow the focus of what you teach and deep-six a healthy amount of ineffective worksheets and basal-based activities to create space to implement new and more effectives practices and activities. Simply put, it's time to put the tired metaphor of the heaping plate to rest. Teachers simply cannot continually add new items to their reading plate while simultaneously producing high degrees of student performance, especially with those students who struggle the most in reading and writing. Implementing the most effective reading practices, such as guided reading groups and thorough instruction in metacognitive reading strategies, demands getting rid of some core program content, activities, and worksheets.

In addition to time, you'll need a wide range of interesting books that are leveled appropriately for each student. For students to become fluent readers, they need exposure to a range of texts with high volumes of words in meaningful contexts (Kuhn, Schwanenflugel, & Meisinger, 2010). Therefore, teachers must provide students with a multitude of books. This seems readily apparent, yet I fear that teachers lose sight of this truth when they teach from basal manuals year after year.

This variety of books goes well beyond the leveled readers that some core reading programs provide. In addition to the anthology story, your basal program may supply a set of theme-related books with labels like "struggling," "on-level," and "enrichment." This can be the beginning of a book collection, but it is by no means adequate. An adequate variety of books is multiple book bins, each containing 30 books labeled with guided reading levels, Lexiles, or DRA levels. An adequate variety of books means classroom libraries stocked with multiple levels of different genres, such as nonfiction about animals, nonfiction history, adventure, fantasy, and poetry. An adequate variety of books is a communal book room stocked with hundreds, if not thousands, of books that a teacher can quickly borrow for use in his or her classroom.

Why are a variety of books on a variety of reading levels and extended blocks of time valuable classroom commodities? Over and over again, it's been found that when academic tasks are matched to students' instructional needs and ability levels, students are much more likely to remain engaged for periods of time and experience academic success (Gambrell, Marinak, Brooker, & McCrea-Andrews, 2011; Treptow, 2006; Vygotsky, 1978; Wyne & Stuck, 1979). In other words, when students read texts on their independent reading levels, they practice more, and when students practice more, they learn more. It's the Matthew effect: The rich get richer (Stanovich, 1986).

The two girls in Figure 1.2 are examples of students getting richer. They've chosen a book on their independent reading level and found a comfortable spot to read. While the teacher works with a guided reading group, these students are reading quietly by themselves. As they read, they encounter new vocabulary words, solve reading roadblocks, build their fluency skills, and learn facts about coral reefs, all without the teacher having to directly instruct them.

Ironically, providing time to read and providing a choice of books on a student's independent and instructional levels are two things that basal programs do poorly (Allington, 2011). Too much time gets eaten up with workbook pages, isolated skill drills, and activities like listening to a story on a CD. To add insult to injury, the difficulty level of the weekly anthology story is often well above some students' instructional levels, especially if the students are struggling or if the class is homogeneously grouped into a collection of below-grade-level readers. And basal anthologies don't give students choices. Choice is vital to reading engagement because choice builds enthusiasm and excitement. Just like adults, children want to have a say in what they read.

Figure 1.2. Independent Reading

Here's the good news: Even the most constrictive basal program can make room for extended reading. You'll find many thoughts on this in Chapter 6, which is devoted to the idea of extended reading and what you'll need to do to create it.

Value 2: Extended Writing

When it comes to writing, Super Core suggests carving out time for extended writing on independently chosen topics rather than sticking to a basal program's prescribed writing prompts, sentence completion worksheets, and writing projects.

Children love to write—but not about prompts pulled from a manual. Children love to write about the people they know and the things they're interested in. They experience flow in writing when they share information about their best friend, retell a funny story, or describe a favorite hobby or sport. It's all about communication. Kids want to tell teachers, their friends, and their classmates about their lives. When they write about objects, events, and people they know and love, children understand the purpose for writing, and they learn to love writing.

Writing plays an important part in a child's reading development. The flip side of reading and decoding, writing allows children to encode.

In other words, it gives them practice in matching individual letters, word families, and patterns to the sounds they hear in a word. Figure 1.3 shows a young writer busily encoding words. If you look closely, you'll notice that he's circling a word that he doesn't know how to spell. Rather than looking up the word immediately after he writes it, which would break the flow of his creative process, he spells the word as best as he can, circles it, and then goes back at a later time to check it in his student dictionary.

Writing does more than allow students to practice their spelling. When reading their writing quietly to themselves or out loud to a buddy, a small group, or the whole class, students practice their reading skills. Writing can be a wonderfully sneaky way to get kids to reread a piece of text three or even four times. Finally, when they write to give a summary of a story, predict what will happen next, compare two characters, or tell why they enjoyed a book, students have multiple opportunities to practice reading comprehension strategies, such as making connections, summarizing, predicting, and answering questions.

Recently, when four days' worth of April reading lessons were almost entirely canceled due to schedule changes (meetings, teacher training, school renovations, physicals, an assembly...you name it, we had it), my third-grade reading group had only 40 minutes to meet. What were

Figure 1.3. Independent Writing

we to do but write?! The students got out their composition books and Good Writers' Checklist (discussed in Chapter 6) and went at it, choosing topics of their choice. Highlights of the writing session included well-constructed paragraphs of 8–10 sentences. The four best paragraphs recounted a surprise birthday party and the big brother who almost ruined it, a salamander that may or may not have imprinted on the little boy who picked it up (to quote the boy, "Maybe the sally just liked the warmth of my hand"), an "I can't wait to go fishing with my dad" story, and a dramatic listing of all the reasons Mrs. Draksler is a little girl's favorite teacher. All of this wonderful writing came from students who, in October, struggled to write two sentences, rarely used proper punctuation or capitalization, and had no idea what a paragraph was.

Although authentic writing is valuable, an uninterrupted block of writing time of at least 30–40 minutes twice a week is equally valuable. To become a better writer, whether child or adult, one must practice, practice, practice. And practice takes time, time, time. In Chapter 5, we'll explore ways to find adequate time for writing. It should be noted that writing instruction encompasses handwriting and printing, spelling, grammar, reading, and speaking and listening. If you think of writing broadly—a way of teaching multiple components of reading simultaneously—carving out big blocks of time becomes more palatable to any teacher who must accomplish a lot in a short amount of time. Hmm, I guess that would be all of us!

I end the introduction of the first two values with a story from the classroom. Toward the end of her educational career, my mother left her coaching position and took command of a first-grade classroom. She taught in upstate New York, and the city school in which she taught stayed in session through most of the hot and humid month of June. On one especially muggy day, when the school year, patience, and sanity were all nearing their end, my mother promised the kids that the next day would be a fun day. "You can do anything you want," she said to her squirming students, "as long as it's related to something that we learned this year."

Before I finish the story, I must add that my mother was an exceptional teacher. After working for years as a team-teacher, mentor, and trainer and teaching both undergraduate- and graduate-level courses at the local college, her classroom teaching was a gifted blend of deep knowledge and practical application. On her list of educational values, extended time for reading and writing were at the top. If you were to walk in on her reading block on any given day, chances are you would see students curled up with a book or busily engaged in some type of writing activity.

In any case, my mother asked her first graders to go home that night and think about what they wanted to do tomorrow. The next day rolled around, again hot and humid, and the kids took their seats at their tables. "So," my mother asked, "what would you like to do today?" One little girl instantly raised her hand. "Tianna," my mother asked, "what would you like to do today?" Without missing a beat, Tianna replied, "Mrs. Weakland, can we read and write *all* day long?" Upon hearing this question, the other students erupted in cheers and applause. My mother still loves to tell this story.

Value 3: The Big Ideas of Reading and Writing

When I was an educational consultant charged with providing staff development to teachers in local school districts, I spent a great deal of time becoming knowledgeable about reading and instructional practice. I attended conferences, workshops, and presentations and put tens of thousands of miles on my car, all to bring back pertinent information to teachers in local school districts. Early on in my staff development gig, perhaps in 2003, I attended a wonderful presentation by Sharon Vaughn of the University of Texas at Austin. Her topic was the big ideas in reading, as handed down by the 2000 National Reading Panel (NICHD, 2000a). Her clever graphic organizer was a reading quilt.

Vaughn's presentation was short, concise, and engaging, and I remember it to this day. She pictured each big idea as a panel of the quilt: phonemic awareness, phonics and the development of the alphabetic principle, fluency and its various subcomponents, vocabulary, and comprehension. A sixth quilt panel was devoted to spelling and writing. The quilt binding was instructional practice and student grouping.

In 20 minutes, she simply and elegantly presented the essence of reading instruction: the five big ideas of reading plus writing and spelling bound together with effective instructional practice. I believe her presentation encapsulated the basics of everything that a reading teacher needs to know. Table 1.1 summarizes and paraphrases how I remember that reading quilt.

Phonemic awareness, phonics, fluency, vocabulary, comprehension, spelling, writing—call me a total reading nerd, but I recite these terms like a mantra. As an elementary school reading specialist and classroom teacher, I press them into practice every day. Whether I'm teaching a kindergarten, third-grade, or fifth-grade lesson, I'm always asking myself, Which big idea am I focusing on? What aspect of the big idea am I working on? and How am I teaching it? To me, these big ideas are the foundational bedrock of reading theory.

Table 1.1. The Big Ideas of Reading and Writing Instruction

Big Idea	What Teachers Need to Teach Students
Phonemic awareness	• That spoken words consist of individual sounds (phonemes) • How words can be segmented (pulled apart) into sounds and how these sounds can be blended (put back together) and manipulated (added, deleted, and substituted) • How to use their phonemic awareness to blend sounds to read words and to segment sounds in words to spell them
Phonics	• The accurate and rapid identification of the letters of the alphabet • The alphabetic principle (an understanding that the sequence of sounds or phonemes in a spoken word is represented by letters in a written word) • Phonics elements (e.g., letter–sound correspondences, spelling patterns, syllables) • How to apply phonics elements while reading and writing
Fluency	• How to decode words (in isolation and in connected text) • How to automatically recognize words (accurately and quickly with little effort) • How to increase speed (or rate) of reading while maintaining accuracy • How to read in smooth and long phrases • How to read with proper inflection and expression (prosody)
Vocabulary	• Knowing the meanings of most words in a text so they can understand what they read • How to apply a variety of strategies to learn word meanings • How to make connections between words and concepts • How to accurately use new words in oral and written language
Comprehension	• How to read both narrative and expository texts • How to understand and remember what they read • How to relate their own knowledge and experiences to texts • How to use comprehension strategies to improve their comprehension • How to communicate with others about what they read
Spelling and writing	• How to segment words into sounds to spell them • How to remember and reproduce exact letter patterns (e.g., letter–sound correspondences, syllables, word parts) • Rapid and accurate letter formation • How to notice reliable spelling patterns and generalizations • How to write fluently • How to apply grammatical rules in writing • How to write for different purposes and audiences in various forms • How to critique and evaluate writing • How to communicate with others about what they know and experience

Although the big ideas bear simple labels, they are rich and nuanced in meaning. So, don't let the simple labels fool you. Each idea is like the center of a semantic web, intimately connected to other equally important ideas. When you discuss comprehension, for example, you also touch on fluency, background knowledge, motivation, metacognitive strategies, time to write, and time to read. Taberski (2010) builds a case for this extensive type of thinking. I find, however, that the big ideas as presented by the National Reading Panel are the easiest way to get acquainted with what is most foundational to reading. So, don't put the cart before the horse; I suggest you know and understand the basics before you dive deeply into each idea.

I also suggest that you should have on hand a PDF or free hard copy of the summarized National Reading Panel report (NICHD, 2000a). Sneak a peek at the summary when you're sitting in a staff development meeting, peruse it while you're waiting in line at the bank, or sit down with it for an hour over the weekend. If you're unfamiliar with the big ideas, the information in Super Core is only a start. But it's a good start! If you're already familiar with the big ideas but their emphasis in your classroom has faded over time, then Super Core is here to remind you of their importance.

Value 4: Teaching Chops (Instructional Expertise)

All teachers possess instructional techniques. Monitoring students as they practice, using proximity or graphic organizers, writing the lesson objectives on the board, using worksheets to practice skills, keeping a brisk pace of delivery, and speaking in funny dialects or with a stern tone of voice are all techniques for getting information across to students. But some are more effective than others.

When I see a teacher using effective teaching techniques regularly and effortlessly, I say that teacher has teaching chops. The term *chops*, like the word *gig*, is one that we musicians throw around regularly, as in "Eric was killer on the gig last night. That guy has some serious chops!" In the music world, *chops* refers to a musician's technique. Thus, a great guitarist fluently plays scales, arpeggios, and chords and masterfully combines these skills to create music with great soulfulness, beauty, or energy. In other words, the guitarist's chops are a means to an end: great music.

A great teacher has chops, too. He or she quickly analyzes a task and breaks it down into its most basic parts, then uses explicit instruction and modeling to introduce the skill or information. The teacher effortlessly hands out positive reinforcement, instantly assesses learning, and deeply engages the class with clever and effective instructional techniques. The teacher uses these teaching techniques as a means to an end:

student achievement and performance. When a teacher uses techniques masterfully, he or she has some serious chops.

Your method of instruction is every bit as important as the information you're attempting to impart. If information or content is a stack of cardboard boxes, your instruction is the big delivery truck that efficiently delivers those packages. Without instruction, content just sits in the warehouse gathering dust. Of course, some delivery trucks are more efficient than others. To become a master teacher, you'll need a truck that delivers the goods quickly, easily, and dependably.

Instructional technique is important because the way that you instruct is a huge factor in whether students attend and behave well in class, become more independent, and effectively organize, store, and use what you're trying to teach them (Leinhardt, Zigmond, & Cooley, 1981). Unlike school funding levels, poverty, and bad student attitudes, your instructional practice is one variable that's completely within your control, so make sure you choose the best instructional techniques.

My quest to become a more effective teacher began in my special education days when I was trained in a variety of teaching models, most notably Hunter's (1994) instructional theory into practice. I needed effective tools in my instructional toolbox because my students were always one step away from ripping up the floorboards and tearing down the walls. I still use many of the techniques I gathered during those early years.

Later, when I left the classroom and became a consultant, I learned other instructional techniques and models, including cooperative learning, Socratic questioning, and direct instruction. Now that I'm back in the classroom, and when I'm having a good day, I feel as if my teaching is better than ever. Why? Because I've mastered a handful of highly effective teaching strategies that I use regularly to engage students. The six techniques I love are time tested, relatively easy to perform, and highly effective. One thing they are not is new. I didn't invent the techniques or prove their efficacy. Researchers and educational innovators such as Marzano, Pickering, Archer, and Slavin did this for me.

Here's a final word before I list and unpack the techniques: *flow.* As an artist who loves to sit and practice the drums or guitar for hours at a time, I'm captivated by Csíkszentmihalyi's research on flow. Flow, which is somewhat analogous to engagement, is the mental state of a person who, when involved in an activity, is fully immersed in a feeling of focus, involvement, and success. When a person feels flow, he or she feels content and alive. Csíkszentmihalyi (1993) describes the feeling as "being carried away by a current, everything moving smoothly without effort" (p. xiii). What I love about teaching is that it's an opportunity to experience flow. Everyone in your classroom experiences flow when you

---
Figure 1.4. The Six Teaching Chops

Use the following instructional techniques and practices to supercharge your reading program:

1. Direct and explicit instruction
2. Social and cooperative learning
3. Whole-class physical response

4. Task analysis and mastery learning
5. Explicit modeling and practice
6. Formative assessment
---

teach a great lesson. Your teaching is strong, and your kids are engaged and happy. You and the students are engrossed and having fun, and the time just flies by. I believe that when you teach with effective instructional techniques as your foundation, you're much more likely to get into a state of flow.

In an educational world bursting with techniques and strategies, I've chosen to focus on six that are especially effective and engaging. Figure 1.4 provides my six teaching chops in a list, each of which I briefly explain next. In upcoming chapters, I explain in greater detail how each is used in reading and writing instruction.

Direct and Explicit Instruction. A staple of the instructivist camp, direct instruction is highly effective and time efficient (Archer & Hughes, 2011). Modeling and mastery learning is intimately connected to this instructional routine, as is explicit modeling and practice. Like social and cooperative learning and whole-class response, direct instruction is a way to more fully engage students in whatever information or skill you're trying to teach. It's often referred to as "I do, we do, you do."

Social and Cooperative Learning. This type of instruction is student centered, easy to do, and effective (Marzano, Pickering, & Pollock, 2001). I love to use think-pair-share, buddy reading, small-group brainstorming, and other types of social and cooperative learning groups. The three specific activities that I listed are only the tip of the iceberg, of course. It's possible to make cooperative learning the focus of your classroom or even school, and some people choose it as their number one value. I choose, however, to focus on a few simple techniques. I'll elaborate on each as they occur in later chapters.

Whole-Class Physical Response. If you frequently teach to the whole class, make all the students respond via some type of physical signal. This keeps the kids engaged and helps you monitor their understanding. Plus, it's fun! Options for ways to respond include response cards, vocabulary cards, whiteboards, and body signals, such as thumbs-up/thumbs-down, fist of five, and head-shoulders-knees-toes.

Task Analysis and Mastery Learning. When teaching a complex task, such as writing a haiku or reading a poem, it's easy to overload struggling learners with too many unknowns. Therefore, you want to analyze the larger task and make sure you teach only one unknown aspect at a time. My wife, a fabulous music educator (and yes, I'm biased), swears by task analysis. She calls it the law of one unknown. Her mentor, Dawn Baker, formerly of Kent State University, called it making tea. Whatever the name, it's all about explicitly introducing one piece of information or one skill at a time. This increases the student's chance of mastering the information or skill (Rosenshine, 2012). The idea of mastery is critical to teaching and central to this book. Teachers and school systems must decide what content and skills are essential for students to master.

Explicit Modeling and Practice. Students learn more when you explicitly model everything that you expect them to do, make them practice everything you model, and motivate them as they practice it multiple times (Rosenshine, 2012).

Formative Assessment. Formative assessments are ongoing and frequent assessments that occur throughout the teaching and learning process. They're foundational to good teaching because they provide real information about students' knowledge, habits, and thinking. Formative assessments are fundamentally different from traditional end-of-the-week summative assessments (on story elements, spelling, grammar, etc.), which, by comparison, give teachers a score and confirm a student's self-impression as smart or not so smart but do little to help a teacher move the student toward mastery in critical areas of reading and writing.

Not only do formative assessments guide your future instruction, but they also validate your current instruction. When your assessments show that 85–90% of your students are at or above the critical reading benchmarks, then your instruction is working. Shine your halo and give yourself a pat on the back! If your classroom scores are below this level, your instruction has yet to take hold. As you know, because of reading difficulties, impaired cognitive functioning, lack of motivation, or a terrible home life, some students need a long time to fully master the meaning of dozens of vocabulary words, read passages of grade-level text fluently, or write well-constructed paragraphs. Therefore, it's best to collect data every two to four weeks on each student's progress toward the most important reading and writing benchmarks. Only formative assessments allow you to collect this kind of data.

Content and Instructional Mastery

If values 1 and 2 are the culmination of my years as a teacher of children, then values 3 and 4 are the culmination of my years as a teacher of teachers. During my 10 years as a trainer, I visited and observed many excellent teachers, all of whom demonstrated a combination of content and instructional mastery. Now that I'm back in the classroom as a Title I reading teacher, I strive to combine my valued big ideas and instructional techniques every time I teach, be it a 30-minute intervention session or a two-hour core reading class.

Chetty, Friedman, and Rockoff (2011) found that the knowledge a masterful teacher imparts to students impacts them not only immediately but also over a lifetime. But what makes for a masterful teacher? It's difficult to pin down. More and more researchers, though, say that effective teachers are a combination of big ideas and teaching chops. I agree with David Chard (2011), dean of the School of Education at Southern Methodist University: "High-quality teachers must have two things: knowledge of content and effective instructional strategies" (para. 8). I value the big ideas because as a reading teacher, I feel it's important to understand the theories that are foundational to reading and writing. Mere knowledge, however, is not enough. You've got to be able to walk the walk. This is why I also value teaching chops. Skillful teachers are like doctors: Doctors use their knowledge to diagnose and cure health problems, and teachers use their knowledge to diagnose and cure learning problems.

Combining content knowledge and instructional pedagogy is where the rubber meets the road. When I'm working with "cute as a button" but "fidgety as a squirrel" kindergartners, some of whom are struggling to master the sounds of individual letters, I must thoroughly understand the alphabetic principle *and* have the chops to hold their attention and impart some information. This aspect of teaching—the art of blending knowledge and performance—is also what I love about performing music. My hope is that you'll see my passion for this blending and be moved to master content and instruction, too.

Not to go off the rails here, but I see the lack of teacher-clinicians as a big problem for the field of education. Many master teachers leave the field, migrating to administration, consulting, or private industry. They have knowledge and expertise, but they're no longer "doing" in the classroom. In other cases, expert teachers are in the classrooms but can't exercise their knowledge and skills because they're restrained and confined by scripted basal programs, controlling school boards, and/or untested educational models championed by administrators.

Finally, many public school systems aren't very good at creating effective classroom reading programs. Why? In some cases, it's because district administrators and university professors who consult with them have little K–12 classroom experience, and their demanding jobs prevent them from immersing themselves in classrooms for any meaningful length of time. This limits their pragmatic and practical knowledge and creates an excess of book knowledge (theory, policy, frameworks, etc.). Because they haven't lived where "the rubber meets the road," these folks don't truly understand how a particular model, assessment, or curriculum unfolds in the classroom. Thus, untested and unworkable models and programs are implemented and then abandoned when it becomes apparent that they don't work in the reality of the classroom. The cycle always begins again, though, because there's always something new to try, even if it's really not worth doing.

In other instances, teachers aren't very good at implementing an effective reading and writing program. These teachers are doing something, but it's not exemplary teaching. Some years ago, during a training session, I chatted over a break with a man who had been teaching reading for almost 17 years. I was shocked when he asked me to slowly restate the big ideas in reading. "Could you repeat those?" he asked. "I want to write them down. I really don't know reading very well." At another time, I observed a teacher using the Wilson Reading Program with a group of four struggling readers. When I talked briefly with the teacher after her lesson, she told me how happy she was to be using the Wilson materials. "Finally," she said, "after 30 years of teaching reading in special education, I feel like my teaching is effective!" As Charlie Brown would say, "Good grief!" I don't know if these comments were born of a breakdown in professional development, a lack of motivation to take the reins and teach themselves what they needed to know, or a combination of the two. Regardless, I was left wondering about teacher effectiveness.

The most effective reading teachers have mastered both content and instructional practice.

All of this leads me back to Waldorf and Montessori. I believe schools need to develop a philosophical foundation of educational values that's strong enough to exist over time. What could this foundation consist of? The big ideas in reading and writing, for starters, and the effective instructional strategies needed to teach them to children. Every reading teacher must have (or should be working toward) a deep understanding of what the big ideas are, how they work together as students move from emerging to established readers, and how to teach the big ideas by using effective and efficient instructional strategies.

How Do the Common Core State Standards Apply?

Unlike Waldorf and Montessori schools, many public schools never establish an essential baseline of content and instruction values that persists over time. Guided reading programs come and go. Heterogeneous groups in a full-inclusion program exist for a short time and then flip to homogeneous groups and pull-out programs. A basal series gives way to a readers' workshop model, only to return to a core reading program a few years later.

The implementation of competing assessments, curricula, and programs also inhibits the establishment of a philosophical baseline. Students are subjected to too many tests (e.g., DIBELS, DRA, 4Sight, Terra Nova, InView) and summative basal assessments, which suck up huge amounts of time but lead to little instructional change. State standards and core program content compete with essential reading program standards, many of which may be out of sync with a school's report card. Attempts are made to combine Response to Intervention with professional learning communities while, at the same time, essential learning and vision statements are created and rolled out via a collaborative teaching model and differentiated curriculum mapping. Huh? Trying to make sense of this educational gobbledygook is more difficult than developing a grand unified theory in physics!

These schools are like barnacle-ridden boats, slowed by the weight of ever-accumulating programs, curricula, and standards. Much is added, but little is ever scraped away. After years of no scraping, the poor little school boat is so encrusted that it can barely glide through the water. So, why bring the Common Core State Standards into the picture? Isn't the Common Core just another barnacle to cement onto the hull?

First of all, states expect to see district curricula based on standards. These standards are the focus of high-stakes tests. Although the worst of that era may be drawing to a close, accountability is important, and accountability tests will continue to be a part of our teaching lives in the foreseeable future. Second and more importantly, reading standards, when they aren't ridiculously broad or laden with minutia, provide a summary of the most important content and instruction. A few focused and well-stated standards provide the essentials of what to teach.

Constructed from past standards from multiple states and informed by the standards of other countries, the Common Core State Standards are designed to provide a strong, focused, and cumulative set of standards that every district in every state can use. Compared with the reading and writing standards of Pennsylvania (my state), I find the Common Core to be more lean and muscular.

When it comes to reading, the Common Core provides 10 reading standards for literature per grade level and 10 for informational texts. I love the idea of focusing on 10 essential standards and four foundational skills. Why? Teachers cannot thoroughly teach the dozens of standards found in state documents and core reading programs. Simply put, when everything is expected, nothing is essential. The word *essential* is by definition a limiting term.

To draw a musical analogy, an orchestral violinist strives to do a few things really well. His or her performance standards are to accurately play pitch, rhythm, tempo, and dynamics. Add general musicality to the list, and you come up with five music standards. These standards guide the violinist regardless of whether he or she is playing Bach, Brahms, or the Beatles. That's what makes them so powerful, so essential.

Thankfully, many of the Common Core State Standards, such as "ask and answer questions," "know and apply grade-level phonics," and "read with sufficient accuracy and fluency to support comprehension," mirror what I already value. This means that when I teach, I'm not struggling to integrate competing standards. My core values are found in the Common Core language, and vice versa. When I use a comprehensive reading program *and* the ideas in this book, I know I'm teaching many of the Common Core State Standards. In each of the upcoming chapters, you'll see how the Common Core and the big ideas of reading and writing intertwine and overlap, and you'll come to a better understanding of how to focus on a few concepts to cover many standards.

Asking and Answering Questions

Once you accept the four values and agree to give them a try, questions will begin to form in your mind: How do I create opportunities for extended reading and teach more authentic writing? Which activities do I use to teach phonics in my spelling and writing block? Which instructional techniques do I focus on first? These questions and many others are answered and discussed in upcoming chapters.

In a general sense, though, you move the four values into a core reading program by carrying out the actions at the top of the four values graphic (see Figure 1.1), namely:

- Make it so by first creating time (i.e., get rid of basal "stuff") and then picking an idea presented in Super Core and doing it.
- Keep track of how it's working, mostly through formative assessments but also through anecdotal notes and the occasional summative or benchmark assessment.

Pretty simple, yes? Of course, it's easier to talk about a process than actually do it. But if you start small and make a commitment to taking action, you'll have a slightly more effective program in three months, a moderately more effective program in two years, and a much more effective program in three to four years.

However, if you want to go for the gusto, you can rocket to a very effective core reading program in two years. Don't fool yourself, though. Current wisdom says it takes 10,000 hours of practice to become a masterful musician, basketball player, or painter. Running a highly effective reading program is no different. It may not take 10,000 hours, but it will take considerable time and effort to get an extended reading and writing program up and running.

Getting the Go-Ahead

Regardless of whether you take action incrementally or in one giant leap, you'll first need to get the blessings of an administrator. It's important that your principal and/or curriculum director gives the go-ahead to make changes in your basal program. Basal programs are often treated like sacred cows. Some administrators enforce a program's fidelity with an iron fist, and others consider interpretation and modification to be big no-nos. If the latter is your district's position, work to convince your administrator to take a leap of faith, for basal programs are not and never will be the be-all and end-all. Core programs alone will never provide students with the extended, real-world reading and writing experiences that are necessary to accelerate their reading achievement.

This book provides you with the facts, activities, and action steps that you'll need to make a case for change. I suggest you start the change with a relaxed summer meeting between you and your principal. In the past, you've probably received informational articles and books from administrators, so perhaps you'll want to return the favor and give them a copy of this book prior to your meeting. Then, armed with knowledge and determination, go into that meeting, look your administrator in the eye, and say,

> Ms. Administrator, I'd like your permission to modify the core reading program. Why, you ask? Well, let me tell you! I want to make my reading program more engaging and effective. I want to see greater growth in my students' reading scores. I want to give my students books on their independent and instructional levels so they can read, read, read. I want to give them opportunities to write about what they know so they are motivated to write, write, write and spell, spell, spell. I want my students to leave the classroom with skills and strategies so fully learned that they'll automatically employ them in later grades. And, yes, I want my program to be more fun!

Press your administrator (politely, of course) until you hear her say, "Yes, yes, a thousand times yes! Please make it so. You have my permission!"

Reading Winners

The space race of the 1950s and 1960s was a contest between the United States and the U.S.S.R.: Who had the best rocket? Who would launch the first orbiting satellite? Which country would be the first to land a man on the moon? Although we are also engaged in rocket building—in this case, a reading rocket—our vehicle isn't part of a contest or competition. In our endeavor, there should be no losers, only winners. Reading winners are students who successfully rise to meet the benchmarks of decoding, fluent reading, and comprehension. And reading winners are students who successfully land in first or third or fifth grade with feelings of facility and confidence.

As you read through the upcoming chapters, I hope you'll see how the four values can transform your basal program into a supercharged reading rocket, one powerful enough to push all of your students into reading orbit. But don't just take my word for it. Tens of thousands of teachers, possibly many more, have embraced these types of values for decades. Talk to the teachers you most admire, and I bet you'll find that they've been working to incorporate these values into their reading and writing programs all along.

CHAPTER 2

Grammar With Gusto

· Your teacher's manual with its scope and sequence of grammar skills
· A selection of response cards (discussed in this chapter), one for each
student in your classroom
· A Writers Think About... poster (discussed in this chapter)

· · · · · · · · · · · ·
You will...
· · · · · · · · · · · ·

· Consolidate and categorize your grammar scope into seven categories
· Decide what grammar skills and concepts are most essential
· Teach essential skills to mastery
· Refrain from using most grammar worksheets and practice book pages
· Use direct instruction to introduce grammar concepts
· Use whole-group physical response activities to teach concepts more
deeply
· Allow students to practice grammar concepts (mechanics, parts of
speech, etc.) in authentic ways (i.e., writing sentences and paragraphs)
· Weave the teaching of grammar concepts and skills into spelling,
vocabulary, and comprehension instruction
· Formatively assess students over time

I f you're an ambitious person with boundless energy, you could
implement this book's instructional routines and ideas in one fell
swoop. As the Nike ads say, "Just do it!" A more relaxed, humane,
and probably more effective approach is to adopt one or two ideas every
year over the course of three or four years. If you opt for this approach,
grammar instruction is a good place to start.

To begin, make a commitment to decrease the number of worksheets
and workbook pages you assign. In the place of inauthentic worksheets
and workbook pages, use authentic writing activities, such as writing

sentences and paragraphs. Another substitute for workbook pages are engaging whole-class activities, such as word sorts and response cards.

In this chapter, I discuss categorizing and consolidating the concepts and skills presented in your grammar scope and sequence so they're easier to present, to teach to mastery, and to infuse into the other big idea areas, such as vocabulary, comprehension, writing, and spelling. We'll also take an in-depth look at instructional practices, such as modeling, direct instruction, and whole-group physical responses, that make whole-group instruction more effective and engaging. Finally, we'll look at opportunities to formatively assess student progress. Couple all of this with more extended writing opportunities (see Chapter 6), and you'll enable your students to thoroughly learn the most essential grammar skills and concepts.

The ideas presented in this chapter will lead to parents who are happy to have their children doing more active learning and fewer worksheets and a teacher—yourself—who more thoroughly enjoys teaching grammar lessons.

The Importance of Grammar

If you read the Common Core State Standards for the English Language Arts K–5, you won't see the words *worksheet* or *workbook* anywhere. Nor will you see phrases such as "use conventions of language in isolated fill-in-the-blank activities" or "demonstrate conventions of spelling by completing a word find puzzle." What you will see are phrases like "use knowledge of language and its conventions when writing," "demonstrate command of the conventions of standard English grammar...when writing or speaking," and "demonstrate command of the conventions of standard English capitalization, punctuation, and spelling when writing."

It's easy to see that the Common Core stresses writing and speaking, not worksheets. You should stress writing and speaking, too. Why? Grammar worksheets are contrived, they crowd out a student's chance to practice real-life activities such as reporting the news or telling a story, and they don't naturally engage students. In a nutshell, workbook pages and worksheets are inauthentic and uninteresting. If students are going to *use* grammar skills rather than merely practice them, they've got to be given the time to speak in grammatically correct sentences and then put those sentences to work in their own letters, poems, stories, and reports.

During my first year back in the classroom, my grammar instruction followed the teacher's manual closely. I was working in a cotaught classroom as a Title I reading specialist, and I volunteered to teach the daily grammar segment of the core reading curriculum. What did this look like? On day 1, I would introduce and teach to the whole group the topic of the week (as dictated by the scope and sequence of the core program). On day 2, and sometimes on day 3, I'd have all the students practice the skill in isolation using grammar workbook pages. By day 4, we were typically running out of time, so I didn't touch on grammar at all. Finally, on day 5, at the end of the week, I'd assess the skill with a summative assessment sheet from the core program's assessment book. The following week, I'd move on to the next topic regardless of whether the students had mastered the previous one. I repeated this sequence over and over again until I reached my ultimate goal: the end of the workbook or the end of the school year, whichever came first.

Comparing that routine with my current grammar instruction is like comparing bologna and filet mignon. My current routine looks like this: After introducing the skill or concept using direct and explicit instruction, I move the students immediately into guided practice using brainstorming and oral and written sentences. The students practice the skills and concepts via a few engaging group physical response activities and authentic writing activities (writing phrases, sentences, and paragraphs). I review the skills and concepts by weaving them into spelling, vocabulary, and guided reading groups. I formatively assess the skill in multiple ways, circling and spiraling back to reteach and review the skill as needed, and I introduce the next skill or concept only after most of the class (around 85%) has mastered the former. This routine helps ensure that my students are building and using an accumulating body of grammar knowledge.

Of course, there are times when you want to assign a worksheet. Perhaps you'll give it as homework or seatwork. A worksheet just might fit the bill if you want your students to see numerous examples of one particular convention, such as irregular plural nouns. Worksheets and workbook pages provide ready-made sentences for students to practice error identification. Additionally, worksheets work well when you have to be out of the classroom and you're planning for a substitute. The majority of your students' practice time, however, should be devoted to a combination of engaging whole-group practice and review activities (e.g., orally brainstorming, speaking sentences, word sorts, think-write-share, response cards) and authentic individual writing activities (e.g., writing a word, sentence, or paragraph). As the teacher, you shouldn't be spending your valuable time correcting worksheets. Instead, use your instructional

Teach grammar in small doses, first directly and explicitly and then through guided practice within engaging whole-group activities and authentic speaking and writing activities.

time to coach grammar and correct errors in real speaking and writing activities.

Think about something that you learned to do recently. Maybe you learned to play volleyball, speak French, or wire a light switch. Or perhaps you're working on playing the tuba. Did you buy a book of worksheets about volleyball, French, wiring, or tubas? I suspect that you got some information (from another person or from books or video demonstrations) and then practiced doing your new skill. Humans learn through doing, so don't make your students circle a word or fill in a blank; make them write and speak.

Scope: What Grammar to Teach

Because my cooperating teacher and I are still required to expose our students to most of our core reading program's curriculum, I teach the grammar scope and sequence, but I've become selective about how much time I dedicate to each skill or concept. Foundational areas get more time, nonessential areas get a lot less time, and I use whatever wiggle room I have to totally ignore grammar topics that are unimportant or trivial, especially for primary-grade learners who are struggling to read and write.

How does one decide what grammar topics are unimportant and trivial? I suggest you compare your teacher knowledge against what you see in the Common Core State Standards, run your thoughts past other teachers in your building, and consult with your principal and curriculum director. During this time of communication and consultation, people may push you to teach everything that's in your core's scope and sequence or to carve out time for pet projects. If your goal is to teach essential skills to mastery, you'll need to politely but firmly push back. Teaching that values all skills equally will result in the brightest kids continuing to do well (because typically they do well no matter what), the average kids holding their own or slipping a bit, and the struggling learners failing to master the most basic reading and writing skills.

The Common Core does a pretty good job of identifying what is essential. But even though the standards are presented as core, you'll still need to prioritize them and decide how much teaching time to devote to each standard. To me, the Common Core State Standards are like Russian matryoshka dolls, those wonderfully clever wooden figures that nest one inside another. Within the Common Core's language standards for K–5 are three categories: conventions of standard English, knowledge of language, and vocabulary acquisition and use. Nested inside each of these categories are numerous standards. Knowledge of language is all about using language and its conventions to create voice, style, and effect and convey ideas while writing and speaking. You can address these standards during writing and speaking activities. As for vocabulary acquisition and use, a category that contains everything from context clues and metaphors to root words and affixes, you can cover most of these standards during vocabulary, spelling, and comprehension instruction.

This leaves conventions of standard English. I like to group these standards into the following categories, especially in grades 2–5:

- Sentences and sentence structure, including simple, compound, and complex sentences, sentence fragments and run-ons, conjunctions, and prepositions
- Mechanics, including capitalization, spelling, and punctuation of all types
- Nouns, including common, proper, singular, plural, possessive, irregular, and pronouns
- Verbs, including regular and irregular, tense, and subject–verb agreement
- Adjectives
- Adverbs

There are a few standards I haven't mentioned, such as modal auxiliaries (and if you know what they are, you win a silver dollar), but my list captures the gist of the Common Core's list of convention standards. The point is that you should distill the Common Core State Standards so they seem manageable and, most importantly, teachable. I suggest you make a poster like the one in Figure 2.1, label it "Writers Think About...," and then hang it in your classroom. This poster will serve as a daily reminder to all writers: Every time someone writes a sentence, he or she should think about these seven essential topics.

The major grammar topics listed on the poster are constants in writing. I wondered about them even as I wrote this book: Do I say "categories" or modify the noun with an adjective and say "major categories"? Should I write a long, complex sentence strung together with commas or stick to shorter sentences? Do I say, "We will discuss," "We will address," or "We'll talk about"? Are my commas and colons used in the correct way?

As a teacher, keeping the seven categories of sentence structure, nouns, verbs, and so forth in mind throughout the day makes it easier for me to weave in grammar concepts regardless of what reading routine or component I'm currently engaged in. For example, during guided reading

Figure 2.1. Writers Think About... Poster

When they write, writers think about...

1. Sentences and sentence structure

2. Mechanics

3. Nouns

4. Verbs

5. Adjectives

6. Adverbs

7. Paragraphs

or anthology reading time, I can teach, reteach, and review adjectives or point out the author's use of commas in a series (mechanics). When we encounter dialogue, I can ask questions like, "Why didn't Jacob say 'Momma and I *is* going to make this the best day ever!'? Why did he say, 'Momma and I *are* going to make this the best day ever!'? And why did the author use an exclamation point at the end of the sentence?" During spelling I can teach the formation of plural nouns, such as *train/trains*, *plane/planes*, *branch/branches*, and *fox/foxes*. This type of weaving creates synergy: The combined effect of teaching grammar within writing, spelling, and comprehension is greater than the sum of the parts.

In the third-grade classroom where I spend the bulk of my afternoons, my grammar instruction follows the cumulative scope and sequence shown in Figure 2.2. Of course, if you teach first, second, fourth, or fifth grade, the chart you construct will look different, but it won't be all that different. In general, the Common Core is a document that shows the threads of common knowledge running through the grade levels. Although these threads become increasingly rich and complex as they wind their way from the primary grades to the intermediate grades, I'm struck by how much overlap exists within and between the grade levels.

Figure 2.2. Grammar Scope and Sequence for Grade 3

Month	Sentences, Sentence Structure, and Paragraphs	Mechanics	Nouns	Verbs	Other
September	• Complete sentences • Fragments	• Capitals and periods • Neat handwriting			
October	• Same • Writing a paragraph with three or more sentences • Exclamations, questions, and run-ons	• Same	• A noun is a person, place, or thing. • Common and proper nouns		
November	• Same • Writing a paragraph with five or more sentences	• Same • Commas • Correcting your spelling	• Same • Singular, plural, and irregular plural nouns		
December	• Same	• Same	• Same	• Verbs show action.	
January	• Same • Writing a paragraph with seven or more sentences	• Same • Using quotation marks	• Same	• Same • Tenses • Irregular verbs	
February	• Same	• Same	• Same	• Same	• Pronouns • Contractions
March	• Same	• Same	• Same	• Same	• Same • Adjectives
April	• Same • Writing two paragraphs, each with six or more sentences	• Same	• Same	• Same	• Same
May	• Same	• Same	• Same	• Same	• Same • Adverbs

Teaching Chops: How to Teach Grammar

Teaching chops are instructional techniques that, when applied in a mindful and masterful way, increase student learning. As you teach grammar, you can use all the chops mentioned in Chapter 1, such as whole-group response, task analysis, and formative assessment. You'll do this to get information to your students in the most efficient and effective ways possible and to ensure that your students are mastering the content.

Although I won't ask you to change your schedule, institute small grammar groups, or create learning centers that emphasize grammar, I will ask you to free up time so you and your students can engage in physical response activities and authentically practice skills (in other words, speak and write) during whole-group instruction. Therefore, you'll need to jettison most workbook pages and many of the teaching activities that are outlined in your teacher's manual. This will make time for teaching chops and the activities that go with them.

What follows are descriptions of how teaching chops can be pressed into the service of teaching concepts (e.g., What is a proper noun?) and skills (e.g., identifying the parts of speech within a sentence or, better yet, writing a complete and interesting sentence).

Direct and Explicit Instruction

As I think about direct and explicit instruction, I'm reminded of the student who told his teacher, "I ain't got no crayons." The teacher responded, "I *don't have any* crayons. You *don't have any* crayons. We *don't have any* crayons. They *don't have any* crayons. Do you understand?" "Well," replied the student, "what happened to all the crayons?"

In this situation, the teacher is alluding to what she wants the student to learn. Asking questions at the start of a lesson is another common teaching technique that is less than effective. For example, I might start a lesson by asking the students, "Who knows what a noun is?" or more absurdly, "Who knows what the function of a conjunction is?" Even Schoolhouse Rock! explicitly answers its own question: "Conjunction Junction, what's your function?" "Hooking up words and phrases and clauses."

To avoid allusions, confusion, and tangential teaching situations, make your instruction explicit and teach new parts of speech directly. For example, write, "A noun is a person, place, or thing," on the board, read it aloud to the students, and then have them read it back to you. Practice with a little script that sounds something like this:

Teacher:	Here's a new word: *noun*. Say it.
Students:	Noun.
Teacher:	A noun is a person, place, or thing. What is a noun?
Students:	A person, place, or thing.
Teacher:	What is a person, place, or thing?
Students:	A noun.
Teacher:	Here is an example of a noun: *apple*. An apple is a thing, therefore it's a noun. Here's another noun: *chair*. What is *chair*?
Students:	A noun. (If they don't answer correctly, say *noun* and ask the question again.)
Teacher:	Why is *chair* a noun?
Students:	Because it's a thing.
Teacher:	Here's another word: *pencil*. Is *pencil* a noun?
Students:	Yes.
Teacher:	How do you know it's a noun?
Students:	Because it's a thing.
Teacher:	Here's a third word: *grab*. Grab is not a person, place, or thing. *Grab* is an action. Therefore, *grab* is not a noun. What about *speak*? Is *speak* a noun?
Students:	No.
Teacher:	Why not?
Students:	Because it's not a person, place, or thing.

In explicit instruction, there's no student exploration or guessing involved. You tell the students what they're learning, you do it directly and explicitly with a brisk pace of presentation, and if a student makes a mistake, you instantly correct that mistake in a direct and explicit fashion. The brisk pace of this instructional routine serves two important purposes: It engages students (they do something physical and must pay attention to keep up), and it saves you time. In a busy school day full of crowded schedules and numerous disruptions, direct and explicit instruction allows you to get your teaching in and helps ensure that your students are learning.

Here's what an instructional routine might sound like during a lesson that introduces adjectives. Assume that *adjective* and its definition (expressed in kid-friendly language) are already written on a whiteboard, smartboard, or easel paper.

Teacher:	I have a new part of speech to share with you today. Today we will learn what an adjective is. Say the word.
Students:	Adjective.
Teacher:	Tyshel, say the word.
Tyshel:	Adjective.
Teacher:	An adjective is a word that describes a noun. Everyone, what is an adjective?
Students:	A word that describes a noun.
Teacher:	Listen to this sentence: "There is an empty house on our street." *Empty* is an adjective. It's a word that describes a noun. *Empty* describes the noun *house*. What part of speech is *empty*?
Some Students:	An adjective!
Other Students:	A noun! [Others who are unsure sit without speaking.]
Teacher:	*Empty* describes *house*, and *house* is a noun. *Empty* is an adjective. Everyone, what is *empty*?
Students:	An adjective.
Teacher:	What is *empty*, John?
John:	It's an adjective.
Teacher:	Correct! And why is it an adjective?
John:	It describes a noun. Like *house*.
Teacher:	Good! Now tell me, is the word *blue* an adjective? Can *blue* describe a noun like *eyes*, *shirt*, or *whale*?
Students:	Yes.

The routine is short, sweet, and powerful. Remember to keep your pace of instruction brisk. Once you get good at remembering the routine, you can effectively introduce any part of speech in five minutes or less. You'll want to quickly move from your initial teaching to guided practice of the concept, such as identifying adjectives in a sentence. If you need or want to use a worksheet that explicitly helps your students understand what an adjective is and practice its identification, then go for it. However, quickly move from that to the application of the skill, such as using adjectives during the writing of complete sentences.

It's a good idea to learn the routine and follow it rather faithfully for your first forays into this type of instruction. Thereafter, you can create your own pattern as long as you follow the basic structure and principles.

You can also supplement the routine with a bit of rhyme and rhythm. Motion, music, and rhythm are effective tools for teaching information that needs to be stored permanently in memory, so add a bit of chanting to your explicit instruction routine. I'm not talking about the Benedictine monks' type of chanting but rather rhythmic and energetic little verses such as these:

> A noun is a naming word: a person, place, or thing.
> A verb is a doing word, like *hop*, *jump*, or *sing*.

Social and Cooperative Learning

Once you've directly taught a concept to students, you'll want to give the kids multiple opportunities to fully understand or master the concept. Instead of using worksheets for my guided practice, I like to use think-pair-share, either orally or written, and response cards (discussed later in this chapter). Think-pair-share is a great activity for grammar instruction because it's social (i.e., fun for kids), it maximizes student engagement time, and it helps spread the information around to those who may not know it at first. Let's consider think-pair-share and the concept of plural nouns as our first example.

Think-Pair-Share Modeling and Practice. After introducing the concept of a plural noun with direct and explicit instruction, I model how I generate examples of plural nouns. First, I simply look around the room and name nouns: *desks*, *globes*, *finger*, *hands*. Next, I pick a topic, such as farm, and model my thinking: I stand quietly for five seconds, look up at the ceiling, and say, "Hmm." Then, I generate a bunch of nouns associated with the topic, such as *chickens*, *eggs*, *feathers*, *horses*, and *hay*. Finally, I have the students brainstorm examples. When I allow them to do this orally and then give them a chance to share, the routine sounds something like this:

Teacher: You know that plural nouns name more than one person, place, or thing. I've already given you examples: *farms*, *buildings*, *singers*, *nostrils*, and *fingers*. Your challenge is to come up with as many plural nouns as you can. Don't raise your hands yet! For the next seven seconds, I want you to look around the room and find examples of plural nouns, like *desks*. Store them in your brain and get ready to recall them when the seven seconds is up. [Nick raises his hand.] Do you have a question, Nick?

Nick: No, I've got a plural noun.

Teacher:	Remember, don't raise your hand yet! I want you to *think* about plural nouns. I'll give you seven seconds. At the end of the seven seconds, I'll say, "Beep!" So, start looking! [mentally counts to 7] Beep! Wow! I love seeing all of these hands, but I'm not going to call on you just yet. [Students groan.] It's all good. I want you to share with your buddies first. I'll set my timer for one minute. You have one minute to share. [Buddy pairs gather and share, and the timer goes off one minute later.] OK, who has a plural noun to share with the group? Brian?
Brian:	*Books.*
Teacher:	Correct. Let's hear from Kaitlynn next.
Kaitlynn:	A bunch of chairs.
Teacher:	Yes! Kaitlynn, what part of speech is *chairs?*
Kaitlynn:	Um, a noun?
Teacher:	It's a special kind of noun called a...
Kaitlynn:	Plural noun!
Teacher:	Correct, it's a plural noun. It names more than one person, place, or thing. OK, Morgan! Tell me a plural noun.

If you're going to regularly run think-pair-share routines, I suggest you create two lists of pairing options. One is a list of teacher-created pairs. This list matches students who complement each other. Perhaps you pair one student with a bit more cognitive ability with another who has slightly less ability, or maybe you pair one student who can stay on task with another who has less ability to focus, and so forth. Another list is buddy pairs created by the kids. This list gives the kids choice and allows them to work with friends. Most of the time, I'll tell the students to "pair up in your teacher pairs," the pairs that I've created. Every now and again, though, at random intervals, I'll tell the kids to "pair up with your buddy."

Power Writing. Oral brainstorming addresses the speaking end of the Common Core. It's a good place to begin learning brainstorming routines because it's one step removed from the more difficult task of written brainstorming. After you do a number of oral brainstorms, move into written ones. During a written brainstorm, instead of just saying plural nouns, the students think for five or seven seconds and then write as many plural nouns as they can in two or three minutes. You'll need to adjust the length given for writing based on the age and abilities of your students. If you have a classroom of high-ability kids, one minute for written brainstorming may be enough. Struggling writers may need two or three minutes.

Before the students write, I encourage them to spell the words with as many correct letters as possible. They can do this by zapping out the sounds of the words and applying the spelling rules and patterns that they've learned in spelling (more on this in Chapters 5 and 7). I don't, however, have the students correct their spelling. The task here is grammar, not spelling.

I frequently use a timer in these types of activities because it frees me to circulate among the writers. As I circulate, I try to nip incorrect answers in the bud and then reteach. Practice makes permanent, so do everything you can to ensure that your students are practicing correctly. When the timer beeps at the end of the thinking and writing, I reset it and then ask the kids to buddy share for two minutes. As the pairs share, I meander through the room and monitor responses, listening to hear if the kids are on task and giving correct answers.

I call these intense two- or three-minute sessions of thinking and writing Power Writing. It's a thinking and writing thunderstorm—boom! As the students write past tense verbs, adjectives, or whatever else, I praise them for their efforts. My past and present students, kindergarten to fifth grade, love to do this type of brainstorming, writing, and sharing. Why? They're eager to come up with ideas on their own and show off their many examples. I, of course, am eager to say, "Wow, your brain must be supercharged! I see that you've written 10 plural nouns!"

During the sharing part of this activity, you can crank up the engagement by drawing student names randomly from a stack of index cards. No student is allowed to raise his or her hand; you simply draw a card. Whoever is picked reads his or her brainstorm list aloud. If the list is long, have the student read only part of the list aloud. Called random reporter, this technique is based on a more complex management technique that I learned when I became certified to teach PowerTeaching (from the Success for All Foundation). I like the concept of random reporter for a number of reasons. First, I don't have to remember which students I've called on because the cards help ensure that all students have an equal chance. Second, and more importantly, random reporter makes all students accountable, especially the ones who are prone to daydreaming or laziness. Students can't sit back and tune out while others do all the work. Finally, using index cards allows me to set a limit on the number of students who will share if we're running out of time. For example, I might say, "We only have a couple of minutes left, so I'm going to pick five cards and then move on." If a student is disappointed because he or she didn't get called on to share, well, it's not my fault. Blame it on the cards!

Whole-Group Physical Response

Whole-group physical response is an engaging way of practicing and refining conceptual knowledge. After I've introduced the term *plural nouns* via direct and explicit instruction, and after the kids have generated examples via oral and written brainstorming and think-pair-share activities, I use whole-group physical response activities to practice one more time.

Thumbs-Up/Thumbs-Down. At its most basic level, whole-group response might be a simple thumbs-up or thumbs-down. For example, I can put a list of words on the board, such as *shoes, airplane, chairs, teachers, pencil, eat, rabbits,* and *Burger King*. After modeling thumbs-up for plural nouns (e.g., *shoes*) and thumbs-down for anything else (e.g., *airplane*), I ask the class to respond with thumbs-up or thumbs-down after I read each word.

One way to determine whether your students have mastered a grammar concept is to quickly present a number of trials, asking for seven or eight responses in a row. Just like random reporter, a whole-group physical response like thumbs-up/thumbs-down engages every student. Everyone has to think and move his or her thumb. Most importantly, it allows you to instantly assess your group and determine who has mastered the skill, who's a bit shaky, and who's completely clueless. Students who instantly and correctly respond have mastered the skill, students who respond slowly but correctly have mastered the skill but need more processing time, students who make some errors either lack confidence or need more practice (or both), and students who respond quickly but incorrectly most or all of the time (or look to the "smart" kid before they hoist their thumbs) don't know what they're doing and need a strong dose of reteaching.

Another way to determine student mastery is to ask students about their thinking. It's important to know why someone is showing you thumbs-up or thumbs-down. In this example, you might ask, "Why do you think *shoes* is a plural noun?" or "If *airplane* isn't a plural noun, then what is it?" Questions like these help you identify which students truly know the material, which have partially mastered it, and which are either guessing correctly (they've got a 50/50 chance, after all) or looking around at others and simply copying the answer. A student who has mastered the concept of plural nouns should be able to quickly reply, "Because there's more than one shoe," or "*Airplane* is a singular noun." If you find that your students can't quickly and correctly answer the probing questions you ask, take the time to reteach the concept.

Response Cards. Like thumbs-up/thumbs-down, response cards engage all students and give them opportunities to actively demonstrate their understanding of a concept or skill. A more sophisticated form of whole-class response than thumbs-up/thumbs-down, a response card is a coded card that allows each student to respond with a physical response. In other words, you ask a question, and the students answer with their cards.

There's more than one road to Rome, and there's more than one type of response card. Response cards can take the form of a simple double-sided green and red card, a triangle-shaped card, or even a double-sided rectangle that allows for four answers. The cards can display either generic symbols (e.g., 1, 2, 3, 4; a, b, c, d) or the actual words of the concepts you're teaching (e.g., *plural, singular, common, proper*). For younger students in grades 1–3, I suggest you use words. Don't make young students try to remember that 1 = noun and 2 = verb. For older students, however, one card with numbers or letters can be used in the service of many concepts, such as 1 = noun, 2 = verb, and 3 = adjective, or 1 = past tense, 2 = present tense, and 3 = future tense.

As with many concepts, it's easier to give an example than to use a lot of words to describe these cards. Figures 2.3 and 2.4 show examples, beginning with a simple two-answer version and then a more complex three-answer version.

There are a few things to keep in mind as you use response cards. First, be sure to model responses so the students understand how the cards are to be used. Younger students can be confused initially about

---

Figure 2.3. Sample Two-Answer Response Card

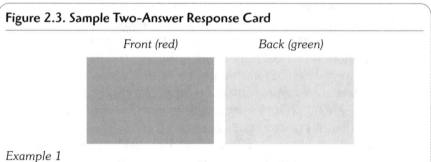

| Front (red) | Back (green) |

Example 1

Teacher: Everyone has a response card. Show me the green side. Good! Now show me the red side. OK! We're going to play a little game called Is It a Sentence? In this game, I'm going to show you a group of words. If the words form a complete sentence, hold up the green side of your card. Green means, "Yes, it is a sentence." If you don't see a sentence, hold up the red side. Red means, "No, it is not a sentence." Remember, a sentence is a group of words that expresses a complete idea. What is a sentence?

(continued)

Figure 2.3. Sample Two-Answer Response Card (*continued*)

Students: A group of words that expresses a complete idea.

Teacher: Right. A sentence always tells you that a person, place, or thing is being or doing something. OK, here's your first one. Is this a sentence, yes or no? [holds up a strip: "The hungry lion chased the deer."] Think in your head: Is there a person, place, or thing in this sentence, and is that person, place, or thing doing something?

Students: [They show the green side of the card.]

Teacher: You got it! That's a sentence. A thing, "the hungry lion," did something, "chased the deer." All right, here's another one. Is this a sentence, yes or no? [holds up a strip: "My cat Buster"]

Students: [They show the red side of the card.]

Teacher: Correct! This isn't a sentence. There's a thing, "my cat Buster," but Buster isn't doing anything. In your heads, think of an ending that will make this phrase a complete sentence. Ready, think. Don't raise your hands yet! [waits a few seconds] OK, who can make this phrase a complete sentence?

Elaine: My cat Buster is running around the house.

Teacher: Great! Anybody else?

Aaron: My cat Buster is eating pizza.

Teacher: Funny! OK, Elaine and Aaron gave our subject, Buster, something to do. Now we have something, my cat Buster, doing something, running around the house or eating a pizza. OK, let's try another one. [The lesson continues.]

Example 2

Teacher: I'm going to show a list of words, and then I'll point to each word. If the word is a noun, show me the green side of your card. Green means noun. If the word is a verb, show me the red side. Red means verb. Here's the first word [points to *table*].

Students: [They show the green side of the card.]

Teacher: Correct, *table* is a noun. Here's the next word [points to *fly*].

Students: [Some show red, some show green, and others look confused.]

Teacher: Brianna, you're showing me green. Why do you think *fly* is a noun?

Brianna: It's an insect, you know, like a fly that buzzes around you.

Teacher: Excellent. *Fly* is a noun. But wait, Jay, don't turn yours to green. You had red. Did you make a mistake, or were you thinking something else?

Jay: Well, I was thinking *fly* like you fly in an airplane. *Fly* is like something you do. It's not a noun. I think *fly* is a verb.

Teacher: This may sound crazy, but you're both right. *Fly* can be either a noun or a verb. It depends on how you use it in a sentence!

Figure 2.4. Sample Three-Answer Response Card

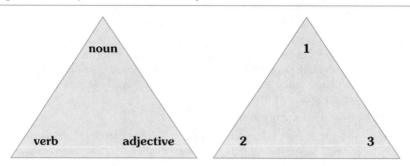

Example 1

Teacher: I'm going to show a list of words. I'll point to each word and say the word. If the word is a noun, pinch the word *noun* on your card. If the word is a verb, pinch the word *verb*. And if the word is an adjective, pinch the word *adjective*. Remember, don't show your pinch until I count up and show you three fingers. Here's the first word: *table*. [waits and then counts silently by holding up first one, then two, and then three fingers]

Students: [They pinch *noun*.]

Teacher: Correct, *table* is a noun. Here's the next word: *eat*.

Students: [They pinch *verb*.]

Teacher: Correct, *eat* is a verb. Here's the next word: *fly*.

Students: [Some pinch *noun*, some pinch *verb*, and others look confused.]

Teacher: Brianna, you're pinching *noun*. Why do you think *fly* is a noun?

Brianna: It's an insect, you know, like a fly that buzzes around you.

Teacher: Excellent. *Fly* is a noun. But wait, Jay, don't change your answer. You're pinching *verb*. Did you make a mistake, or were you thinking something else?

Jay: Well, I was thinking like you fly in an airplane.

Example 2

Teacher: On the smartboard, you see that 1 on your pinch card equals past tense, 2 equals present tense, and 3 equals future tense. I'm going to show you a sentence on the smartboard. If the sentence is in the past tense, pinch number 1. If the sentence is in the present tense, pinch number 2. And if the sentence is in the future tense, pinch number 3. Let's review. Pinch the number for a past tense sentence.

Students: [They pinch 1.]

Teacher: Good. Show me the pinch for future tense.

Students: [They pinch 3.]

(continued)

> **Figure 2.4. Sample Three-Answer Response Card (*continued*)**
>
> Teacher: Correct! OK, I think you know what you're doing. Here's the first sentence: "Tomorrow I will go swimming."
>
> Students: [They pinch 3.]
>
> Teacher: Correct! Brianna, how did you know that sentence was in the future tense?
>
> Brianna: Because you're going swimming tomorrow.
>
> Teacher: Brianna, you are right on the nose! OK, here's the second sentence: "The family went to Florida on vacation." [The lesson continues.]

what part of the card they're supposed to pinch. Match the difficulty of the card to the age of the students. Red and green double-sided cards go to kindergartners and first graders. Second and third graders can handle the triangular cards if words are used instead of symbols. Reserve symbols and four-answer cards for the oldest kids.

It's also important to model how students should display the cards. Because they're prone to waving their cards wildly about with outstretched arms, I model how to hold a card calmly in front of me, at chest or chin level with the number or letters facing the teacher. Then, I have the kids practice this. First, we simply practice the behavior. Then, we practice the behavior using easy examples of the content. Only then do we move on to more difficult content. I've found that when my students have difficulty managing their response behaviors, it's typically because I haven't adequately modeled the behavior and had the kids practice it. You'd think that after all my years of teaching, I'd learn to always model, practice, and look for mastery. However, I get impatient and tired, and this leads to sloppy teaching. When this happens, I typically pay for it with poor student performance. Luckily, teaching is a forgiving profession. I know I can always go back and reteach, model, and provide more opportunities for practice.

You should provide clear instruction about when the students are to show their cards. After asking a question or showing a visual prompt, give the kids three or four seconds of think time. During this time, they should not show their cards. After think time, give a snap or a verbal prompt, such as, "Show me," or "Go!" This is the signal for everyone to simultaneously show his or her card to the teacher. You can also silently count to 3 by holding up your fingers. Of course, you can be looser about this and simply have the kids respond as the answer occurs to them. However, giving think time and having everyone show their cards at the same time really challenges the kids to think, it gives slow-processing students a chance to respond at the same time as the fast processors, and because there is little time to look around the room prior to making a decision, it gives you a better indication of who has and hasn't mastered the concept.

Speaking of looking around the room, don't be concerned if some students first look around to see what the majority of the class is showing before they give their response. Some kids want to slyly hedge their bets. Others lack confidence in their answers and are prone to following the majority, even when the majority is wrong. Still others don't know the answer and need to look to others for an answer. Although some teachers might view this as cheating, I prefer to see it as all the kids participating and engaging in the activity. Responding as a group offers opportunities to talk to kids about when it is appropriate to change an answer or how it's OK to be different if you really think you're right. It also gives you the opportunity to quickly assess the class and then guide and reteach those who don't know the skill or concept.

Vocabulary Card Sorts. A vocabulary card sort is another whole-class physical response activity. In this instance, you'll use vocabulary words from an anthology story to review grammar concepts. If you want to learn about word sorts in depth, jump ahead to Chapter 3 and read through the section entitled "Vocabulary Word Sorts." Take your time; I'll check my e-mail and pour a cup of coffee while you're gone. Otherwise, it's enough to know that vocabulary word sorts make use of the numerous word cards that your students will accumulate after weeks of vocabulary instruction.

For this example, let's imagine that your students have the following vocabulary words written on index cards and collectively stored in a small ziplock bag:

ache	*dim*	*solar system*
admire	*entertainment*	*splendid*
bother	*object*	*telescope*
concentrate	*passion*	

If nouns are the current focus of your grammar instruction, have your students pull their vocabulary cards from their bags and sort them into two piles: words that are nouns and words that are not nouns. You can have the kids work in groups of two or three if you like.

My guess is that it'll be relatively easy for your students to identify *object*, *solar system*, and *telescope* as nouns. Those words are concrete; it's easy to form a visual image of each as a specific place or thing. It will probably be more challenging for them to identify *ache, entertainment,* and *passion* as nouns. A challenge like this, however, provides an opportunity for students to learn and calls on you to really guide and teach. *Ache* functions as both a noun and a verb, and *passion* provides you with an opportunity to expand their understanding of a noun to an idea or feeling.

Later in the year, after you've introduced verbs and adjectives, you can do a word sort with the same words, only this time you'll have your students sort the words into three piles: nouns, verbs, and adjectives. Once they've sorted the words, challenge them to use them in complete sentences, either orally or in writing. This type of activity allows typical students to generate basic sentences, such as "I saw the moon in my telescope," and brighter students to generate more complex sentences, such as "My dad couldn't concentrate on the dim object because he had a headache."

To organize and manage all of these vocabulary cards and response cards, you may want to store them in manila envelopes or plastic bins. Break out the bins when you have 10 minutes for a quick whole-group grammar lesson and let the kids have fun responding physically. Another organizational option is to give each student a two-pocket folder. Students can place their bags of vocabulary cards and their various response cards into one pocket of their folder. A composition book, a Good Writers' Checklist, and a thin student dictionary can go in the other pocket. I'm getting ahead of myself, however. We'll discuss all of these materials in detail in Chapter 6.

Explicit Modeling and Practice

When it comes time to have your students apply their grammar knowledge by writing complete sentences, model everything that you expect the kids to write. Don't assume that they'll already know how to do a skill or will remember from one month to the next. If you expect them to write a neatly written sentence with a capital letter at the beginning, a period at the end, a noun in the subject, and a verb in the predicate, then you should first stand in front of the class, write a sentence, and discuss what you're doing as you do it. Your modeling might sound something like this:

> Today we'll continue to practice writing complete sentences. Watch as I write a complete sentence. First, I'm going to think about what I want to write. I'm thinking that I'll write the sentence "My uncle likes to work on his truck." I'll say the sentence softly under my breath: "My uncle likes to work on his truck." Now I'm going to write it. [writes] OK, I've written it.

Now I'm going to go back and check my sentence. Watch and listen: Does it have a capital letter at the beginning? Yes. Does it have a period at the end? Yes. Is my writing neat? Yes. Does my sentence tell me about somebody or something doing or being something? Let's see, I have a noun in the subject, "my uncle." That's somebody. Is he doing or being something? In this case, yes, he's doing something: He's working on his truck.

This extended and explicit modeling is necessary while students—our emerging writers—are learning to construct sentences. Once students can fluently write sentences, this level of modeling might be necessary only with the small groups of kids who have not yet reached proficiency, or perhaps you'll need to do just a quick review now and again. In the end, it all depends on the makeup of your class.

Once students are regularly generating solidly constructed written samples, share well-written sentences and paragraphs with the whole class. Project them on the wall with an overhead, show them on a smartboard, write them on a whiteboard or on easel paper—whatever you happen to have on hand. What's important is that you show your students that their peers are capable of reaching the writing goals that you have set out for them. At some point, you may want to have one of the students come up to the board and model writing an excellent sentence. Or, after much modeling of positive comments related to student work, you might want to give students the opportunity to positively critique student work: "Kayla, what did Jeremy do that shows he understands how to write a good sentence?" Kids love to be the teacher, and the students in the classroom will appreciate a chance to observe someone other than you.

There are two important rules for using student work as models:

1. Always ask the student writer for permission to use the work. I usually do this privately before class begins. Most kids are thrilled that you want to show everyone their good work.

2. Always use student work as a positive example. If you need a negative example, create your own sentence to use as the negative example.

Task Analysis and Mastery Learning

My two biggest beefs with basal grammar programs are that grammar skills and authentic writing are rarely connected and that too much information is presented in too short a time frame, thus thwarting a teacher's efforts to get students to mastery level on essential skills. I address the first beef later in this chapter and again in Chapter 6. As for the second beef, we can address it by mapping out a sequence for concept introduction, creating a Writers Think About... poster, and introducing and teaching only one essential skill or concept at a time.

Task analysis and mastery learning are not instructional techniques like direct instruction or explicit modeling. Rather, they're concepts that manifest in your teaching. You bring them alive as you first analyze the grammar sequence of your basal and then teach and review the most essential skills and concepts over and over again. Teaching one important piece, such as how to use quotation marks when writing dialogue, and providing multiple opportunities to practice it allows the majority of your class to master what you're teaching.

Let's use the concept of a complete sentence, often the first concept taught in a core reading program's grammar sequence, to further discuss task analysis and mastery learning. My school's core program, Treasures, defines the concept of a complete sentence as a group of words that tells a complete thought, which is a rather difficult concept for struggling readers and writers to wrap their minds around. In third grade, after presenting a few workbook pages that have students analyze but never write sentences, Treasures moves quickly into three different types of sentences: statements, questions, and commands. Each sentence type is explained via examples and nonexamples (an instructionally effective thing to do), and each can be orally read and heard by the whole class. However, this skill practice is unrelated to real-world speaking and writing. Instead of writing or speaking sentences they construct, students underline sentence parts, fill in blanks, and make corrections to incorrect sentences presented in a workbook. When it comes to writing skills/daily writing prompts, the component of the core program where real writing is actually practiced, the teacher's manual says to have the students write a persuasive paragraph or create an acrostic poem. These activities have little to do with the grammar skill or concept being taught. Rather, they introduce an entirely new and different skill. The end result is the presentation of more information than a third grader can possibly digest, or a teacher, even an extraordinary one, can teach in a week's time.

To rectify the situation, I have my students generate their own spoken and written sentences. I don't heap on a bunch of additional skills, such as teaching them about persuasion and acrostics, and I don't teach the concepts with workbook pages. I simply have the kids generate sentences on their own (with varying degrees of support), first orally and then in writing. As they speak and write, I monitor and guide them to understand the grammar concept that we're currently practicing. In the case of complete sentences, I directly teach what a complete sentence is and personally model the speaking and writing of many examples of each. We collectively discuss why the sentences are complete. Next, the students practice speaking and writing their own complete sentences. We practice identifying examples and nonexamples with response cards, and then the kids practice writing complete sentences again. Each sentence must be short and neatly written with a capital letter at the beginning and a period at the end, and each sentence must tell about someone or something doing or being something. From there, I can weave in instruction on nouns, adjectives, spelling, and mechanics.

When young students first begin to write sentences, I support them with sentence starters, such as "My teacher...," "I love...," "The crazy dog...," and "Do you like...." I also provide topic categories, such as horses, video games, family, sports, and whatever else I know they're interested in. Students who need more support simply use the sentence starters. Others with more ability or creativity say things like, "Mr. Weakland, can I start my sentence with 'My Uncle Ray's old dog...'?" I use informal observation and assessments to ensure that the students have mastered speaking and writing basic sentences before I begin to teach them about exclamations and questions, and I spend almost no time at all on commands. Why? Kids typically don't use commands in their writing. Furthermore, is identifying a sentence as a command an essential skill? For me, that's an easy one: no.

As I said earlier, whenever possible, I downplay or totally ignore grammar topics that are unimportant or trivial, especially for primary-grade learners who are struggling to read and write. I argue that for any subject you teach, be it grammar, science, or math, it's crucial that you discriminate between what is essential and what is merely interesting. The discrimination must, of course, be based on something other than "my opinion versus yours." You'll need to know your scope and sequence, observe and test the depth of knowledge of your students and their capacity for learning and retaining new information, and hold some probing conversations with experienced teachers and administrators in your district.

Once you have a handle on what's basic and essential, I believe you'll have the responsibility to advocate for having kids master it even when state test preparation books and basal programs say struggling students need to move on to topics such as consonance or the correct order of adjectives. Likewise, this argument should be brought to administrators who want their teachers to expose struggling learners to every skill and concept listed in core reading programs. Masterful teachers who care about teaching foundational concepts and skills to all students, even the most struggling ones, must speak truth to power—respectfully, of course!

It's crucial for teachers to jettison nonessential stuff because this is the only way to free up time to write in grades K–5. Simply put, writing takes a lot of time. In my elementary school, we run the Kid Writing program in kindergarten. Even the most accomplished kindergarten writers need at least 10 minutes to think of and then write just one sentence, such as "I am playing with my brother," or "My mom and dad are at the beach." The students who are struggling to learn may take 15–20 minutes to write a solid sentence. As for my third graders, they need at least 20–30 minutes to think of, write, and refine an interesting and well-written five-sentence paragraph. You won't be able to create the time that kids need if you're constantly assigning workbook pages and teaching every "piddly little skill" (as my father would say) mentioned in the basal program and written in the state test prep book. Again, it's about essentials. Becoming a competent writer is an essential skill, and we need to find the time to let beginning writers grow into skilled writers.

I have one last word on mastery: *weaving.* I free grammar and language concepts from the constraints of dedicated grammar time by reviewing and even teaching them during spelling, vocabulary, and comprehension instruction, as well as during extended writing and guided reading time. The Wilson Reading System calls this type of instruction weaving, and I think it's a wonderful word to use. It reminds me that the metaphor for both reading and teaching is a finely woven tapestry, not a collection of spools of thread.

I weave the concept of a complete sentence into October lessons on nouns and December lessons on verbs. I review and sometimes reteach complete sentences (and terms like *question, statement, exclamation, run-on, subject,* and *predicate*) when we have time for extended writing, before the students do independent writing, and sometimes during a guided reading group. It is only through constant weaving, reviewing, and reteaching that my struggling students will master the essential skills of writing.

Formative Assessment: Is It Working?

Assessment is what enables you to know whether your students have mastered the skills and concepts that you've taught them. When it comes to assessing grammar (or any subject), I prefer a combination of formative and summative assessments, with the emphasis on the formative. The beauty of thumbs-up/thumbs-down, response cards, and vocabulary card sorts is that they serve double duty as formative assessments. When you conduct a word sort or ask your students to respond with a response card, you'll instantly know which students have mastered, partially mastered, or failed to master the information that you've presented. Instantaneous assessment is one of the many advantages that a whole-group physical response activity has over a workbook page. There's no need to go back to a written page and spend time checking to see whether the students are correct or incorrect. With an activity like response cards, you instantly see which students identify a complete sentence and which do not, or which ones know the difference between a verb and a noun.

If the majority of your kids bomb the answers or hesitate to show the answers on numerous trials, you'll know that they have yet to master the skill or concept. At this point, stop the activity and go back to reteach and repractice. Remember that practice makes permanent, so don't allow the kids to practice giving wrong answers trial after trial. If students learn incorrect information, you'll spend a lot of time and energy getting them to unlearn the incorrect stuff (a difficult thing to do) and relearn correctly.

Finally, don't pass up the opportunity to translate some of this informally gathered physical response information into written information that you can use to guide your future instruction. My mom is a big advocate of using labels and a clipboard to accomplish this feat. Let's say you've given your 25 fourth graders triangular pinch cards with *past*, *present*, or *future* written in each corner. You show them sentences like "Last night I went to the mall," "She will wash the dishes if you ask her," and "I love to write," and after each sentence, you ask them to pinch the appropriate tense. As you observe your students responding, you notice that Cassandra, Emily, Logan, and Tyler consistently give the wrong response. You also notice that Mark never pinches until he looks to see what David is pinching, and you know that Mark is a struggling learner, whereas David picks up things quickly.

If you have a clipboard with blank labels on it, simply title one of the labels "Verb Tense," write in the date, and list Cassandra, Emily, Logan, Tyler, and Mark's names. At the end of the day, when you have a minute to breathe, peel off the label and slap it on a sheet or in your lesson plan book. You might have another label from another day that says, "Capitals and periods, 11/14/13, Mark." This label reminds you that you recently tagged Mark for not using capitals and periods. Labels are easy to use, cheap to buy, and give you ongoing information that you can use to plan future instruction. Let's say you're planning to have your 20 students write complete sentences in the future tense. While they're doing that, you can pull Cassandra, Emily, Logan, Tyler, and Mark aside and reteach them how to determine the tense of a sentence.

Make It So

Many styles of grammar instruction are possible within a core reading program. On one end of the spectrum sits an instructivist style. This type of instruction champions the direct and explicit teaching of grammar and mechanics, often in short, isolated bursts and repetitive doses. On the other end of the spectrum sits the constructivist style, best represented by the writers' workshop model. This type of instruction, put forth by writers such as Graves (1994) and Calkins (1994), teaches grammar through writing.

The Common Core State Standards affirm the explicit teaching of grammar, as do most core reading programs. Rather than sticking to one style of instruction or another, though, I suggest a middle-ground approach that blends the two. This approach involves, as you've probably guessed, some direct instruction and teaching of skills in isolation and some constructivist teaching of grammar through writing. Teach your students grammar concepts and skills by using short bursts of instruction that's direct, laced with immediate corrective feedback, and based on what students have already learned and mastered. Then, as soon as possible, link these specific skills to authentic speaking and writing tasks. Connect your grammar and mechanics instruction to speaking, writing, and reading, and you'll be staying true to the standards, true to your district's wish to use a basal program, and true to your own desire to bring more effective and engaging practice to the students you teach.

In a busy day with too much to do, grammar instruction may get the short end of the instructional stick, and sometimes it's left out of the mix altogether. The good news is that by focusing on speaking, writing, essential content, and teaching chops, you can easily strengthen and deepen your grammar instruction, even when you don't have the luxury of time. Combining content and instruction in a masterful way will certainly increase the chance that your students will use grammar skills successfully as they construct an answer to a test question, compose a paragraph that describes their favorite hobby, or spontaneously pen you a letter that begins, "Dear Mr. Flubwidget, thank you for being such a wonderful teacher!"

CHAPTER 3

Supercharged Vocabulary Instruction

. . . .
You will need...
. . . .

- Your teacher's manual with its lists of vocabulary words
- Anthology stories from your core reading program
- Small index cards or 2" × 3" cards cut from card stock

. . . .
You will...
. . . .

- Give vocabulary instruction an extra 5–10 minutes on specific days
- Refrain from using most vocabulary worksheets and practice book pages
- Sort your list of vocabulary words into Tier I, Tier II, and Tier III words
- Pick a shorter, more focused list of words
- Make sure all words are base words
- Use direct instruction to introduce the words
- Use the vocabulary card method to teach the words more deeply
- Formatively assess your students over time

Vocabulary instruction is another place to ease into core program changes. Through the use of a few simple routines, you can teach scores of vocabulary words over time and actually have the words stick in the minds of your students to the point where they can use the words in writing and speaking long after they were introduced.

To supercharge your vocabulary instruction, you don't need to make major changes to your program or schedule. Minor changes will include adding a few new materials, decreasing the number of worksheets and practice book pages you assign, and adding 5–10 minutes to your vocabulary instruction on specific days. The biggest change involves how you instruct your large group.

In this chapter, we'll begin with a look at why vocabulary instruction is important and then segue into a method for picking the most appropriate vocabulary words. Next, we'll move on to ways of instructing, also known as teaching chops. Specifically, we'll look at how you can make whole-group instruction more effective and engaging through the use of modeling, direct instruction, and whole-group physical responses. We'll dive deeply into direct and explicit instruction and thoroughly discuss the vocabulary card method, an instructional routine that makes use of numerous teaching chops. The chapter wraps up with ways to use formative assessment to increase the effectiveness of your instruction.

The Importance of Vocabulary Instruction

To be successful in school, students must know the meanings of many words. More specifically, vocabulary knowledge is crucial if a child (or adult) is going to comprehend the meaning of any given word, sentence, paragraph, or story (Nation, 2008). Also, reading comprehension improves when vocabulary instruction is present (Adlof, Perfetti, & Catts, 2011; Graves & Watts-Taffe, 2002). Thus, vocabulary acquisition is a crucial component of learning to read, and teachers must teach word meanings if they want to improve their students' comprehension.

Vocabulary acquisition is especially important for at-risk students. Why? When compared with the general school population, at-risk students are less likely to hear a wide variety of words used in their homes and are more likely to have smaller vocabularies and read fewer words in context (Graves & Watts-Taffe, 2002). In addition, Stahl and Shiel (1992/1999) have said that 300–400 word meanings can be taught with direct instruction during a typical school year. Therefore, if you're teaching at-risk students, the 300–400 words you teach will be a significant portion of the total number of words these students will learn that year.

In addition to direct teaching, vocabulary acquisition occurs naturally as students actively process the words they hear (listening), say (speaking), and see (reading). In reading, most vocabulary is gained during periods of extended reading in connected text (Graves & Watts-Taffe, 2002). Typically this interaction with vocabulary words occurs during independent and guided reading time. However, most basal reading programs don't give students the opportunity to read for long periods of time from a variety of books on their instructional and independent reading levels, and some families don't promote reading at home. Thus, it's possible that many students don't encounter a wide range of words.

Core reading program problems that pertain to vocabulary extend beyond a lack of reading time in extended texts and a lack of reading materials. Basal vocabulary routines are ineffective for a number of reasons, including initial instruction that's not direct and explicit enough, a lack of opportunities for students to review and use vocabulary words over time, and word selection that's not based on student needs specific to your classroom (Dewitz & Jones, 2013). With a lack of effective instructional routines in the teacher's manual and a dearth of extended reading opportunities in the basal-centered classroom, it's especially important that teachers take it upon themselves to supercharge their vocabulary instruction. So, let's consider some new ways to introduce, practice, and cumulatively review vocabulary words so students actually remember the meanings of most, if not all, of the words and begin to use them when speaking and writing.

Scope: What Vocabulary to Teach

Typically, when you open a teacher's manual to any lesson for any grade, you see materials, supplemental books, activities, scripts, and workbook pages that address phonemic awareness, phonics, fluency, vocabulary, and all manner of comprehension skills and strategies. In core reading programs, the big ideas of reading, such as vocabulary, are incorporated into the foundational design of the program. That being said, it's not enough that the big idea of vocabulary is simply mentioned in your manual, and it's not enough that the basal gives you ready-made lists of vocabulary words and a generic routine of how to present the words to the students.

Teaching is the art of combining instructional technique with content knowledge, so let's dig a little deeper into vocabulary content knowledge before we look at instructional technique. We'll start by examining the weekly word list.

Word Selection

You don't need to teach *every* vocabulary word presented in the teacher's manual. Conversely, you may want to add a few words to the weekly list. To determine which words to keep, subtract, or add, it's helpful to think of vocabulary words in terms of three categories.

In their classic work on vocabulary, Beck, McKeown, and Kucan (2002) categorize vocabulary words via a three-tiered system. Tier I words are basic words, such as *happy*, *dangerous*, and *mountain*. These words are familiar to students and are best handled through conversation. They don't need to be taught directly by a teacher.

Tier II includes words that might be less familiar but that readers and speakers will see, hear, and have the opportunity to use often. Once mastered, the use of Tier II vocabulary words is a hallmark of a mature speaker, reader, and writer. Recently, my guided reading group was reading Judy Nayer's *The Lost and Found Game*, a guided reading book in Modern Curriculum Press's First Chapters series. While reading a passage, Skyler came upon the word *ancient*. As she attempted to sound out the word, she applied the syllabification rules that she'd been taught: "an-si-ent." Because this "word" was nonsensical, I encouraged her to try to think of a word that made sense and matched the letter sounds. Skyler drew a blank. "The word is *ancient*," I told her. Upon hearing this, Edward immediately piped up: "I know the meaning of *ancient*, Mr. Weakland." "OK, Edward," I replied, "tell Skyler what *ancient* means." "It's what Mr. Weakland is!" Edward said with a smile.

Edward demonstrated his more mature vocabulary by showing his command of the word *ancient*. I'd classify it as Tier II. Tier II words are often called high-frequency or utility words. *Absurd*, *splendid*, *ache*, and *concentrate* are all examples of Tier II words.

Finally, Tier III words are low-frequency words that are typically limited to specific categories or areas of study. *Echolocation*, *isotope*, *theocracy*, and *peninsula* are examples.

I suggest you look through each anthology story's recommended list of vocabulary words and concentrate only on those that are Tier II. You don't need to teach Tier I words, so weed out the ones that most kids already know. You may want to teach an occasional Tier III word or two, but don't get bogged down with them. At the elementary level, you'll have plenty of general academic words to teach. If you're teaching words more deeply, it won't hurt to have fewer words on the list, so don't include Tier III words in your vocabulary lists. They're too technical and narrow in their definitions. If some Tier III words are essential for understanding the story, teach the students to use appropriate resources to determine the words' meanings, but don't expect that these words will soon become a part of the students' core vocabulary. It may be helpful to think of Tier III words as extension, enrichment, or even challenge words. You can expose your students to these types of words, but you shouldn't hold an expectation that the majority of your kids will master them.

To give a more concrete example of sorting words into Tier I, Tier II, and Tier III, I offer two vocabulary lists that come from two third-grade anthology stories (from Treasures). Each story title is listed in bold, and the corresponding vocabulary word list follows:

- **Wolf!** by Becky Bloom: ached, admire, bothering, concentrate, dangerous, passion, splendid

- **What's in Store for the Future?**: computers, entertainment, objects, predictions

When I taught these lists of words, I immediately got rid of *dangerous* and *computers*. I consider these to be Tier I words because most students in third grade know them. It's possible that some students might have only a cursory knowledge of *dangerous*. Perhaps with a bit of probing, I would have found that some didn't understand the nuances of the word, but when time is of the essence, I can't afford to teach Tier I words that 95% of the kids already know well.

I don't feel there are any Tier III words in the above lists, so there's nothing to eliminate from a Tier III perspective. This leaves me with a final list of nine words from two stories, all of which I think of as Tier II words: *ached, admire, bothering, concentrate, entertainment, objects, passion, predictions,* and *splendid.*

Base Words

Once you have a list of Tier II words, make it a habit to teach *only* base words. The tendency of some core reading programs is to present vocabulary words that have an ending on the base word. I think the basal programs do this because these are the words that actually appear in the story. This really irks me!

In the list above, you'll see the word *ached.* The word has limited usage because of its tense. Using the word *ached* as the instructional word, you might be able to ask questions such as, "Have your feet ever ached?" but you can't ask, "Have you ever had a stomachache?" or "Why did the wolf's head ache?" So, just teach the base word: *ache.* Using base words allows you to explore all the various forms and tenses of any vocabulary word. In this case, once you teach *ache,* you can also teach *ached, aching, achy, backache, headache, stomachache,* "Achy Breaky Heart," and so forth.

The same goes for the word *bothering.* If you teach *bother* instead of *bothering,* you can explore all the variations of the base word, including *bothered, bothering, bothers, bothersome,* and *unbothered.* Using base words allows you to draw a word web or concept map more easily. Most basals provide large, preprinted vocabulary cards. If some of these aren't in base word form, it's well worth five minutes of your time to make new cards that show only the base words.

After filtering out Tier I words and changing the remaining words to a base word form, I'm left with the following list of Tier II vocabulary words: *ache, admire, bother, concentrate, entertain, object, passion, predict,* and *splendid.*

Teaching Chops: How to Teach Vocabulary

Direct and Explicit Instruction

What It Isn't. Teacher's manuals often introduce story vocabulary with a routine that goes something like this:

- Hold up a preprinted vocabulary word card.
- Read the manual's definition of the word.
- Read the manual's "word in a sentence" example.
- Ask the manual's question, something like, "What is the opposite of ___?" or "What does ___ mean in this sentence?"

This routine is an ineffective way of introducing vocabulary. Another routine that's even more ineffective looks and sounds something like this:

- Hold up a vocabulary word card.
- Use the word in a sentence.
- Ask the kids, "What does ___ mean?"

Pointing out the words as they arise in the story and then assigning two "fill in the blank" vocabulary worksheets are also less than effective routines.

To strengthen vocabulary instruction, let's get rid of ineffective routines and add an effective teaching chop: direct and explicit instruction, which is both an instructional technique and a routine. It's also the instructional underpinning of reading programs such as SRA's Corrective Reading. In Corrective Reading, direct instruction is one of a number of instructional techniques woven into each scripted lesson. When you open a Corrective Reading teacher's manual, all you have to do is read the script for 45–60 minutes, week after week, month after month.

I must admit that when I first learned about this repetitive and mechanical form of instruction, I would have preferred to stick a fork in my thigh than to teach this way. However, the tight instructional design of Corrective Reading leads to a high degree of student success, especially for struggling readers. Why? Components of the program, such as brisk pacing, instant error correction, and the aforementioned direct instruction, are highly effective teaching techniques in and of themselves. When combined, they work synergistically to produce a powerful effect.

For the purposes of this book, I'm not advocating, or even talking about, using a direct instruction program like Corrective Reading. I'm simply focusing on instruction that directly and explicitly teaches students what they need to learn.

In direct and explicit instruction, there's no student exploration, not much transactional construction, and certainly no guessing involved. You tell the students what they're learning, and you do it directly and explicitly. In its pure form, direct instruction is easy to use, time efficient, and highly effective in getting kids to initially learn basic information. It's a perfect routine for teaching vocabulary words. Perhaps the best way to describe direct instruction is to give you a nonexample first.

Let's say a teacher is planning to teach the meaning of the vocabulary words *enrage* and *tyranny*. Using an anthology story, she draws attention to a sentence and then reads it aloud to the class: "The tax plan <u>enraged</u> the colonists and united them against British <u>tyranny</u>." In nondirect instruction, this teacher might hold up a card with one of the words on it and launch into an instructional technique that I call Can You Guess What I'm Thinking? The student–teacher exchange might sound like this:

Teacher: Who knows what the word *tyranny* means? [Four students raise their hands, and the other 19 sit quietly.] Tywan?

Tywan: It's like someone is always telling you what to do.

Teacher: OK, that's part of it. Who can tell me more? Martin?

Martin: I think... Is it a type of dinosaur?

Teacher: You're thinking of a *Tyrannosaurus rex*. *Tyrannosaurus* and *tyranny* have the same base, so you're on the right track. Let's keep thinking. Does anyone else know what *tyranny* means? [Two kids raise their hands.] Chandrea?

Chandrea: It's like you're mean.

Teacher: Well, that's part of it but not quite. [She scans the room. Students slouch in their seats and try to avoid eye contact.] How about you, Valeria? Do you know what *tyranny* means?

Valeria: Nope.

Teacher: OK, I guess I'll just tell you. *Tyranny* means...

In this teaching scenario, the teacher is off to a good start because she has correctly identified the story's Tier II words, such as *tyranny*. She assumes that her students either don't know anything about the word or that their knowledge is incomplete or erroneous. Therefore, she needs to teach the word's meaning. So far so good. The lesson takes a turn for the worse, however, when the teacher tries to teach the students an unknown word by first asking them what it means. When the questioning strategy doesn't work with the first student (and why would it?), she proceeds to ask other students, over and over again.

In this "guessing game" method of vocabulary instruction, a few knowledgeable and engaged students attempt to guess the meaning of the word. Maybe one of them will hit the jackpot. Meanwhile, the rest of the class is sitting quietly, staring into space, fidgeting, or worse. Of course, the clock is ticking. The teacher has used up two minutes of instructional time, and no one knows what the word means. Multiply these two minutes by five vocabulary words, and we find that this teacher will spend 10 minutes of instructional time on what amounts to a game of 20+ questions. Although a guessing game can be fun for students who know the answer, it isn't an effective way to teach the meaning of a word to those who don't. A more effective way is to teach the meaning directly, without guessing, and in a time-efficient fashion.

What It Is. Here's what an effective direct instruction routine looks like: First, write the word and its definition on a blackboard, smartboard, or poster. Make sure you translate the dictionary language into kid-friendly language. Then, use a script like the one below to teach the meaning of the word. Finally, repeat the process, using a brisk pace of instruction, for the remainder of the five words.

- The teacher says, "Here's a new word: ___. Say it." The students say the word.
- The teacher says, "___ means ___. What does ___ mean?" The students repeat the definition.
- The teacher uses the vocabulary word in a sentence and then asks, "What does that mean?" If the students don't know, the teacher quickly and directly supplies the answer and has the students repeat it.
- The teacher provides another example and asks, "What does that mean?" The teacher follows up with a request for clarification.
- The teacher gives a nonexample.

Here's what the script will sound like using the word *tyranny*:

Teacher: The vocabulary word is *tyranny*. Say it.
Students: Tyranny.

Teacher:	John, you say the word.
John:	Tyranny.
Teacher:	Tyranny is exercising total power over others in cruel and unjust ways. Everyone, what does *tyranny* mean?
Students:	Exercising total power over others in cruel and unjust ways.
Teacher:	Say it again.
Students:	Exercising total power over others in cruel and unjust ways.
Teacher:	Listen to this sentence: "The students dreamed of escaping the <u>tyranny</u> of their teacher." Use the definition and tell me what *tyranny* means. [No one responds.] Tyranny is exercising total power over others in cruel and unjust ways. Everyone, what does *tyranny* mean?
Students:	Exercising total power over others in cruel and unjust ways.
Teacher:	Listen to this sentence: "The students dreamed of escaping the <u>tyranny</u> of their teacher." Use the definition and tell me what *tyranny* means.
Suzy:	The teacher was cruel and unjust. She had total power.
Teacher:	You used the definition of *tyranny* well. Great answer. Everybody, can a mean and demanding coach exercise tyranny over her players?
Students:	Yes.
Teacher:	Good! That's because *tyranny* means…
Students:	Exercising total power over others in cruel and unjust ways.
Teacher:	Do you think I'm tyrannical? Is my classroom a tyranny?
Students:	Yes!
Teacher:	Why?
John:	Because you have total power over us.
Suzy:	No, you're not cruel and unjust.
Teacher:	So, this room isn't a tyranny?
Suzy:	I don't think so.
Teacher:	Can a baby exercise tyranny over its mother?
Suzy:	No, because a baby isn't cruel and unjust. It doesn't have total power.
Kaitlynn:	My little sister acts like she has total power.

The routine is short, sweet, and powerful. Remember to keep your pace of instruction brisk. Once you get good at remembering the script, you'll be able to effectively introduce five to seven new words in about 10 minutes.

Notice that I said *introduce* the new words. To truly master the definition and usage of any new vocabulary word, students need many exposures to the word and time to process it deeply. Background knowledge, attention to the task, the ability to remember, and motivation to learn are just a few factors that impact how many encounters are needed to memorize and understand a word and its meaning. Because of these many variables, it's difficult to give the definitive number of repetitions that it takes until a student learns a new word, and the number of necessary exposures varies according to the abilities of each student. Estimates in the literature vary from six to 20 exposures, but at least 10 is the number that I'm most familiar with (Webb, 2007).

Regardless of the actual number, you must assume that your students will need a lot of exposures to each word, certainly more than the three that are gained when you first introduce it, point it out in the story, and review it before the test. This means you'll need more than just direct instruction. You'll need the vocabulary card method! This method is one way to create opportunities for exposure and deep processing and to teach, assess, and review vocabulary words.

The Vocabulary Card Method: Many Teaching Chops, One Method

If you're currently using a teaching routine that asks students to memorize vocabulary words for a week, take a test on them, and then never use those words again (because you're moving on to a new story and a new set of words), I think you should put that routine on a high shelf and quickly walk away. My suggestion is that you replace it with a card-based routine that allows students to regularly interact, week after week, with an ever-increasing number of words. As students repeatedly encounter vocabulary words over a long period of time, they'll learn and remember the meanings of dozens of words. More importantly, they'll have the chance to develop working vocabularies. That is, they'll be more likely to use a variety of nuanced words when they speak and write, and they'll be more likely to understand these words when they hear them in conversations and read them in a book.

The vocabulary card method is an instructional routine that my mother introduced to me two decades ago, although over the years, I've tweaked it in various ways. The fourth and fifth graders in my learning support room loved this regularly occurring activity, and my current crop of third-grade regular education students enjoy it, too.

The vocabulary card method is a number of well-researched and highly effective instructional techniques rolled into one. In the method, you'll find direct and explicit instruction, whole-group physical response, task analysis and mastery learning, explicit modeling and practice, and formative assessment. Add a think-pair-share routine (from the social and cooperative learning category), and you will have covered every one of the six teaching chops. The vocabulary card method is like the amazing Ginzu knife of the 1970s: It slices, dices, chops, and minces!

At first, you'll use the vocabulary list from your basal's anthology story. (Remember that you've already modified this list to include only Tier II base words.) Later, you can expand the method to include words from your guided reading books. If you like, you can even include words from other subject areas, such as science and social studies.

Remember, this method takes the place of vocabulary activities that are outlined and scripted in your teacher's manual. More importantly, it takes the place of vocabulary worksheets and practice book pages. Thus, do *not* assign the worksheets and practice book pages that you assigned to students in past years! You must create time to do the vocabulary card method, and one way to free up time is to jettison workbook pages and less than effective manual activities. You'll also need time to choose the most appropriate words. Do this during your planning time rather than spending time correcting worksheets and practice book pages.

The vocabulary card method is an effective way to teach vocabulary words because it teaches vocabulary words to mastery by giving students repeated opportunities to see, say, and use the words; it's visual, verbal, and kinesthetic; and it provides multiple opportunities for students to deeply process the meanings of the words. This deep processing, in which students concentrate on word meanings and the words' relationships to one another, is extremely important.

Write It, Draw It, Bag It. First, chose your five or six vocabulary words for the week. Teach them using the direct instruction routine described previously. Make sure the definitions are kid friendly. Basals often do the work for you and give easily digestible definitions, but watch out for definitions that are too wordy or complex or contain words that demand additional definitions.

Next, have the kids write each word on a 2" × 3" index card. Then, ask them to copy your corresponding kid-friendly definition onto the back of each card. The students should leave enough room to include a small picture that illustrates the definition. These pictures, illustrating some of the more difficult words, can be drawn later in the week, perhaps on day 2 or 3 of your instructional sequence.

A picture is especially important when the vocabulary word is an abstract one like *astonish* or *tyranny*. When a student connects the word to a visual image, the abstract is made more concrete. Thus, a student may draw a surprised-looking face for *astonish* or a mean-looking king for *tyranny*. An additional benefit comes from the act of drawing. The vocabulary card method is multimodal instruction (which helps build more neural pathways) that includes writing, drawing, physically manipulating, and orally reading the cards.

When your students draw pictures, some of them will want to go all Michelangelo or Georgia O'Keeffe on you. To use your instructional time more efficiently, model stick figure drawings and set a time limit for each illustration. Likewise, you may need to offer suggestions for an illustration. The kids only need of couple of minutes to draw a simple picture on each card. The main focus should be on a simple visual that conveys the meaning of the word.

Cards at various stages of completion (word, definition, simple drawing) are placed in a ziplock bag with the student's name on it. These bags are then placed into the student's reading folder, a common bin, or some other easily accessible place.

Read, Sort, and Assess. In the future, the kids will pull out their cards and practice reading, arranging, and sorting their words. At first, you'll need to repeatedly model and practice the process (see value 4: teaching chops [instructional expertise].) Students are expected to take out their cards, quietly read each word, turn over the card, study the picture, and quietly read the definition. Practice this during a specified time in whole-group instruction.

Also teach the kids, through modeling and guided practice, how to order the words alphabetically and conduct various types of word sorts, such as sorting the cards into piles based on the number of syllables, parts of speech, and story theme. Later, after your guided reading groups are up and running and you've thoroughly taught your students the vocabulary card routine, the students can independently practice their words during independent reading and writing time (see Figure 3.1). All you have to do is write, "Study vocabulary words," on your I Can... chart. For more on all of this, see Chapter 6.

Each week, when new words are introduced, the students create the word cards and add them to their bag. As the weeks go by, the kids build up an ever-increasing pile of vocabulary words. Every two or three weeks, assess the words. Use a checklist to keep track of who has read his or her words and how many words each student knows. Whenever I have a couple of minutes, I pull a student aside and say, "Please read your vocabulary words to me." For some words, I spot-check meaning by

Figure 3.1. Students Doing Word Sorts

asking the student to tell me what the word means or to use the word in a sentence. I often double-check the words that are more abstract or that I know may be difficult.

Words correctly pronounced and explained go into a stack that's secured with a rubber band. Unknown and mispronounced words stay loose. These loose cards become the focus of future study. I call these words the "practice makes perfect" pile. Once a month or so, I ask for volunteers to read through their entire rubber band stack. Kids beam when they fluently read and define 50 or more vocabulary words!

Vocabulary cards are great for whole-group activities. I'd suggest you start by teaching your students how to order them alphabetically. If the students have a low number of cards, such as 15 or fewer, they can alphabetize every card. If they have a lot of cards, have them alphabetize the words that they need to practice (only the loose cards). Another option is to have the class count out 10 random words from their rubber band stack and alphabetize these words. When the kids all have their words in alphabetical order, randomly call on a student to read his or her words, or ask for a volunteer.

One of the many beauties of alphabetizing vocabulary words is that every student can have different words. Thus, this activity expands into differentiation. You can further differentiate by having some students work with a buddy. You will, of course, need to meander and monitor. This movement is critical to the collection of formative assessment data. Note on a sticky note, checklist, or teacher data sheet which students have mastered the skill and which have not.

Closed and Open Word Sorts. After you've taught your students the process for alphabetizing their vocabulary cards, teach them how to conduct a word sort. Word sorts help students recognize linguistic or semantic relationships among words. In a word sort activity, no paper or pencil is used. Kids read, think, and physically move cards to show skill-based or meaning relationships among the words for any given category, such as verbs and nouns, words with two or three syllables, or words related to stories or themes.

Word sorts can be used in two ways: closed or open. In a closed word sort, the teacher provides the categories. In an open word sort, students group words into categories that they construct. I'll first describe a closed word sort, using select words from three stories (*Wolf!*, *What's in Store for the Future?*, and Franklyn M. Branley's *The Planets in Our Solar System*) in the Treasures third-grade anthology.

Other than *solar system*, which I consider to be a Tier III word, I chose the following words because they're Tier II words (words that are seen and used frequently and have a high degree of utility). Each word, regardless of how it first appeared in the manual, is written as a base word.

- *Wolf!*: ache, admire, bother, concentrate, passion, splendid
- *What's in Store for the Future?*: entertain, object, predict
- *The Planets in Our Solar System*: dim, farther, solar system, telescope

Let's pretend that your class has read all three stories. You've directly taught the meanings of all 13 words, and the students now have 13 vocabulary cards in their ziplock bags. To do a closed word sort by story, your students will need to have the same cards, or at least mostly the same cards. Ask the students to sort their cards into three piles: one for *Wolf!*, one for *What's in Store for the Future?*, and one for *The Planets in Our Solar System*. Although some students may sort the cards exactly as listed above, I bet many won't. One thing you should not do is automatically identify a card as incorrectly sorted when it doesn't match the original list from its associated story. Word sorts are never a brute memorization task.

When you see that some students have created sorts that don't match the initial story lists, ask questions such as these: "Tywan, why did you put *object* here?" and "Sarah, you put *object* in a different pile. Why?" If you've done a good job of teaching your students that learning is about thinking deeply and explaining their thought processes, rather than just about memorization, your kids will enter into these discussions with eagerness.

If a student places a word from one story in the pile of another story *and* can justify that word's inclusion with a well-reasoned explanation, then count it as correct and praise the student's thinking. After all, you want the kids to understand the nuances of meaning and the multiple relationships that each word has to key concepts.

Here's an example of one student's sort (by story title):

- *Wolf!: ache, admire, bother, entertain, passion, splendid*
- *What's in Store for the Future?: predict*
- *The Planets in Our Solar System: concentrate, dim, farther, object, solar system, telescope*

You'll notice that the words *concentrate* and *object*, originally found in the *Wolf!* and *What's in Store for the Future?* stories, are now sorted into the pile for *The Planets in Our Solar System*. Additionally, the word *entertain* has migrated from *What's in Store for the Future?* to *Wolf!*

As you go around the room and have the students read their sorts, follow up with *why* questions. Here's what a sort discussion might sound like:

Hunter: Angel has *object* in the category for *The Planets in Our Solar System*. It's supposed to be in *What's in Store for the Future?*

Teacher: Angel, tell us why you put the word *object* in the pile for *The Planets in Our Solar System*.

Angel: Planets are objects. You can see them with a telescope.

Teacher: Planets are indeed objects. Good answer, Angel. You can keep that word there. I see you have *concentrate* in your pile for *The Planets in Our Solar System*, too. Does anyone else have *concentrate* in that pile?

Emily: I do.

Teacher: Emily, why is *concentrate* in your pile for *The Planets in Our Solar System?*

Emily: Because you have to concentrate to look through a telescope. The planets are really small.

Teacher: Good reasoning, Emily. Keep that word there.

Another type of closed word sort is the skill-based sort: Students sort their words into piles based on the number of syllables (one, two, three, four, or more), parts of speech (nouns, verbs, adjectives, and others), or phonic patterns (open syllable, closed syllable, short vowel sound, prefix/suffix, etc.). Figure 3.2a shows two examples of closed word sorts, one for syllables and one for parts of speech, and Figure 3.2b shows what the cards actually look like.

Notice that even though a sort for parts of speech is technically closed, it has an open quality to it. Why? Because words like *ache* and *bother* are, according to use, both nouns and verbs. These words, and how students have sorted them into different categories, can be points of discussion and opportunities for learning when you discuss the sorts with your students.

In an open word sort, students create their own semantic constructions. An open word sort is useful when you want to assess how students impose organization onto words that belong to a particular semantic network (or category). In this type of sort, you'll give the students a choice of how many categories to create. Usually the choice is provided as a range, such as two or three, or three or four. This provides support for a challenging task.

To begin an open word sort, say to your class, "I want you to think about the meanings of your words and how they relate to one another. If you were to sort your words into two or three categories, what would they be?" After you give them 10–15 seconds of think time, say, "I want you to sort your vocabulary words into two or three piles. Each pile should be a specific category. When you're done, you'll have to tell me why you sorted your words into those particular piles."

If you've already taught your students how to perform closed word sorts (phonic elements, parts of speech, syllables, etc.), some students will automatically go there. For example, some students might sort *ache*, *admire*, and *object* into one pile because they all begin with a vowel. The words in the second pile would typically all begin with consonants. Other students will think more deeply about the sort. Either way, open word sorts provide a wealth of learning objectives to talk about.

There are numerous opportunities to include more teaching chops in the vocabulary card method. When your students take out 15 of their vocabulary cards and put them in alphabetical order, they're responding as a group in a physical manner. If all of your students have the same words, have them do a choral read or an echo read. This type of repeated word

When you give students multiple opportunities to read, say, and explore the relationships among vocabulary words, you increase the chance that they'll use the words during writing, understand the words during reading, and remember the words over time.

Figure 3.2. Closed Word Sort Examples

a.

ache	*concentrate*	*farther*	*predict*	*splendid*
admire	*dim*	*object*	*solar system*	*telescope*
bother	*entertain*	*passion*		

Syllable Sort

Number of Syllables	Words
1	*ache, dim*
2	*admire, bother, farther, object, passion, predict, splendid*
3	*concentrate, entertain, telescope*
4	*solar system*

Parts of Speech Sort

Nouns	*ache, bother, object, passion, solar system, telescope*
Verbs	*ache, admire, bother, concentrate, entertain, predict*
Adjectives	*dim, farther, splendid*

b.

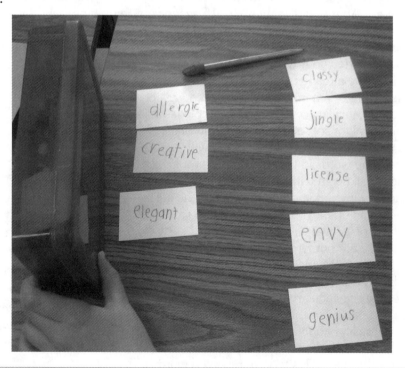

reading not only builds vocabulary but also gives the kids another shot at practicing their reading, and it's another opportunity to build in group response.

As you teach the vocabulary card method, don't forget to explicitly model each step. If you want the kids to put the words in alphabetical order, model that for them, directly and explicitly. Simple closed word sorts, such as a sort by syllables, won't take much modeling, but more complex sorts, such as by theme or parts of speech, will take multiple modeling sessions.

Modeling should be followed by several sessions of guided group practice. Then, make sure you give the students numerous opportunities to practice independently. Multiple opportunities to practice are crucial for mastery learning. One of my beefs with basal vocabulary instruction is that few, if any, vocabulary words are ever taught to mastery. There's simply no way that a fourth or fifth grader, let alone a first or second grader, is going to master 20 vocabulary words introduced over four weeks (and by *master*, I mean recall 90% of their words, truly understand their meanings, and even use some in authentic speech and writing) unless those words are repeatedly pronounced out loud, linked to definitions, sorted by category, applied in written sentences, and spoken in conversations. Unlike the traditional basal instructional method of minimal discussion, a couple of worksheets, and a summative weekly test, the vocabulary card method gives students many exposures to multiple vocabulary words week after week.

When you teach vocabulary with more refined word lists, direct and explicit instruction, and the vocabulary card method, you'll do more than practice your instructional teaching chops. You'll also naturally and effortlessly address many of the Common Core State Standards. In some cases, you'll directly teach to a standard, such as the grade 3 craft and structure literature standard that states, "Determine the meaning of words and phrases as they are used in a text" (National Governors Association Center for Best Practices & Council of Chief State School Officers [NGACBP & CCSSO], 2010, p. 12), or the grade 5 craft and structure informational text standard that states, "Determine the meaning of general academic and domain-specific words and phrases in a text" (NGACBP & CCSSO, 2010, p. 14). At other times, you'll indirectly address the standards, such as when the words your students learn enable them to "read and comprehend informational texts" or "read with sufficient accuracy and fluency to support comprehension." In these cases, you'll have addressed range of reading standards and foundational skills standards through vocabulary instruction.

In my eyes, reading is more akin to a cake batter than a salad. Its component parts inform and influence one another and are not separated out easily. Thus, when you teach to vocabulary standards, you're also teaching to many other English language arts standards simultaneously.

Formative Assessment: Is It Working?

The vocabulary card method is formative assessment at its best. Because formative assessments are ongoing—essential skills must be monitored multiple times over the course of each quarter, semester, and year—they need to be quick and easy to give and score. In the case of vocabulary cards, you can assess your students' mastery of word pronunciation and meaning every time they have their cards out. And because the cards don't go away, assessment is available at any time. To assess how many words a student knows, simply pull a student's rubber band stack and count the cards. These spot-check assessments can occur as often as you like. I try to formally record each student's progress at least once every three weeks. A simple way to manage this is to divide your class into thirds and assess one of the three groups each week.

Make It So

Like grammar, vocabulary can be an area of instruction that gets shortchanged week after week. There seem to be so many tasks to complete each day. With direct and explicit teaching and the vocabulary card method, however, you can easily strengthen and deepen your vocabulary instruction while simultaneously saving time and materials.

Remember that the vocabulary card technique takes the place of the vocabulary activities and workbook pages outlined in your basal manual. You have to give up to gain, and what you are looking to gain is 10–15 minutes to do the vocabulary card method every couple of days. Actually, you may need just a bit more time when you first teach the process, but once you have it up and running, students will learn the routine and then be able to do much of it on their own.

In the end, this new type of cumulative and kinesthetic vocabulary instruction is well worth the time. The method actually leads to vocabulary mastery. Your students will enjoy the process, and best of all, they may actually remember and use the vocabulary words when they write and speak, something that rarely occurs when you review a set of vocabulary words, assess them once, and then move on to a new set of words.

Boosting Comprehension Instruction

You will need...

- Your teacher's manual with its list of comprehension strategies
- Anthology stories from your core program
- Additional trade books
- A Good Readers' Fix-It-Up and Clarify Strategies poster (discussed in this chapter)
- A Good Readers' Metacognition Strategies poster (discussed in this chapter)
- Think-aloud and talking to the text strategies

You will...

- Take note of the many comprehension strategies in your teacher's manual
- Decrease the number of comprehension strategies you teach from dozens to 12
- Display the strategies in your room
- Teach the strategies to mastery over time by using modeling, direct instruction, repeated guided practice, and independent practice
- Model how the strategies are used in different texts
- Formatively assess your students' use of the strategies via think-alouds and talking to the text

Comprehension of a sentence, paragraph, or story is the ultimate goal of reading. Therefore, it makes sense for a teacher to focus on strengthening his or her instruction of comprehension strategies. The teaching of these strategies is another logical place to begin making changes to your core reading program. Big changes aren't necessary at first. Just as I proposed in the previous chapters, there's no immediate need to change your basal schedule or your whole-group instruction. You can continue to use your anthology, and you can use some of the comprehension strategies listed in your teacher's manual. However, you should hang posters that list specific strategies on your classroom walls and decrease the number of worksheets and practice book pages that you ask the students to complete. And I'll ask you to make important changes to the number of comprehension strategies you teach as well as the way that you teach them.

What's the Matter With the Manual?

The typical basal teacher's manual practically bursts with teaching and reteaching ideas, enrichment and remediation activities, connections to standards, notes to the teacher, scripts for the teacher, writing prompts, reading strategies and their explanations, and references to supplemental books. This list is by no means exhaustive. If you page through your teacher's manual carefully enough, you'll probably find some loose change, your missing sunglasses, and Jimmy Hoffa.

Administrators and teachers sometimes confuse "teach everything" with "teach effectively." When a teacher chooses, or is expected, to do every activity and workbook page listed in the manual, the effectiveness of his or her teaching diminishes. Student learning decreases as well. On the flip side, when a teacher is given permission to teach fewer concepts and less content, allowing him or her to focus on the most essential concepts and content, the teaching becomes more effective, and student learning increases.

Regarding comprehension skills and strategies, it's no secret that the typical core reading program tries to cover more ground than the research literature suggests. For example, according to Dewitz et al. (2009), basals introduce 18–29 comprehension skills and strategies per program per year. Meanwhile, research literature, from the National Reading Panel report (NICHD, 2000a) to the writings of Pressley (2006) and Duke and Pearson (2002), has consistently endorsed the use of 7–12 highly effective strategies.

Stated simply, more is less, and less is more. This is why I suggest that you cut way back on the number of comprehension strategies that you teach throughout the year, choosing only ones that are inclusive and encompassing of other strategies and especially effective and powerful.

Manual Strategies

One of my pet peeves is that a typical teacher's manual purports to effectively teach a dozen different strategies over the course of one story. To be blunt, this simply can't be done. The following is a list of 12 student-used reading skills and strategies outlined in one anthology story from a basal series teacher's manual. By the way, because the terms *skills* and *strategies* are used somewhat interchangeably in manuals, I'll stick to the term *strategy*, regardless of what the manual calls it. The list is from a third-grade story introduced in mid-October. As the teacher and students read through the story, the teacher is directed to stop, point out, discuss, and model the bulleted strategies.

1. Understand the genre of fantasy and distinguish between fantasy and reality
2. Generate and answer questions
3. Preview and predict
4. Make predictions during reading and confirm predictions
5. Use illustrations to gain meaning
6. Understand and retell the beginning, middle, and end of the story
7. Analyze characters
8. Monitor and clarify by reading ahead
9. Study the author's word choice and use of humor
10. Analyze characters and plot
11. Make inferences
12. Understand multiple-meaning words

Is it really possible to thoroughly teach 12 comprehension strategies over the course of one or two weeks? In a word, no. In defense of the core program, it doesn't think so either. Many of these strategies were taught in first and second grades. Also, the manual spirals around in third grade to reteach many of these strategies in future stories. This spiral construction allows students and teachers to come into contact with each strategy multiple times. Supposedly, this leads to a gradual mastering of each strategy. I argue, however, that there are simply too many strategies for this type of instruction to be effective. The strategies aren't taught explicitly and deeply enough, nor are they modeled and practiced thoroughly enough, to create mastery. Researchers who have studied the instruction of reading comprehension skills and strategies as taught in basal programs say much the same (Dewitz et al., 2009).

As the weeks go by, the list of strategies builds. Here are nine more from subsequent stories:

1. Summarize the story
2. Put events into a sequence
3. Identify the genre of historical/realistic fiction
4. Identify the narrator's point of view
5. Identify figurative language: simile and idiom
6. Analyze character development
7. Draw conclusions
8. Identify topic sentences and the supporting details of a paragraph
9. Identify word parts

Now, don't get me wrong. I'm not saying that these strategies aren't important. I'm simply saying that even a great teacher cannot teach this many strategies to mastery level. By the end of 14 weeks of instruction, third graders, many of them struggling to read and comprehend, have been exposed to over 21 comprehension strategies! Does this strike you as a "mile wide and inch deep" way of teaching? It does to me.

Strategy Assessment in Published Programs

Another problem with a core reading program's comprehension instruction is that when students read mainly or exclusively from an anthology, they aren't called on to apply the strategies in a variety of texts. Will the 21 strategies generalize to trade books and magazines? No one knows because the students aren't expected to read from a wide variety of texts, and the teachers aren't expected to assess the strategies in these texts.

As difficult as it is to teach the manual's long list of comprehension strategies, it's more difficult, if not downright impossible, to gauge which students are applying a specific strategy. Why? Basal assessments, such as story and end-of-unit tests, rarely provide accurate assessments of a student's strategy use. Because basals most often use multiple-choice items, the teacher is rarely sure that the student actually knew the answer. Perhaps the kid simply made a good guess. Also, story and unit tests are summative in nature. This means that even when a basal assessment tests a skill such as "predict and then answer your prediction," it rarely measures the application of the strategy over time.

The Importance of Comprehension:
What Good Readers Do

A good reader is active when reading. The reader isn't simply decoding words and spouting streams of sentences. Rather, a good reader thinks about the words and sentences that he or she is reading. Provoked by the text, his or her brain generates thoughts: "Wow, I wonder what happens next?" "Ha, ha, that description was funny!" "Hmm, I'm not sure what *oligarchy* means." "What? I don't get it. Who's Abigail? I guess I should go back and read that again." The reader notices, remembers, and then acts on these thoughts. As his or her eyes scan the words, an accomplished reader simultaneously visualizes images, asks questions (and often answers them), and acknowledges confusion about a word or passage.

This thinking about reading (or in a more general sense, thinking about thinking) is known as metacognition, which is one of the defining cognitive processes of human beings. Because we can think about our thinking, we can take action as we read. As accomplished readers, we know when we stumble over a word, and we know how to correct that stumble. We know when we're confused about the meaning of a word or passage in a story, and we know how to clarify our confusion. As accomplished readers, we make predictions about what comes next in the text. Then, we check in with ourselves to see if our predictions were correct. We make connections to the text before, during, and after we read, and we visualize or see pictures in our heads as events in the story unfold. We also focus on important points and facts, review them as we read, and paraphrase, retell, or summarize passages after we read them (Duke, Pearson, Strachan, & Billman, 2011).

In my description of metacognition, I've used the phrases *accomplished readers* and *good readers*. It's important to note that many poor readers engage in few, if any, metacognitive behaviors. Many poor readers don't reflect on what they read, don't think about their thinking, and aren't active participants in the act of reading. Why? For some, the struggle lies in the decoding. Because poor decoders haven't mastered the code, their reading is hesitant, disconnected, and full of word errors. As they struggle to read the words, they lose sight of what the story is about, and their comprehension fails. For others, a lack of attention to meaning may simply be a bad habit. Some students read fluently but fail to comprehend the meaning of a passage. Fluent readers who lack comprehension may cruise through extended passages of text like professional newscasters but respond to critical thinking questions with "deer in the headlight" stares. It's possible that these students really don't understand that the words they read should mean something. If this is the case, they must be taught that the goal of reading is to understand the text.

It's possible that teachers are part of the problem. Over the years, we may have pushed comprehension strategies to the sidelines as we pulled fluency to center stage. A heavy emphasis on fluency assessments (e.g., DIBELS) and fluency programs (e.g., Read Naturally) may have contributed to this sidelining. Typically, the kind of instruction that builds fluency neither teaches nor assesses comprehension and metacognition. Fluency is important and must be practiced, but we cannot and must not sideline comprehension instruction.

Strategies that enable readers to derive meaning from a text should be center stage because understanding is the ultimate goal of reading. All other reading skills, such as decoding, applying the meanings of vocabulary words, and fluency, are pressed into service as a student strives to understand a text. The same is true for adults. Think about your own reading for a moment. Can you summarize the gist of what you've read so far? Do you remember having made a few connections from this text to your reading program? While reading this text, did you run into any problems in understanding what you just read, and if you did, did you go back and reread the passage? If you engaged in any or all of these actions, you're employing cognition strategies that help you understand the text.

As accomplished readers, it may be hard for us to imagine a reader who doesn't see pictures in his or her head, fix up a mistake, or make predictions while reading. For some readers, however, nontransactional word calling is a way of life. Therefore, it's up to us to teach those readers how to become metacognitive thinkers. Only then can they more fully understand and enjoy the texts they read.

In my first years of teaching my learning support kids, I had little sense of how to teach comprehension. Looking back on those days, I now understand why. First, the reading component of my special education training was lightweight. My program included only one course on how to teach reading to students with learning disabilities. Yikes! More importantly, the field of reading was still forming opinions about how metacognitive strategies could and should be taught. Today's reading researchers know a lot more than was known 20 years ago and have greater insight into how the brain works to derive meaning from text. A review of the literature clearly shows that both children and adults can be taught to think about their thinking (Lai, 2011). More specifically, researchers and writers, such as Schraw, Halpern, Kuhn, and Dean, who have been delving into metacognition for decades, have described how teachers can teach students to gain knowledge about themselves as learners and use specific strategies to improve their learning and understanding (Lai, 2011). Some researchers, such as Paris, have looked into ways to teach both children and adults how and when to use metacognition strategies (Paris & Parecki, 1993; Paris & Winograd, 1990), while others, such as Palincsar and Brown (1984), have developed effective teaching tools (in this case, reciprocal teaching) by combining strategies such as summarizing, questioning, clarifying, and predicting.

Scope: What Comprehension Strategies to Teach

Mile-Deep Comprehension Instruction

To teach comprehension strategies to mastery, Super Core advocates pulling back from a manual's "mile wide and inch deep" list of strategies. A more reasonable approach is to focus on two groups of highly effective, time-tested strategies. I'm talking about teaching five or six useful fix-it-up strategies and five or six high-impact comprehension strategies. This means you'll only teach 10–12 strategies for the entire year! This is "mile deep and inch wide" thinking.

In addition to narrowing the number taught, I advocate teaching the strategies with modeling, direct instruction, task analysis, and formative assessment. In other words, combine the big ideas of reading and writing with teaching chops (instructional expertise). Talk about getting some bang for your buck!

Fix-It-Up and Comprehension Strategies

In my mind, metacognitive strategies fall into two categories: fix-it-up and comprehension. The first category, fix-it-up (and clarify), is taught so students can independently monitor their decoding and comprehension and adjust their reading process as difficulties arise. When students employ fix-it-up strategies, they become stronger and more confident readers who are willing and able to tackle more difficult text. My favorite fix-it-up strategies are shown in Figure 4.1.

The second subset, comprehension strategies, is brought to bear so a reader can comprehend texts in a deeper way. To me, these strategies seem more complex and nuanced than the fix-it-up strategies. When employed correctly, readers use comprehension strategies to gain greater understanding and enjoyment of a story. My favorites are shown in Figure 4.2.

The strategies that I picked for my teaching (and for this book) are time tested and powerful. The National Reading Panel stated, "comprehension can be improved by teaching students to use specific

Figure 4.1. Good Readers' Fix-It-Up and Clarify Strategies Poster

Good readers...

- Stop, go back, and get a running start

- Skip ahead and then reread

- Sound out the word

- Cross-check (Does the word make sense? If no, what word does make sense? Does that word match the letters?)

- Adjust their reading rate (Go a little faster or a little slower.)

- Read with fluency (Read smoothly and steadily, with long phrases. Read with expression.)

Figure 4.2. Good Readers' Metacognition Strategies Poster

Good readers...

- Use prior knowledge

- Make connections to personal experiences, to other texts, and to the world

- Retell and summarize

- Visualize (see a movie in their heads)

- Ask and answer questions (right there, seek and find, and author and me)

- Predict and check (What will happen? Did it happen?)

cognitive strategies or to reason strategically when they encounter barriers to understanding what they are reading" (NICHD, 2000a, p. 4). More recently, members of the International Reading Association's (2012) Common Core State Standards Committee observed the following:

> Research shows the effectiveness of summarizing text as it is read, asking oneself questions about text and answering those questions, recognizing and using narrative and informational text structures to help make sense of and to remember text information, visualizing, comprehension monitoring, and other active ways of thinking about the ideas in a text. The use of such strategies is especially helpful with texts that a reader finds challenging. (p. 2)

I've witnessed metacognition and fix-it-up strategies at work in numerous elementary school classrooms. During my years as a trainer, I got to know teachers who ran reading classes based on strategies, especially metacognitive reading strategies. These teachers told me that their strategy-based programs were especially effective with poorly performing readers (who were not in special education programs).

Roll Out the Strategies

There are many ways of presenting your fix-it-up and comprehension/ metacognition strategies in your classroom. Whiteboards, easel paper, bulletin boards, and posters all come to mind. I prefer turning them into posters on either small whiteboards that I can haul with me to whatever classroom I'm visiting or on large sheets of paper.

At the beginning of the year, hang the strategies posters in your classroom. Then, kick back, relax, and watch the magic happen! Uh, just kidding. There's a bit more to it than that. However, if you make the posters and get them up on your wall, you're off to a good start.

I suggest that you teach one strategy from each poster every two weeks. As you move down the list, review each previously taught strategy. Thus, by the time your class is moving into the winter break, you will have introduced and modeled (and your students will have practiced) 10–12 strategies. Because of the constant review, there's a good chance that come December, 80–90% of your students will have mastered at least four or five strategies.

When it comes to displaying strategies, a pocket chart is even better than a poster because it allows you to construct a cumulative list. Put each strategy title on an index card. Then, add a new index card onto the poster as you introduce that strategy.

When you return from the winter break, begin to review, reteach, remodel, and practice, practice, practice the strategies. Concentrate on the ones that most students haven't mastered. Formative assessments, such as teacher observations, student writing samples, and checklists, will guide you as you decide which strategies need more practice. If you introduce all the strategies by late December, you'll have plenty of time to reteach those that haven't taken root, and the kids will have plenty of time to practice.

As time goes by, you'll discover that many strategies listed in your teacher's manual are simply variations on those listed on your posters. For example, the "ask and answer questions" strategy, especially when it's taught as Raphael and Au's (2005) question–answer relationships strategy, can easily encompass these five strategies listed in the basal manual: fact and opinion, inferencing, drawing conclusions, generating and answering questions, and identifying the author's point of view.

That being said, you may still want to teach minilessons on some of the manual's strategies, such as using figurative language, identifying genre, or analyzing characters. As you teach those strategies, try to relate them to the ones listed on your posters. Categorizing and explicitly connecting strategies helps create schemata in the minds of students. If your entire building or district embraces teaching with these posters, the students will get practice on the same strategies year after year. Just think of how deeply a student could understand and apply strategies if every teacher, regardless of grade level, focused on the same 12 fix-it-up and comprehension reading strategies. By the time a first-grade reader hit fifth grade, the student would be a metacognitive genius!

Here's another upside of a yearlong focus on 12 strategies. When upper-grade students truly master the strategies, they'll be able to put them to use on high-stakes, year-end reading tests. According to Guthrie (2002), it takes at least three months of practice for reading strategies to be mentally accessible to and usable by students. Just what strategies lead to success in high-stakes testing? They include the following:

1. Searching to locate information, a skill found in the asking and answering questions strategy
2. Summarizing, a strategy already on your poster
3. Self-monitoring, which is part of the fix-it-up and clarify strategies
4. Self-questioning, which is an integral part of using prior knowledge, predicting and checking, and asking and answering questions (Guthrie, 2002)

There's one more important reason to teach select lists of strategies throughout the year and across the grade levels. The strategies listed on the two strategies posters, as well as all of those mentioned in the previous list, are key to the Common Core State Standards. When you teach these reading strategies, you'll be teaching the standards. But don't take my word for it. Pick up the Common Core document and see for yourself.

A quick look under the heading "Foundational Skills" and the subheadings "Phonics and Word Recognition" and "Fluency" reveals that students are asked to apply word analysis skills and "use context to confirm or self-correct word recognition and understanding, rereading as necessary." In other words, students need to fix up their reading problems. Look under the headings "Key Ideas and Details" and "Craft and Structure" for both literature and informational texts, and you'll find standards that ask students to summarize text, retell stories, ask and answer questions, and "determine the central message, lesson, or moral and explain how it is conveyed through key details in the text." Take a peek at the all-important heading "Range of Reading and Level of Text Complexity" for both literature and informational texts, and you'll see that students are ultimately asked to read and comprehend. How do they get to the point where they comprehend the text they're reading? By using strategies such as summarizing, making connections, asking and answering questions, using prior knowledge, predicting and checking, visualizing, and solving a reading roadblock as they encounter one.

Focus on a small number of powerful comprehension strategies and teach students to apply them in all manner of texts.

To summarize, it pays to explicitly teach students a small repertoire of powerful comprehension strategies. I feel so strongly about this that I'll say it once more with feeling: It pays to explicitly teach students a small repertoire of very powerful comprehension strategies!

Teaching Chops:
How to Teach Comprehension Strategies

Comprehension strategies and how to teach them are the subjects of entire books. Some are broad in scope and address dozens of strategies in general detail. Others focus on just a few categories of strategies and examine each strategy within the category in great detail. There are seemingly endless permutations of some of the most meaty strategies. For example, the question and answer strategy alone has numerous names, such as thick and thin questions and question–answer relationships, and it's possible to spend years perfecting the teaching of just this one strategy. Therefore, it's beyond the scope of this book to

Table 4.1. Sample of Books That Delve Into Strategies More Deeply

- Harvey, S., & Goudvis, A. (2007). *Strategies that work: Teaching comprehension for understanding and engagement* (2nd ed.). Portland, ME: Stenhouse.
- Keene, E.O., & Zimmermann, S. (2007). *Mosaic of thought: The power of comprehension strategy instruction* (2nd ed.). Portsmouth, NH: Heinemann.
- Kelley, M.J., & Clausen-Grace, N. (2013). *Comprehension shouldn't be silent: From strategy instruction to student independence* (2nd ed.). Newark, DE: International Reading Association.
- Miller, D. (2013). *Reading with meaning: Teaching comprehension in the primary grades*. Portland, ME: Stenhouse.
- Oczkus, L.D. (2010). *Reciprocal teaching at work: Powerful strategies and lessons for improving reading comprehension* (2nd ed.). Newark, DE: International Reading Association.
- Schoenbach, R., Greenleaf, C., Cziko, C., & Hurwitz, L. (1999). *Reading for understanding: A guide to improving reading in middle and high school classrooms*. San Francisco, CA: Jossey-Bass & WestEd.

delve into the particulars of how best to teach each strategy, especially when it comes to tweaking each one so it works for the developmental level of students in various grades.

For specific and in-depth ideas on how to teach various strategies, refer to Table 4.1 for a number of excellent texts on the subject. For the purposes of this book, however, I touch on a number of general points regarding the teaching of comprehension strategies.

General Points for Teaching Strategies

Explicitly Model and Explain Each Strategy. Here we rely on teaching chops 4 (task analysis and mastery learning) and 5 (explicit modeling and practice). If you use direct instruction to introduce the strategy, you'll also use teaching chop 1 (direct and explicit instruction). Remember, strategies need to be modeled repeatedly throughout the year using a variety of texts. Model, review, reteach, and practice until the majority of students have mastered the strategy. When you first begin, you'll only use anthology stories. Later, model the strategies using books from independent and guided reading time.

Model How the Strategies Are Used Before, During, and After Reading. Some strategies are easily categorized: Predicting is done before reading, a fix-it-up strategy is done during reading, and summarizing and retelling are done after reading. Other strategies are not so cut-and-dried. A reader can ask questions before reading by scanning the title and cover art. The reader can also ask questions during or after reading the text. Although predicting and summarizing are usually done before and after reading, they can also be used during reading, such as when a reader predicts what will happen in upcoming pages or summarizes a chapter before moving on to the next one. While teaching, explicitly point out when and how students should use the various strategies.

Teach Your Students to Verbalize the Strategies. Next, teach your students to jot down thoughts that demonstrate their use of a strategy. You'll do this via think-alouds and by modeling examples of talking to the text. Think-alouds come first. Once students are able to orally describe what's happening in their head, they'll be ready to talk to the text. Both of these are described more fully in the following section.

Give Your Students Ample Opportunities to Use the Strategy on Their Own. This is most easily done during guided and independent reading time. During guided reading, you can monitor and coach your students' use of strategies. In small groups of three to six students, it's much easier to see how they use (or don't use) the strategies. Extended reading time is an opportunity for independent practice in the use of strategies. All of this is touched on in Chapter 6.

It's a good bet that your basal series incorporates many if not all of the 12 specific strategies that I identified on the two strategies posters. Basal writers and researchers work hard to get a multitude of comprehension strategies into the manual. Therefore, some of the work has been done for you. All you need do is take note of when and where the 12 strategies occur.

It'll take extra effort, however, to find additional places in the anthology where you can teach, model, and guide the students in the use of any specific strategy. As you read through each anthology story with the posters in mind, you'll find that some passages lend themselves to predicting, others to visualizing, and still others to asking (or answering) questions. Use sticky notes or simply write notes right in your manual each time the text provides you with an opportunity to teach one of the 12 strategies.

Direct and Explicit Instruction + Modeling

I'd be remiss if I didn't relate how to explicitly explain and model at least one strategy, so here's a description of how you might teach the retell and summarize strategies.

First, pick a story that's relatively easy for students to read and comprehend. You could use an anthology story, but I suggest a trade book that's short and easy for your students to read. Using easy books to model comprehension strategies enables your students to focus on the strategy and not the text and reduces the likelihood that the kids will struggle with word identification. So, pick a book that permits every student to easily say the words, understand the vocabulary, remember the details, and get the general gist of the story.

At the same time, make sure the book allows for a genuine (not contrived) use of the strategies, in this case, retell and summarize. You'll want a book that generates authentic questions, lends itself to being summarized, includes passages that promote visualizing, and so forth. For this example, let's use Aliki's (1972) *Fossils Tell of Long Ago*.

To model an inwardly occurring thought process, it helps to have a little gimmick or visual prop. You want your students to understand that as they read a book, sometimes they're reading, and other times they're thinking about their reading. Two squares and a thinking cap are props that work well with elementary and middle school students.

For the two squares, use masking tape on the floor to demarcate the squares side by side. Another option is to lay down two carpet squares side by side. When you read from the text, stand in the left square. When you think aloud about the text, jump to the adjacent square and talk from there. When you return to reading, jump back to the previous square, and so forth.

For the thinking cap, you'll use some type of cap or hat. For elementary school teachers, this should be easy because most of the ones I know have a wacky hat or two somewhere nearby. Begin by reading the text with the cap off. When you think aloud, put the thinking cap on. Here's an example of a think-aloud summary for the first third of Aliki's fossil book. It begins with a bit of direct instruction. The phrases in quotation marks show what I had written on the board.

> "To understand and remember what they read, good readers stop to retell and summarize what they've just read." Let's read that statement together. (The teacher and students read aloud.) Good. Now, you read it. (The students read it aloud.) Nice job of staying together!
>
> "*Summarize* means that you choose the most important details. Many words become just a few words." Let's all read that together. (The teacher and students read aloud.)
>
> I'm going to show you how I summarize what I've read. Remember, good readers stop to retell what they've read, and they summarize what they've read. To show you what I'm thinking, I'm going to use my thinking cap. When my thinking cap is off, I'm reading from the book. When my thinking cap is on (she puts on the cap), I'm thinking about what I've read. First I'm going to read from

the book. (She takes off the cap and reads aloud from the book. Then, she stops and puts on the thinking cap.)

Hmm, here are some of the details that I can retell from memory. First, I remember that there were fish swimming around millions of years ago, the fish died and sank to the bottom of the sea, and then they turned to stone. They became fossils. I also remember that fossils started to form when the fish died and sank into the mud at the bottom of the sea. Most of their bodies rotted away, but the bones were still there. Now I'm going to read a few more pages. (She takes off the thinking cap and reads aloud from the book. She stops and then puts the thinking cap back on.)

Hmm, I remember that the fish bones got covered up with mud, the mud got pressed down, and minerals seeped into the bones. *Seep* means that the minerals oozed into the bones very slowly. *Seep* is one of the vocabulary words that we talked about in class. After millions of years, all the mud, pressure, and minerals seeping into the bones created a fossil. Later, the land changed, and the seas dried up. Now the fossils can be dug up.

Now I'm going to summarize all that I've said in my retell. I'll summarize by telling you the most important details of the story in just a few short sentences. Here comes my summary! When animals died millions of years ago, some of them got covered with mud. The flesh of the animals rotted away. Only the bones were left. Pressure pushed on the bones, minerals seeped into the bones, and a fossil was made. Later, when the land changed, the fossils could be dug up.

Together, we'll read 10 more pages of the story. As you read, I'm going to ask you to stop every so often, put on your thinking cap, and retell the story out loud. When we're done reading the 10 pages, I'll give you think time to summarize what you read. We'll do a quick think-pair-share, and I'll ask for volunteers to summarize with a think-aloud.

As with any strategy, the think-aloud strategy should be modeled and practiced numerous times. And you'll need to coach the students' responses as the class learns this strategy. Over time, you can gradually fade the coaching away (Pearson & Gallagher, 1983).

Differentiation and Enrichment

As a final note, if some students master the strategies early, differentiate and provide enrichment as you reteach or provide guidance to those who haven't yet mastered the strategy. For example, teach the following buddy routine to the entire class and use it whenever you have students who have thoroughly mastered a strategy, such as predict and check.

- Put the mastery-level kids into teams.
- During the 15 minutes that you spend on reteaching the strategy to other students, have the teams of mastery-level kids silently read a very short book (or part of a book) on their independent level.

- At a designated stopping point, have each member of the team write down two predictions of what will happen next in the story.
- Have each person in the team share his or her predictions with the teammates.
- Have the team collectively read on and check to see whether any of the predictions occur.

Another possibility for differentiation makes use of the making connections strategy. As you reteach or provide guidance to students who haven't yet mastered the strategy, have mastery-level students do the following.

- Have each student read a short, independent-level nonfiction book or paragraph on a specific subject, such as dolphins, seeds, or Helen Keller. To make the experience enriching, choose subjects that they haven't learned about in your class.
- Have each student read a second short book or paragraph on the same topic.
- Have each student find connections between the two books or paragraphs, such as they both mention that dolphins are mammals or show a picture of Helen Keller reading braille.
- Have the students note their connections on sticky notes and place one note in each book.
- At some point, allow the students to present their connections to the rest of the class or to one another.

Finally, when you group students for activities such as the two just mentioned, group them by reading level, approximate or exact. Then, give those who are upper-level readers upper-level books to read. You've now provided instant differentiation and enrichment!

Formative Assessment: Are Your Comprehension Strategies Working?

To get students to the point of mastering any content or skill, I must keep track of their achievement and performance over time. For example, by the end of the school year, I want my kindergarten readers to use multiple reading strategies, such as "look at the picture," "think about what the book is about," and "get your mouth ready to say the first sounds of the words," to figure out the unknown words that they encounter in texts. In order to decide where to put my instructional energies, I need to keep track of which strategies the kids use and which they don't. While taking notes on their reading habits, I may find that one student typically tries to sound out an unknown word but rarely thinks about the meaning of the text. This information provides an instructional focus and tells me that in upcoming guided reading lessons, I should draw the student's attention to the meanings of words and sentences. Specific strategies to review and reteach might be doing a picture walk, using picture cues, thinking about the title of the story, and thinking about the meanings of the words in a sentence.

Formative assessments not only inform your instruction but also validate it, and it pays for a reading teacher to assess students' progress well before important benchmark or summative tests. Formative assessments are tremendously useful because they tell you where your instruction and your students' learning stand at all times. To bring this point home, here's an analogy:

Imagine that you're flying your private jet 2,000 miles, from Washington, DC, to Seattle. Now imagine that your jet has a digital control panel (air speed, fuel gauge, radar, chronometer, altimeter, etc.) that's ultimately controlled by two big buttons, one labeled "summative" and one labeled "formative." Finally, imagine that after takeoff, a large screen rolls down and covers your plane's windows. You can't see anything! Suddenly, the summative and formative buttons begin to blink. Which one should you press?

If you press the summative button, your control panel remains blank for the next 1,990 miles. You are, for all intents and purposes, flying blind. Throughout the trip, you won't know your altitude, your air speed, or if a giant thunderhead looms directly in your flight path. You won't know how much fuel is left in your tank. If you press the summative button, your control panel clicks on only during the last 10 miles of your journey. Only then will you know whether you will arrive on time and have enough fuel to finish the trip, or are heading straight into the Cascade Mountains.

If you want to plan ahead, keep abreast of your progress, and avoid thunderheads along the way, pressing the summative button is not the way to go. Formative is a much better way to fly. With a formative control panel, you'll know your air speed at all times. You'll know whether you're running low on fuel over Minnesota and need to land at a Midwestern airport, and you'll know whether you must fly around a thunderhead or increase your altitude to get over the Cascades well before you get there.

For subjects such as writing, spelling, and oral reading, formative assessments are easy to implement. For example, to assess spelling, give students a cold list of pattern-based words or look at an authentic writing sample. To assess writing, use a writing rubric and note the student's strengths and weaknesses (e.g., focus, voice, idea development, mechanics). For oral reading accuracy and fluency, give a running record or DIBELS progress monitoring passage and do a bit of error analysis (e.g., omissions, substitutions based on meaning, substitutions based on first letter, gets lost, never corrects for meaning).

Assessing a student's use of fix-it-up and metacognition strategies is a bit trickier, though. How does one assess thinking about thinking? Performing a functional MRI scan is probably not an option, and telepaths are hard to come by, so I suggest a low-tech checklist.

The Checklist

Start with a checklist that assesses a student's use of the fix-it-up strategies. This type of checklist lets you generally know if the student is aware of whether or not his or her reading makes sense. At a specific level, you'll know what fix-it-up strategies the student is employing during the reading. An example of a strategy checklist is given in Figure 4.3.

To use this checklist assessment, sit down with a student for two minutes and listen to the student read from a book that's on his or her *instructional* reading level. You don't want to use a book on his or her independent level because you want the student to struggle a bit so you can assess the use of fix-it-up strategies. The percentage of accuracy that defines independent and instructional changes depends on which reading guru you're consulting (more on this in Chapter 6), but for now let's consider a book to be on a student's instructional level if he or she can read it with 93–97% accuracy. Perhaps a story from your basal anthology is appropriate. If not, choose a book from your classroom library, your school's book room, or the library of a friendly teacher in another grade. Note the date, title, and level of the book. Check off the strategies used: Does the student ever misread a word, stop, and go back to the beginning of the sentence? Does the student sound out an unknown word? Are long phrases and expression present? Does the student-substituted word change the meaning of the passage or make no sense at all?

It's important that your checklist of strategies matches the strategies listed on your Good Readers' Fix-It-Up and Clarify Strategies poster. The checklist should note how many times the student uses each strategy and the number of times the student experiences a reading problem but takes no action to correct it. Use a tally mark system to do this. This type of strategy-based checklist tells you which students are encountering problems, what their problems are, and how many times they don't use a strategy to correct a problem. It also gives clear indications of which strategies are being used. If a particular student focuses too much on one strategy, explicitly review another strategy on the list, model what it looks

Figure 4.3. Sample Checklist for Assessing the Use of Fix-It-Up and Clarify Strategies

Student	Date	Stops, Returns, Running Start	Skips Ahead, Rereads	Sounds Out Word	Corrects to Make Sense	Smooth, Long Phrases	Expression	Problem but No Strategy

and sounds like, and then guide the student to use it while reading aloud to you.

Talking to the Text

Talking to the text is another formative metacognitive assessment. I learned about it from the Reading Apprenticeship program, but it's been around for years in other forms (e.g., text rendering). With talking to the text, students make invisible thoughts visible through writing. As they read, they "talk back" to the text by writing on the page, in the margins, or on sticky notes. Talking to the text is a great way to keep track of a reader's thought process. If you use it every two to three weeks, it's formative. It's also an assessment that works as a classroom activity, and vice versa.

This assessment/activity is a form of talking back, so it shouldn't be too hard to familiarize your students to the idea. Oprah and Dr. Phil make a mint by making their thoughts audible. Children also make their thoughts audible, except they don't get paid for the activity (although they sometimes pay a price if they're talking out of turn). Twitter feeds, blogs, and the comments feature of online newspapers (whereby readers can instantly post a response to an article) are examples of thoughts made visible. It's obvious that our culture doesn't have a problem with talking back! People talk back in all types of ways, offering up opinions at the drop of a hat.

In talking to the text, active processing is encouraged as students (and adults, for that matter) jot down notes about the text they're reading. Because I'm old school, I stick to paper and pencil. I'm sure, however, that some of you tech-savvy types will create ways to blog, tweet, or even text message to the text. If you're interested in pursuing options for techies to talk back via hypertext links, blogs, podcasts, QR codes, or tweets, Table 4.2 lists a few websites to explore and some recent articles that you may want to read.

Regardless of how thoughts are recorded, the goal is to enable students to voice their concerns, express their confusions, make connections, ask questions, and generally take close note of the words, sentences, and paragraphs that they're reading. As they write, their thoughts become visible, their reading process becomes more active, and their comprehension grows deeper.

Begin to teach the strategy with a photocopied page from a basal anthology story or from a level-appropriate book. Task analysis is critical in the teaching of this strategy, so pick a book that's easy for everyone to read. You don't want to give the students too many unknown variables at a time. At the same time, the text needs to be rich enough to provoke

Table 4.2. Techie Talking Back Options

Articles	Websites
• Dalton, B. (2013). Engaging children in close reading: Multimodal commentaries and illustration remix. *The Reading Teacher, 66*(8), 642–649. • Kissel, B., Wood, K., Stover, K., & Heintschel, K. (2013). *Digital discussions: Using Web 2.0 tools to communicate, collaborate, and create* [IRA E-ssentials series]. Newark, DE: International Reading Association. doi:10.1598/e-ssentials.8002 • Miller, S. (2005, October 10). *50 ways to use Twitter in the classroom*. Retrieved October 3, 2013, from www.universityreviewsonline.com/2005/10/50-ways-to-use-twitter-in-the-classroom.html	• Start a student or classroom blog on Kidblog (kidblog.org) or Edmodo (www.edmodo.com). • Create a three-minute podcast with Audiboo (audioboo.fm). • Use QR codes to engage students by watching "Black & White Scanned All Over" (www.youtube.com/watch?v=ayW032sKtj8).

questions, comments, connections, and other critical thoughts. Also, make sure there's enough white space around the text for students to write down words and complete thoughts.

To begin the activity, the students read the text silently or track along with you as you read the text aloud. At this point, no one should be writing. You simply want the kids to become cursorily familiar with the passage. After the passage has been read, have the students read it again to themselves. This time they should try to think deeply about the text, reflect on its meaning, monitor any thoughts that arise, and then make these thoughts visible by writing them down on the photocopy. Teach your students how to circle words that are difficult to understand, draw arrows to connect one piece of text to another, and jot down questions and answers in the margins. As always, repeatedly model your own talking to the text, both before your students attempt the strategy and as a review throughout the year. After modeling, repeated guided practice is a must. Finally, make sure you concentrate on the strategies listed on the comprehension strategies poster.

Keep in mind that when you have students interact and reread the text in this carefully considered manner, you're teaching to the Common Core. Close reading is an important concept and expectation of those standards, and it's mentioned numerous times in that document, most notably in the introduction but also repeatedly under the "Key Ideas and

Details" heading for literature and informational texts. Here's a quote from the introduction:

> The Standards also lay out a vision of what it means to be a literate person in the twenty-first century. Indeed, the skills and understandings students are expected to demonstrate have wide applicability outside the classroom or workplace. Students who meet the Standards readily undertake the *close* [emphasis added], attentive reading that is at the heart of understanding and enjoying complex works of literature. They habitually perform the critical reading necessary to *pick carefully through* [emphasis added] the staggering amount of information available today in print and digitally. (NCACBP & CCSSO, 2010, p. 3)

After the students have notated their photocopies, it's time for discussion. Perhaps you'll want to do a think-pair-share first. Have the kids independently review (think) and then pair up and share (and compare) what they've written. Students should talk about the connections they made, the words they found challenging, and the questions they asked (and possibly answered). Finish up with a whole-group discussion. If you're pressed for time, you can bypass the think-pair-share and jump right into the class discussion.

After the discussion, it's helpful to spend five or 10 minutes on showing the class one or two exemplary pieces of student work. Toward the beginning of the year, it's best to focus on only one or two specific strategies. Toward the end of the year, you can point out all the strategies that a student demonstrated. Only show positive examples and only with the student's permission. If your school has technology, scan the student work and display it via a smartboard or computer projector. If you need to go low-tech, photocopy the student work onto a transparency and display it via the overhead projector. Regardless of how you display it, the main goal is to point out what's working well in the student's talking to the text. Your instruction might sound something like this:

> Here's Jeremy's talking to the text passage. Wow! You can see that he has a lot of good things going on because his page is covered with writing, boxes, lines, and arrows.
>
> Jeremy has asked a lot of questions. He wrote, "What does this mean?" "What's *aroma*?" and "Why doesn't she understand?" He's answered some questions, too. That's great. Remember what I said about asking questions: Good readers ask questions, but they also try to answer them as they read. You'll often find the answer to a question if you keep reading. Jeremy answered his earlier question about *aroma* right here where he wrote, "*Aroma* is a smell."
>
> Over here, Jeremy made a connection. This line is connecting two circled sentences, and Jeremy made a note: "They both show where she is going." That particular connection is a text-to-text connection.

Later in the year, after they've mastered talking to the text on photocopied sheets during group lessons, allow your students to write their thoughts down on sticky notes. These notes can be placed right on a text. This cuts down on photocopying and allows students to use the strategy at any point in the text. Once you've initiated guided reading (see Chapter 6), you can monitor the students as they use the strategy in small groups.

Another way to monitor strategy use is to gather the students into a circle at the end of a talking to the text lesson. As you circulate while the students use this strategy, you'll identify those who use their reading strategies in competent and/or interesting ways. Bring these students into the center of the large circle and ask them to share specific sticky notes. This gives everyone opportunities to observe and give feedback. When you identify a struggling reader who's competent in the use of a strategy, ask the student to discuss his or her work. The students will find it very rewarding when you ask them to share a job well done with the entire class.

It's appropriate to teach, model, and practice talking to the text during whole-group shared reading with your anthology story and small-group guided reading with an instructional-level book. Although it's possible to assign talking to the text as students read independently during quiet reading time, I suggest that you don't do this. Too much enforced practice will turn kids off to the strategy. Quiet reading time provides a space for students to incorporate strategies naturally, and kids need time to sit down and simply enjoy the act of uninterrupted reading.

It's easy to use talking to the text as a formative assessment. To assess your students' use of strategies, simply collect the photocopies or sticky notes. Rather than assess all the strategies at once, which is very time consuming, scan over the writing and take note of one or two specific strategies. Circle or highlight examples of them in use. You'll then be able to make a general statement (e.g., "On average, Abdul uses comprehension strategies four times per reading.") or a specific statement (e.g., "During the reading of five paragraphs, Darlene asked two questions, answered one of them, made one text-to-text connection, and made one prediction."). Additional information can be gathered by jotting down brief notes as you circulate through the room during work time.

Whether your benchmark is scoring 18 out of 20 on a writing rubric or using three types of metacognitive reading strategies while reading any given text, you know that some students will take longer to reach mastery levels of writing and reading. You also know that some kids won't achieve benchmark scores by the end of the year. This might be due to a lack of motivation, a poor home life, a disability, or even a piece of the instructional puzzle that you're currently missing. If your formative assessments are showing that 85–90% of your students are using reading strategies at the benchmark levels determined by your district, then count your instruction as successful! If you're not hitting this percentage, create a plan for additional instruction and practice for those students who aren't yet at benchmark.

Finally, remember that just as you jettisoned worksheets and activities to make room for the vocabulary card method, you'll need to jettison something to make room for talking to the text. As before, worksheets are the easy target. Another target is class discussion that entails you asking a question and the students answering it. I encourage you to turn some of your teacher-directed instruction into student-directed activities, such as talking to the text. One final way to save time is to modify or even drop your end-of-the-text assessment. After all, you're now formatively assessing with vocabulary cards, a fix-it-up checklist, and student samples of talking to the text. These assessments give you a wealth of information that can be used to inform and guide your instruction. You know which students are on track and which need additional guided and/or independent practice, and you know which students are ready for more advanced instruction or need to practice with text at a more difficult level. Therefore, give careful consideration to the usefulness, or lack thereof, of the information gathered from your end-of-the-text or end-of-the-unit test.

Make It So

Teach comprehension more effectively by doing the following:

- Narrow your focus to two categories of metacognitive strategies: fix-it-up strategies and comprehension strategies.
- List 12 specific strategies on two posters.
- Teach these strategies through extensive modeling and guided practice.
- Give students opportunities to practice the strategies.
- Conduct formative assessment of the strategies via a checklist and/or samples of talking to the text.

If your assessments show that your students are high achieving, move on to more complex permutations of the basic strategies and provide richer and more nuanced stories to comprehend. If you find that your students are chugging along, learning at an average rate throughout the year, then keep your instruction chugging along. If you find that your students are still struggling to master the basics, provide more teaching and practice. Regardless of which path they're on, your students will benefit from your reimagined comprehension instruction.

Using the ideas just listed, you'll transform your core reading program's comprehension component from one that's shallow and wide (impressive looking but ultimately not that effective) to one that's deeper, more focused, and much more effective.

CHAPTER 5

Power Up With Extended Reading

You will need...

· A revised schedule for your reading block
· A multitude of books of various genres for independent reading
· Sets of leveled fiction and nonfiction books (six to eight per set)
· An I Can... list (discussed in this chapter)
· A table at which you can run a small guided reading group (four to seven students)

You will...

· Refrain from using most practice book pages
· Develop a system for managing independent reading time and independent reading books
· Give students extended time to read books on their independent reading levels
· Spend less time on each anthology story and more time on coaching strategies during guided and independent reading time
· Teach the routines for the I Can... list and allow students to gradually take over ownership of these routines
· Develop a plan for conducting and managing formative assessments
· Formatively assess your students over time and use the information you collect to guide your future instruction

Extended reading is a critical component of an effective reading program because it gives students a chance to practice reading. Just as budding musicians must play their instruments to master a piece of music, and beginning swimmers must repeatedly step into a pool to learn how to swim, students can only become competent readers when they're taught the essential skills and strategies of reading, when they're given adequate time to practice and apply these skills and strategies, and when teachers use student practice time to observe and coach reading behaviors (Allington, 2002). Thus, when you build extended reading time into your classroom schedule, you provide numerous opportunities for your students to interact with the big ideas of reading: They'll use phonics to decode words, they'll apply vocabulary knowledge, they'll learn to read more fluently, and they'll independently use strategies to determine word meanings and comprehend texts.

Just what is extended reading? My definition is simple: a student reading text for 15 or more uninterrupted minutes. The text can be in a magazine or book or on a computer or tablet. The reading can take place independently at desks, in comfy chairs, on carpet squares, or around a table in guided reading groups. Regardless of how and where the reading takes place, the goal is to get students to read real texts, not isolated sentences or worksheet pages, for as much time as possible.

If you're anything like me, you get the warm fuzzies whenever you see a student immersed in a book. I love to see students engrossed in reading, especially when they're the ones who have been labeled struggling readers. Recently, my cooperating teacher, Mrs. Draksler, assigned two cursive writing practice pages as part of the day's independent work. After the students completed their handwriting sheets, they were free to choose either independent reading or independent writing. Connor, however, made a beeline to the book bins as soon as his guided reading group was over. He was excited to read *Walter the Farting Dog* by William Kotzwinkle, a book I had introduced and placed in the browsing bin just two days before. Completely forgetting that he was to complete his handwriting sheets first, Connor snatched up the book and began to read.

For the next 25 minutes, as I ran my second guided reading group at the table in the front of the room, I watched Connor out of the corner of my eye. He was totally engrossed in his book, smiling as he carefully read each page and sometimes chuckling out loud. When he was done, I saw him take a reporting slip from the independent reading folder and intently fill it out, grinning the entire time. But when reading time ended, he suddenly cried, "Oh no, I forgot to do my handwriting!" "No need to worry, Connor," said Mrs. Draksler, "It happens. But you'll have to take the work home and do it for homework." Connor looked crestfallen for a moment. Then, brightening up considerably, he said, "That's OK. That book was funny! I loved every time they said *fart!*"

Oh, the simple joys of a third-grade boy! It's heartwarming to see kids spending time with a book that's interesting, fun to read, and on their independent reading level.

The look of extended reading varies from classroom to classroom. In one room, students read independently at their desks; in another room, they read with a buddy on a carpet square; and in a third room, five students read with the teacher around a kidney-shaped table. Sometimes the books are nonfiction, and at other times, they're fiction. Books vary from the Junie B. Jones series by Barbara Park and the Magic Tree House series by Mary Pope Osborne, to books from publisher-created series such as Ready Readers or First Chapter Books, to classic tales such as *Bronx Masquerade* by Nikki Grimes, *Shiloh* by Phyllis Reynolds Naylor, and *Hatchet* by Gary Paulsen. Formats vary, too, from graphic novels and picture books to massive chapter books such as *Harry Potter and the Goblet of Fire* by J.K. Rowling. Nowadays, you might even find a student curled up in a classroom corner reading from a computer tablet.

The common element of all of these variations is a student in a state of reading flow. When a student is in flow, he or she is captivated by the text, interested in the language and the pictures, and enthralled with the facts or story lines that are unfolding in the pages. Most importantly, that enthrallment and captivation lasts for an extended period, not merely five or six minutes.

If five or six minutes don't qualify as extended time, what does? If you're a hardcore reader like I am, you might lose yourself in a book for hours. My nephews have been known to fall asleep with a book on Friday night and then spend the bulk of their Saturday morning polishing it off. For the purposes of the classroom, however, I define an extended period as at least 15 minutes of totally engrossed reading for first and second graders and 20 minutes or more for third graders and beyond.

The Importance of Extended Reading

"The more you read, the better reader you become" strikes me as a commonsense thing to say. Educators, however, need to justify instructional practices with more than commonsense. Fortunately for us, there's a broad and deep research base that supports the instructional practice of having kids read from many books on a multitude of levels for extended periods of time. So, before I dive into how we make changes that allow for extended reading, I'd like to touch on a few studies and quote a few researchers to support why we should make those changes.

There's an oft-quoted saying that practice makes perfect. What's more, practice makes permanent. After countless hours of practice, Michael Jordan never once forgot how to dribble a basketball or do a layup during an NBA game. After playing Little Feat and Steely Dan tunes three or four nights a week for years on end, I can still remember the melodies, lyrics, and rhythms to songs I haven't played in 15 years.

Gladwell (2008), the author of *Outliers: The Story of Success*, puts a number on just how much practice is needed for those who hope to achieve perfection and permanence. According to Gladwell, it takes at least 10,000 hours of practice to become excellent at what you do, be it high-caliber tennis player, artful jazz drummer, or masterful reading teacher. To put it in terms of learning how to read, that's 4,000 2.5-hour blocks of high-quality reading practice (not worksheets, word puzzles, and state test preparation). Stated another way, that's about 22 years of schooling!

Of course, teachers don't have anywhere near that amount of time, nor do the students. Don't despair, though. The 10,000 hours figure is really just a quick and catchy way of saying that lots and lots of deliberate, dedicated, and focused practice is needed if someone is going to develop a skill or set of skills to a level of mastery. Besides, we're not trying to create reading wunderkinds with reading skills analogous to the tennis talent of Serena Williams or the drumming adeptness of Buddy Rich. We do, however, want to enable all of our students to become competent readers. To create competent readers in much less than 10,000 hours, we must focus intently on how and what we teach. This is why Super Core strongly suggests that you budget as much time as possible for student-centered reading routines. Here are two that are critical:

- Every student in the classroom reads *every* day for at least 15 minutes from a book on his or her independent reading level.
- Every student in the classroom reads *every* day for at least 15 minutes from a book on his or her instructional level.

In a general sense, reading opportunities translate into gains in fluency, comprehension, and even vocabulary (Graves & Watts-Taffe, 2002). Studies suggest that every opportunity to read fosters improved reading proficiency (Allington, 2009). They also suggest that if students are to make reading achievement gains, they need to have access to quality teachers, quality reading experiences, and a quantity or volume of reading (Topping, Samuels, & Paul, 2007). In other words, it takes effort on the part of both the teacher and the student plus a tremendous amount of reading practice if the student is going to become a competent reader. This is especially true if the student is a struggling reader.

I mention the teacher and student specifically because the reality is that teachers can't rely on anyone outside the educational system to provide students with instruction, practice time, or even books. Whereas some parents practice with their children, reinforce reading at home, and set limits on computer and television time, many don't. I'm not judging, merely stating a fact. More and more, students are spending fewer and fewer hours reading outside of the school setting (National Endowment for the Arts, 2007).

Schools have their problems, too. Studies show there is precious little reading going on inside many of our schools. In 1977, Allington wrote an article entitled "If They Don't Read Much, How They Ever Gonna Get Good?" in which he described struggling readers who read very little during regular and remedial reading classes. This lack of reading wasn't due to the students refusing to read. Rather, the teachers and school systems weren't providing opportunities to read.

According to researchers, not much has changed since 1977. Regarding the amount of reading that students engage in during any given school day, Brenner, Hiebert, and Tompkins (2009) say that it "has remained at a relatively low constant over the past 30 years" (p. 125). Throughout the 1980s, 1990s, and 2000s, studies consistently reported that students were reading only 8–14 minutes per day! Imagine trying to become a proficient welder or chef with only 8–14 minutes per day to practice. I can't even whip up a batch of macaroni and cheese in eight minutes.

Today, the question, "If they don't read much, how they ever gonna get good?" is seen in a more nuanced light. Researchers are looking into the nuances, and their answers are concerning. In their analysis of 90-minute reading blocks in core reading programs, Brenner et al. (2009) found that students spent a limited amount of time engaged in reading, either orally or silently. What do they mean by *limited*? On average, the students spent only 20% of their 90-minute block, or 18 minutes, reading any type of connected text. The bulk of the time was spent on activities such as teacher instruction, completing workbook pages, and playing word games. These researchers also found that since No Child Left Behind came into being, many schools had doubled the time they devoted to reading instruction, but the time students actually spent reading had increased by only 15%. This means that if kids read for 18 minutes in school in the past, they're only reading 2.7 minutes more today.

Basal programs simply don't provide the reading routines and text options that allow students to read for any great length of time. When Brenner and Hiebert (2010) looked at various third-grade core reading programs, they found that the programs provided limited opportunities to read, specifically an average of 15 minutes per day (with a range of approximately 10–24 minutes). I wonder how many of these 15 minutes were teacher directed, how many were devoted to independent practice, and how many involved students being actively engaged with the text. If students are reading round-robin style, individual students might read for two to three minutes and then zone out for the rest of the 15 minutes.

Thus, 15 minutes of reading practice could in reality be a mere two to three minutes.

When teachers follow basal or core reading programs faithfully, their students simply don't read much. How can they when, as Dewitz and Jones (2013) noted, the reading text block is crammed full of before, during, and after questions to determine comprehension; differentiation activities to accommodate gifted students and struggling learners; language-building sidebars; and personal response activities?

Eighteen minutes per reading block, 8–14 minutes a day, a range of 10–24 minutes—these amounts don't sound like much, and they aren't. Teachers should be especially concerned about the lack of opportunities for student reading when they consider the following: Ivey and Fisher (2006) recommend that the amount of time spent in reading and writing should be greater than the amount devoted to instruction, and Allington (1983, 2006) placed a number on it, suggesting that a minimum of 90–120 minutes of high-success reading activities be programmed into every school day.

Of course, there are issues beyond what we teachers create. One huge problem is instructional time that's lost due to factors beyond our control. Do you ever feel like you're teaching inside a pinball machine or in the middle of a hurricane (or inside a pinball machine that's being buffeted by a hurricane)? I do! In an elementary school, it seems like something or someone comes through the door every few minutes and disrupts the class. Because I love to think about numbers and trends (or maybe it's just because I'm obsessive-compulsive), I keep a record of every significant event that impinges on my instructional time. Over the last three years, I calculate that 15–50% of my teaching time per month has been disrupted by or lost to schedule changes; snow delays; drug and alcohol assemblies; bullying prevention assemblies; vision and hearing testing; teacher absences; school concerts; holiday activities; professional development sessions; nosebleeds, vomiting, and other student-centered disruptions; 4Sight, DIBELS, Developmental Reading Assessment (DRA), and end-of-unit testing.... I could go on, but I'd rather not.

There's some good news, however. We know that even relatively small increases in the time a student reads extended text can make a difference in his or her reading achievement. For example, Kuhn and Schwanenflugel (2009) looked at second-grade classrooms and found that classrooms of students who made significant gains in reading achievement had more reading time programmed in than did classrooms of students who did not. How much more time? In

To inspire and support reading, give students a choice of texts and plenty of time to read on their independent and instructional reading levels.

the classrooms with significant gains, the students read for an additional seven minutes each day. Seven minutes! Surely, we can make room for this amount of extended reading time in our core reading programs.

Reading research over the past 40 years firmly supports the idea that reading programs should include time for extended reading, whether it's instructional reading in a guided reading group around a table or independent reading on a carpet square, at a desk, or in a cozy chair. In the words of Gambrell et al. (2011),

> It is clear that the amount of time spent reading is a critical consideration in reading development. We have long known that students who spend more time reading are better readers (Allington & McGill-Franzen, 2003; Anderson et al., 1988; Cunningham & Stanovich, 1998) and that students who have more experience with reading are better prepared for reading success than their counterparts with less experience (Allington, 1991; Neuman & Celano, 2001). (p. 155)

With a willingness to change and a bit of planning, you can increase the amount of time that your students spend reading during your reading block, and thereby increase the chances that the kids will make significant gains in reading achievement, and you can do it amid all the insanity that's part of educational life. So, let's get on with a bit of planning.

Scope:
Creating Time and Space for Extended Reading

To make extended reading happen takes planning that goes well beyond gathering up a bunch of books, putting them on a shelf, and telling the kids when they finish a test early, "Find a book and read it until everyone's finished." If students are going to read by themselves or in a small group guided by you, then you must organize the reading so reading errors, wrong learning, and frustration are minimized. Conversely, you want to maximize reading accuracy, proficiency, and success. There are three keys to all of this: teacher expertise, a wealth of leveled books, and time in the classroom for you to teach small guided reading groups and for students to read quietly by themselves.

You've already started down the road of becoming a more knowledgeable and skillful teacher of reading, so let's discuss ways of gathering leveled books and creating time for independent reading and guided reading groups. Both are challenging topics to address within the confines of a core reading program based on "drill the skill" workbooks, one anthology, and a limited number of leveled books. This means it's time to make some major changes. But don't worry! As Kris Kringle sang to the Winter Warlock, "Put one foot in front of the other, and soon you'll be walking cross the floor." We'll take it a step at a time, beginning with your schedule.

To create a classroom environment that fosters the love of reading, you'll need to have time for the kids to read lots of books. Although this chapter is all about reading, I'm going to describe scheduling options that address spelling, grammar, and writing, too, because it's easier to look at the whole and then work backward to the parts. In subsequent chapters, we'll revisit the time allocated to writing, grammar, and spelling. Right now, let's look at a traditional schedule based on a nonmodified core reading program.

A Traditional Basal Schedule

In my school, the primary grades get roughly 120–150 minutes for reading and writing per day (we call it communications), and the intermediate grades get 60–75 minutes. I'd bet that your reading class runs for 60–150 minutes a day, so I'm going to pick a generic figure of 100 minutes. Figure 5.1 shows a 100-minute reading schedule loosely based on a third-grade core reading program as it may exist in schools today.

It's rather cut-and-dried, wouldn't you say? You'll notice that it reflects all the components of a traditional core reading program, namely,

- Spelling, which also includes the phonics scope and sequence
- Grammar, another broad scope and sequence that students learn via whole-group instruction and workbook pages
- A basal story from an anthology that's read in a whole-group setting
- Opportunities for whole-class questioning, discussion, and worksheet practice in a multitude of comprehension and reading skills outlined in the teacher's manual
- A handwriting component

Also included are 15 minutes for writing (during grammar time or perhaps a writing project during one day of anthology time) and a 30-minute opportunity to run a small and flexible reading group or groups once a week.

You may also notice the following. First, an entire reading block is devoted to summative testing and summative test preparation. That's 100 minutes a week, or 20% of the total weekly reading time! Second, instruction is mostly with the whole group. Finally, there's little indication

Figure 5.1. A Traditional Basal Schedule

Topic and Time	Day 1	Day 2	Day 3	Day 4	Day 5
Spelling: 20 minutes	• Pretest • Introduction	• Instruction • Practice book pages	• Guided practice • Practice book pages	• Review • Practice test	• Summative test
Grammar: 20 minutes	• Introduction	• Instruction • Practice book pages	• Practice book pages	• Formal writing assignment	• Summative test
Story from the anthology: 50–55 minutes	• Introduction to the story • Introduction to the vocabulary • The teacher reads the story aloud to the students (if the story is too hard) or with the students. • Class discussion: Comprehension strategies	• Review the vocabulary • The teacher and/or students reread the story for fluency. • Comprehension: The teacher questions the students using the teacher's manual.	• Practice book pages: Vocabulary and comprehension skills • Project from the manual or small-group/ guided reading (30 minutes)	• The students listen to and read along with an audio recording of the story. • Practice book pages or continuation of the project from the teacher's manual • Review for the summative test	• Summative test (30 minutes) • State test skills prep (30 minutes)
Handwriting: 5–10 minutes	• Practice book pages	• Practice book pages	• Practice book pages	• Practice book pages	

that specific students are reading on their independent or instructional levels or engaging in extended reading and writing activities.

As Skippyjon Jones might say, "Holy guacamole!" To me, this schedule is a recipe for mediocrity. Although the core program addresses many of the necessary components of reading instruction, the traditional basal schedule is simultaneously too broad (too many skills and standards in the various scope and sequences practiced via too many workbook pages) and too narrow (one story doesn't fit all, there's a dearth of real books to read, there's little time to write, etc.).

During my first year of teaching with a core program, I calculated that of the reading block time we actually had (remember that 15–50% of it was lost every month by various disruptions), my cooperating teacher and I spent 54% of it giving summative tests, prepping the kids for the state test, and mucking about with one story a week in the anthology. The other 46% of the time was spent on grammar, spelling, and handwriting skills and a tiny bit of guided reading.

Looking back on that first year, I realize how little time the kids spent reading. The basal program, and our instructional focus, was forcing the students down the same path as those students studied by the researchers. On the majority of days, the kids spent less than 10 minutes on reading any type of expository or narrative text. Something had to give, and I was determined that it would be that traditional core program schedule.

A Super Core Schedule

To create a new schedule with a focus on time for students to read and write, my current cooperating teacher, Toni Draksler, and I reduced the time we spent in two major areas: (1) the weekly basal anthology story and (2) workbook pages and skill-based grammar, spelling, and anthology activities.

I want to be very clear here that with Super Core, the basic core reading components will remain. You'll still teach the weekly anthology story and a good portion of your core program's grammar, phonics, and comprehension scope and sequence. Equally important, you'll still cover the Common Core State Standards. However, Super Core suggests you move away from teaching grammar, spelling, and comprehension in an isolated skill-based fashion and move toward teaching them within extended reading and writing routines. This creates synergy. In other words, by teaching skills *within* authentic activities, you create learning that's more than the sum of its parts.

Specific to our schedule, Toni and I first cut back on the time we dedicated to the reading of the weekly anthology story and the teaching of dozens of comprehension strategies. Next, we canned 95% of our workbook pages in all areas. Third, we decreased and reconfigured the amount of time we spent on teaching the memorized spelling list. Finally, we cut back on the time we dedicated to handwriting.

Right about now, you may be exclaiming, "Holy pruning shears, Batman! That's a lot of cutting!" I agree. We pruned away a veritable thicket of basal activities and worksheets. The pruning, however, opened up glorious blocks of time. Into those blocks of time, we placed routines and materials that allowed students to more naturally and thoroughly practice grammar, spelling, writing, phonics, fluency, vocabulary, and comprehension.

Because administrators have come and gone, as have district policies and practices, our Super Core schedule has changed a number of times over the last two years, and it may change again next year. Nothing's *ever* easy in education. The essence of our original schedule is still intact, though, and Figure 5.2 shows what our schedule looks like today.

You can see that the basal basics are still there and that we reserved a block of time every week to coach the students for the spring summative state reading test. If I had my druthers, I'd get rid of that coaching block, but for now, our district policy mandates it. As Yul Brynner said in *The Ten Commandments,* "So let it be written, so let it be done!"

Notice how the time devoted to extended reading and writing has increased dramatically. With a revised schedule, weekly opportunities for students to read on their instructional level in small groups jumped from 30 minutes to anywhere between 50 and 100 minutes. Time to write paragraphs jumped from the occasional 50 minutes to between 40 and 100 minutes every week (depending on how we run the second half of our reading block), and time to read independently or with a buddy (during guided reading time) jumped from 0 to 25, 50, 75, or even 100 minutes.

While time for certain reading and writing activities increased, time for other activities decreased. Explicit handwriting instruction dropped from 20–40 minutes to 10 or 20 minutes. Much more dramatically, and more importantly, the time devoted to whole-group instruction or activities based on the basal story dropped from around 150–200 minutes to 75–80 minutes. Finally, time devoted to whole-group instruction of grammar and spelling, and the subsequent practice of isolated skills in workbook pages, was decreased. We did this by pushing skill work into the guided reading and independent reading and writing blocks.

Even during weeks of multiple classroom disruptions, this flexible and synergistic schedule allots to each student a minimum of 25 minutes of reading in instructional-level text almost every day, 25 minutes of

Figure 5.2. A Super Core Schedule

Day 1	Day 2	Day 3	Day 4	Day 5
• Anthology story (30 minutes): Build background knowledge and schemata, introduce vocabulary, and read the story	• Anthology story (25 minutes): Reread and teach fluency and comprehension via the Good Readers' Metacognition Strategies and the Good Readers' Fix-It-Up and Clarify Strategies posters (discussed in Chapter 4)	• Skills prep for state testing (20–25 minutes) • Handwriting (5–10 minutes)	• Anthology story (20–25 minutes): Reread and teach fluency and comprehension via the two strategies posters • Handwriting (5–10 minutes)	• Modified selection test (formative; 35 minutes): Integrate the Good Readers' Metacognition Strategies poster and writing
• Modified spelling list (20 minutes): Segment and blend for phonemic awareness and phonics	• Word work (25 minutes)	• Grammar skills (20 minutes): From the reduced scope and sequence, direct and explicit, and practiced with writing activities	• Spelling practice test with instant error analysis and correction (15 minutes)	• Formative assessment (15 minutes): Spelling test
• Grammar minilessons (10 minutes): Skills used in writing • Authentic writing (with formative assessment) or guided writing (40 minutes): Every other week in the second semester, write Common Core pieces, task specific or otherwise (compare/contrast, retell, summarize, persuade, narrative, descriptive, etc.)	• Guided reading (four groups, 25 minutes per group, two groups per teacher): Match the basal story theme if possible and teach fluency and comprehension via the two strategies posters • Use the I Can... list (discussed later in this chapter) for independent reading and writing practice (50 minutes)	• Same as day 2 (50 minutes): Guided reading groups and independent reading	• Same as day 2 (50 minutes): Guided reading groups and independent reading • Progress monitoring of oral reading fluency coupled with the I Can... list (30 minutes every other week)	• Guided reading and independent reading, or authentic writing (with formative assessment), or guided writing (every other week in the second semester; compare/contrast, retell, summarize, persuade, narrative, descriptive, etc.) (50 minutes)

reading in independent-level text almost every day, and 35 minutes to write sentences and paragraphs at least two times a week. Additionally, the kids get time to engage in word work activities that build the phonics foundation that so many struggling readers lack.

Have we achieved Allington's 90–120 minutes of daily high-success reading activities? Not yet, but we're getting close. Within the confines of our core reading program and our current district policy, we've created a more student-centered program with a great deal of reading and writing. In a smoothly running five-day week without disruptions, and in comparison with what we had before, the time devoted to extended reading is simply enormous.

As I wrap up this section, I must stress that the third-grade classroom that I work in is a cotaught classroom. You've probably figured this out already. Toni and I have the luxury of running two guided reading groups simultaneously, effectively doubling the amount of instructional-level reading that each student receives (as compared with a typical third-grade classroom). But I must also stress that thousands of teachers across the United States run guided reading groups by themselves each and every day, and if I had my own classroom to run, as I did when I ran a special education learning support classroom for fourth and fifth graders, I'd run it with a schedule much like the one we just discussed. So, I encourage you to create a schedule that allows you to run at least one or two guided reading groups every day.

A 70-Minute Super Core Schedule

If you only have 60–75 minutes for your reading block, you can still make changes that allow for some extended reading and writing. Figure 5.3 shows a schedule based on a 70-minute block of time. It has fewer changes and more traditional basal components, but if you're testing the waters and starting out conservatively, this is a good schedule to consider.

A Super Core Schedule With No Guided Reading

We've talked a lot about guided reading routines and schedules, in which students read on their instructional levels. If you aren't yet ready to jump into running a guided reading group, it's possible to construct a schedule that allows for your core reading program and independent reading time. Figure 5.4 is an example using a 70-minute block of reading.

In this schedule, the students remain in a whole group, but about half of the time typically given to anthology story instruction is replaced with I Can... independent reading and writing activities (described later in this chapter). Teaching students to complete I Can... routines and then

Figure 5.3. A 70-Minute Super Core Schedule

Topic	Day 1	Day 2	Day 3	Day 4	Day 5
Spelling	Introduction (15 minutes)	Word work activities (15 minutes)	Handwriting (10 minutes)	Word work activities or practice book pages (10 minutes)	Formative test (10 minutes)
Grammar	Introduction (15 minutes)	Practice book pages (15 minutes)	• Writing minilessons (10 minutes) • Authentic or guided writing (30 minutes)	Grammar practice (10 minutes): Whole-group physical response	Formative test (10 minutes)
Story from the anthology, or guided and independent reading	Story introduction (40 minutes): • Build background knowledge and schemata • Teach the vocabulary words • Read the story • Fluency and comprehension instruction via the Good Readers' Metacognition Strategies and the Good Readers' Fix-It-Up and Clarify Strategies posters (discussed in Chapter 4)	While others engage in independent reading and writing with the I Can... list (discussed later in this chapter), guided reading group A (most needy group) and then guided reading group B (20 minutes per group)	While others engage in independent reading and writing with the I Can... list, guided reading group A (20 minutes)	• Anthology story (20 minutes): Shared reading for comprehension and comprehension instruction via the two strategies posters • While others engage in independent reading and writing with the I Can... list, guided reading group C (20 minutes)	• Formative assessment (25 minutes): Modified selection test • State test skills prep (25 minutes)

Figure 5.4. A 70-Minute Super Core Schedule With No Guided Reading

Topic	Day 1	Day 2	Day 3	Day 4	Day 5
Spelling	Introduction (15 minutes)	Word work activities (15 minutes)	Handwriting (10 minutes)	Word work activities or practice book pages (10 minutes)	Formative test (10 minutes)
Grammar	Introduction (15 minutes)	Practice book pages (15 minutes)	• Writing minilessons (10 minutes) • Authentic or guided writing (30 minutes)	Grammar practice (10 minutes): Whole-group physical response	Formative test (10 minutes)
Story from the anthology, or independent reading and writing	Story introduction (40 minutes): • Build background knowledge and schemata • Teach the vocabulary words • Read the story • Fluency and comprehension instruction via the Good Readers' Metacognition Strategies and the Good Readers' Fix-It-Up and Clarify Strategies posters (discussed in Chapter 4)	• Anthology story (20 minutes): Shared reading for comprehension and comprehension instruction via the two strategies posters • Whole-group I Can... list (discussed later in this chapter; 20 minutes): Independent reading and writing	Whole-group I Can... list (20 minutes): Independent reading and writing	• Anthology story (20 minutes): Shared reading for comprehension and comprehension instruction via the two strategies posters • Whole-group I Can... list (20 minutes): Independent reading and writing	• Formative assessment (25 minutes): Modified selection test • State test skills prep (25 minutes)

giving them the time to practice means they'll have lots of time to read on their independent reading levels. It also provides time for students to do independent writing, vocabulary word practice, and a host of other reading and writing activities. You can enable all of this by simply decreasing the amount of time you spend on hammering away at the weekly anthology story. You can also use some of the instructional time you gain to listen in on a student's independent reading, quickly assess strengths and needs, and provide feedback or brief instruction.

Teaching Chops: How to Teach Extended Reading in Guided Reading Groups

Simply put, guided reading groups (small, flexible groups of students reading instructional-level texts with the teacher) give teachers the structure to provide supportive and effective reading instruction. It's important to note that various writers and researchers describe the guided reading format in different ways. We can think of guided reading as a method of teaching small, relatively homogeneous groups, as described in books written by Fountas and Pinnell (1996) and others (e.g., Richardson, 2009). For the purposes of this book, I'm using the term *guided reading* to describe small-group instruction with teacher guidance and strategy coaching.

It's beyond the scope of this book to describe all the ins and outs of a guided reading lesson. If you'd like to explore the topic in greater depth, pick up one of the excellent books listed in the References section, starting with *Guided Reading: Good First Teaching for All Children* by Fountas and Pinnell (1996). In the meantime, let's discuss in a general sense how to create and instruct a guided reading group, based on instructional reading levels and the needs of each reader, within your core reading program.

The I Can... List

To make the basic structures of guided reading work, you'll first need to establish a classroom of learners that values independent reading and writing. To do this, you'll need to put into place the I Can... list and teach its routines throughout the year. I learned of the I Can... list from Diller's (2003) work on literacy centers. Figure 5.5 shows two versions of the list, which can easily be made into posters. The first shows routines taught in the first nine weeks of school, and the second adds a few more routines for the second nine weeks.

> **Figure 5.5. Two Versions of the I Can... List**
>
> | *First nine weeks* | *Second nine weeks* |
> |---|---|
> | I can... | I can... |
> | • Read independently | • Read independently and complete a book slip |
> | • Buddy read | • Buddy read |
> | • Repeat reading with my toolbox | • Repeat reading with my toolbox |
> | | • Read, record, and check |
> | | • Review my vocabulary cards |

The purpose of the I Can... list is to have your students read and write independently while you work with readers in a guided reading group. Therefore, it's essential that the kids who aren't in the guided reading group be able to work independently without interrupting you for any reason. A little later on, I'll explain some ways to create this blissful state of noninterruption. Once your independent work routines are established, you can begin to form small, flexible, and leveled groups of readers that meet for 20–30 minutes one or more times a week. These groups are the beating heart of guided reading instruction (along with the teaching chops you bring to teaching the groups). I must stress that these groups should not be formed in the first few weeks of school. It's imperative to your yearlong success (and your mental health) that you form your guided reading groups only after your students have had multiple opportunities to practice independent reading and writing routines without teacher intervention. This means that you may need four to six weeks before you and your students are ready for guided reading groups.

Size Matters

The groups you create can have as few as two students or as many as five, six, or even seven. A group larger than seven can make it difficult for you to hold the attention of every student in the group, prevent you from knowing the individual reading habits of each student, or lead to a lack of differentiation. Conversely, if you have fewer than two students in a group, it's not a group but a one-on-one tutoring session. More importantly, small groups of two or three students means you'll have five to seven groups in your classroom, which leads to management problems, mental breakdowns, and a general gnashing of teeth. Over the years, I've seen teachers struggle and eventually give up on guided reading because they try to manage too many groups. I suggest you shoot for a maximum of four guided reading groups (see Figure 5.6).

Figure 5.6. A Guided Reading Group

Creating a smaller number of groups, each with four to six students, may require you to group students who are on neighboring instructional reading levels. Here's an example: Imagine that you're a fourth-grade teacher who finds at the beginning of the year that you have four students on DRA level 28, three students on level 30, four on level 34, 10 on level 40, and one on level 50. To some, five levels means five guided reading groups. Although some teachers might be able to run five guided reading groups effectively, you might not be that person. I know I'm not. To create four groups, look at your test results carefully to find out which students are stronger in their level and which are weaker. Now imagine that you identify two lower achieving 30s, one higher achieving 30, six lower achieving 40s, and four high-performing 40s. Figure 5.7 shows

Figure 5.7. Sample Groups With Mixed Developmental Reading Assessment (DRA) Levels

Group	Number of Students	DRA Level
1	4	28
	2	30
2	1	30
	4	34
3	6	40
4	4	40
	1	50

how you can group these readers. Reducing your instructional groups from five to four might not seem like much, but it can be a lifesaver.

The 70-minute schedule outlined earlier is based on three guided reading groups. Group A is seen twice a week, whereas groups B and C are seen only once a week. There are other possible permutations, of course. The important thing to remember is that a student who's reading instructional-level text for 25 or 50 minutes a week is much better off than a student who reads *no* instructional-level text.

Instructing a Guided Reading Group

The more you listen to students read, the more you come to understand what they need to learn and practice. As you accrue time with your readers, you'll begin to think thoughts like, "Donnell needs to gain confidence and use basic word attack strategies," "Harley and Katy need to slow down and carefully read through each word," and "Barry needs to think about meaning as he reads; ask himself, Did that make sense?; and then reread and self-correct." During these moments, use formative assessment to help keep track of what you're noticing and sensing.

If you're buying into the Super Core philosophy, the reading strategies you focus on in your guided reading groups are basically the same as those focused on during anthology time, namely, the six fix-it-up and clarify strategies, such as "skip ahead then reread" and "sound out the word," and the six metacognition strategies, such as "retell and summarize" and "predict and check." As you gain practice in running guided reading groups, you'll become more skilled at guiding, supporting, offering feedback, and encouraging students as they encounter and attempt to solve problems related to mastering the big ideas in reading, namely, decoding, fluency, vocabulary, and comprehension. Fountas and Pinnell (2012) put a name to a teacher's ability to guide students as they read: attending to elements of proficient reading.

As students read, they encounter difficulties. It's your job to allow them to make mistakes, and then guide them to apply fix-it-up, clarify, and comprehension strategies. When you're teaching students in a guided reading group, remember these two things: (1) If a student is stuck on a word or a question, don't give the word or tell the answer, and don't let other kids tell either; and (2) teach, model, and guide students in the use of strategies so they can then use these strategies to figure out unknown words or answer questions. If a student begins to read the sentence "He loved to explore the woods and the stream" and gets stuck on the word *explore*, you can encourage the student to read ahead and then come back and use a word that matches the letter sounds of the skipped word and also makes sense in the sentence. Or you can encourage the student to find the vowels in the word, divide it into syllables using the V–C–C–V rule (where blends are not divided), and then decode each syllable. Or if the student says, "explode," instead of "explore," you can ask, "does it make sense to say that he loved to explode the woods and the stream?" Of course, the boys in your group will say yes! Table 5.1 provides examples of what you

	Table 5.1. Samples of Guided Reading Support
Decoding	• Teach phonic patterns and encourage students to apply their knowledge when they encounter words with that pattern. • Teach students to read all the way through the word. Conversely, teach students to use both the letters and sounds of the word and the meaning of the sentence. Some writers call this cross-checking letter–sound patterns and meaning. • Ask questions such as, "Does the way you read that word sound right to you?" "What's another word that sounds similar but makes sense?" "Is that the way we speak?" • When a student solves a word problem, ask, "How did you figure out that word?" This helps students become aware of their own strategy use.

Fluency	• Model fluency to the group by reading a passage and pointing out what makes your reading fluent. For example, say, "Listen as I read this paragraph fluently. I'm going to read in smooth, short and long phrases; I'm going to pause for a second when I come to a period and take a breath; and I'm going to read with expression!"
	• Review the fix-it-up and clarify and metacognition strategies prior to reading.
	• Offer feedback on oral reading and provide opportunities to reread a passage. Possible ways to reread in a guided reading group include the following:
	  • Read a passage chorally and then have a student reread the passage. As students read, offer guidance and feedback about their reading.
	  • Echo read the selection. This means that you read a passage in the text, and then an individual or the group echoes back what you read. I suggest echoing at the paragraph level. If students echo at the sentence level, they may be merely memorizing the sentence and then parroting it back to you.
	  • Reread the text as Readers Theatre. After the text has been read again, give the students feedback about what they need to improve on and what they did really well.
	  • After you read a story, have the students go back through the book, pick out their favorite event and/or page, silently reread it to themselves, and then read it aloud to the group with as much accuracy, flow, and prosody as possible. After the passage has been read, give them feedback about what they did really well.
	  • Ask the kids to describe what they or others did well, such as, "What did Janella do that demonstrates her fluency?"

(continued)

Table 5.1. Samples of Guided Reading Support (*continued*)

Comprehension	• Have students retell information about characters, the setting, and events. • Teach students that reading is always about making sense. Guide them to constantly monitor their reading to make sure they're making sense. Ask questions such as, "What does that mean?" "Does that sentence make sense to you?" "Does the word ___ make sense in that sentence?" "What you just read doesn't make sense to me, and I wonder if it makes sense to you." "What's another word that sounds similar to the word you just read but makes sense?" • Practice boiling down what was just read into a summary. • Ask questions that can be answered by looking right there in the text, inferred by thinking and searching, or inferred by combining previous knowledge with text information. • Guide students in the use of strategies that lead to greater comprehension, such as asking and answering questions, making and checking predictions, visualizing, and making connections.

might do and say as you guide, support, and encourage your students as they work on the big ideas within their guided reading groups.

Once again, it's beyond the scope of this book to describe all the ins and outs of instructing a guided reading lesson. Guided reading is a complex and rich method of instruction with many years of history behind it. If the method works for you, then, by all means, buy books specifically about guided reading and engage in some professional development in this area.

When I work with students in small groups, I really get to know them as readers. Guided reading groups give me time to praise and support individual strengths and teach strategies to overcome individual weaknesses. According to Gambrell et al. (2011), "teacher guidance and support appear to be critical components of successful reading practice for developing readers" (p. 150). I agree. When given multiple opportunities to practice reading strategies under the guidance of an expert teacher (who provides both support and explicit instruction), students' reading skills can blossom and grow like well-watered flowers.

This is certainly the case for Allie and Jayna, two kindergartners in one of my guided reading groups. My guided reading routine, which supports their emerging reading skills, looks something like this: Before the students read the book, I have them look at the cover page, think about the title of the story, and make predictions about what will happen based on the title and the cover illustration. Then, we complete a picture walk for the entire story. All of this helps the students build schemata about the book topic, be it traveling to the beach or tending a garden. The picture walk also gives me an opportunity to use vocabulary words from the story and clarify word meanings if necessary. While reading the text, I support Allie and Jayna as they perfect their left-to-right tracking; one-to-one matching; and use of picture, meaning, and letter cues to read each word. After reading, the girls might answer a question about the setting or a character in the story, share their favorite event in the story, or go on a word hunt for words that begin with the letter *W* or contain the *-in* and *-at* patterns. Although regularly occurring guided reading instruction (three times a week for 15–20 minutes) isn't the only reason these students are making progress, it's certainly one of the biggest reasons why they've both progressed from knowing a handful of letters and letter sounds in September to reading on DRA levels 2 and 3 (Fountas and Pinnell level C) by early January.

Before, During, After, and Simultaneous Reading

On any given day during any given week, you might emphasize certain skills and strategies during guided reading time. The instructional routines of your guided reading group, however, can remain fairly constant. Table 5.2 provides options for what you can do before, during, and after the kids read their guided reading books.

Here's one final guided reading activity to consider: simultaneous reading. The technique, which works best with emerging readers, involves teaching kids to whisper read their guided reading book at whatever speed is good for them and to go back and reread if they finish before being asked to stop. As the students read, you should coach strategies individually, based on what you notice as you give a quick listen to each student reading. The benefits of the technique include additional coaching time and a chance to formatively assess the students through teacher observations, as well as increased reading time for the kids because every student is actively reading.

All of these activities and techniques dovetail nicely with the Common Core's standards for grades K–5. Because the dovetailing is extensive, I won't list specific standards. Suffice it to say that the Common Core frequently mentions the following, all of which relate to your teaching and the students' learning, and all of which are addressed in a well-run guided reading group: prompting and support; scaffold as needed; ask and answer questions about key details in the text; read and comprehend literature; describe a character, setting, or event in depth; determine the meanings of words and phrases as they're used in a text; read and comprehend informational texts; and read with sufficient accuracy and fluency to support comprehension.

Table 5.2. Before, During, and After Guided Reading	
Before Reading	Develop students' interest, motivation, and purpose for reading and build schemata: • The teacher discusses the title of the book. The students tell what they know about the book topic and/or make a personal connection to it. • The students make predictions about what they might encounter as they read the book. • The students do a picture walk, leafing through the book and discussing concepts, thereby building schemata for the concepts in the book. During discussion, the teacher includes vocabulary words that are important to the story.
During Reading	Model and coach strategies and provide practice time: • The teacher points out text features to the students. • The students read and reread to build fluency. • The teacher points out vocabulary words. • The teacher points out strategies for solving reading problems and guides students as they use them.
After Reading	Develop comprehension and firm up strategy use: • The students summarize and retell the story. • The students answer comprehension questions. If they can't, the teacher coaches the students to go back into the text and visualize a scene, ask and answer questions, use picture or context clues, etc. • The students discuss the strategies that they used to solve problems. • The students discuss connections, surprises, things that interested them, etc.

Where Do I Get Sets of Instructional-Level Books?

To run guided reading groups, you need multiple copies of books on specific reading levels. Educational book publishers, such as Modern Curriculum Press, Celebration Press, and Capstone Press (full disclosure and shameless self-promotion: I'm a Capstone author), put out dozens of books every year on topics that are interesting to kids, relatively short (thus creating a sense of accomplishment: "Wow, we read that book in one week!"), and accurately leveled using any number of leveling systems. I hope a lack of books won't be what keeps you from running guided reading groups, but it might. Multiple copies of numerous titles across many levels are an investment, so begin lobbying your administrators for funds to buy sets of leveled books. If the monies allocated for workbooks can be redirected to the purchase of leveled books, you have a ready source of funding.

Our school is fortunate to have a book room that contains thousands of books on various levels. Our biggest purchases included multiple book sets from the following series:

- Very First Chapters (Modern Curriculum Press) are short chapter books (hence the name) and run from a second-grade level to a fourth-grade level. They cover both fiction and nonfiction topics.

- Ready Readers (Modern Curriculum Press) begin at a kindergarten level and extend into a second-grade level. Each short book addresses a specific phonic pattern. Topics include both fiction and nonfiction.

- Book Treks and iOpeners (Celebration Press) are nonfiction book sets. Each set has multiple copies of books on high-interest topics such as tornadoes, amazing animals, and famous historical figures. Each book is clearly labeled with a Lexile number, a DRA number, and a guided reading letter.

If your students are anything like mine, you know that they're as captivated by books about sports figures and planets as they are by books about dragons and pokey, little puppies. The Common Core State Standards emphasize both nonfiction and fiction texts and clearly expect an extensive use of informational texts at all levels of schooling. With book sets such as the ones just mentioned, you can provide high-interest reading for the boys and girls in your classroom while addressing the Common Core's emphasis on informational texts.

For readers on a kindergarten or first-grade level, you'll need lots and lots of books on levels A–J (DRA levels A–16). Books at these early levels are very short, sometimes just eight pages long with one sentence on each page. This means emerging readers might read three or four books each day during independent reading time. Be aware that although you might find numerous books on levels H and above in thrift shops, it's unlikely that you'll find many on levels A–G. To stock these levels, you'll need to buy books.

If your school has no money, I encourage you to find a few like-minded teachers and see if you can create book sets by pulling books from various classrooms. If you can find like-minded teachers who each have a classroom budget, you might be able to each spend $100 on books and then share the resources. Or you might find grants from your parent association or local businesses.

Thrift shops and library sales can be a treasure trove of books, but the titles tend to exist as stand-alones and not as multiple-copy books. Thus, these options tend to work best for creating a classroom library. However, if you hit enough thrift shops and find enough previously cast-off classroom libraries, you might soon gather up four, five, or six copies of *Miss Nelson Is Missing!* by Harry Allard and James Marshall, *Out of the Dust* by Karen Hesse, or *Fossils Tell of Long Ago*. The booklists in Fountas and Pinnell's (2009) book *Leveled Books K–8: Matching Texts to Readers for Effective Teaching* are excellent resources for finding a guided reading level on almost any book that doesn't have a level of some type already printed on its back cover.

Teaching Chops: Unpacking the I Can... List

The I Can... list is a must for running guided reading groups because while you're working with a guided reading group, the rest of your students need to be reading independently, reading with a buddy, recording their reading, writing in a writing journal, or engaging in a host of other activities. These types of independent routines, which my cooperating teacher and I have repeatedly modeled and practiced, enable us to keep the kids quiet and productively engaged while we run our guided reading groups. Actually, to say that we kept them quiet is inaccurate. Most students keep themselves quiet not through force of will but through the flow they experience as they read engaging stories to themselves, have fun reading with a buddy, and write about events and topics they're interested in.

You don't need to run guided reading groups to use an I Can... list, however. You can use the list for dedicated independent reading and writing time. Running a schedule without guided reading groups leads to considerably less learning than if you run both guided reading groups and independent reading routines, but it's a legitimate place to start. Once you and your students get hooked on the I Can... list, you might find that you're up for implementing guided reading groups, too!

Regardless of how you use it, the list is a device that organizes independent reading and writing routines. We'll look at the reading end of things first and discuss the writing end in Chapter 6. To review what's on an I Can... list, jump back to Figure 5.5. As you teach students additional routines, simply put up the poster that reflects all the routines available to date. Note that the routines aren't grade specific. You can use an I Can... list from kindergarten to eighth grade.

You may prefer to use a pocket chart for your I Can... list. A pocket chart allows for an ever-accumulating list of routines and activities. Teach one routine, model it, have the kids practice it, and then add it to the list. Then, repeat the process. After 10–12 weeks, you'll have six to nine reading and writing activities in the pockets, each designed to keep your students happily immersed in reading and writing for 25 minutes at a time.

The I Can… list comes in handy when you're unexpectedly confronted with a schedule change or classroom interruption. When this happens, run the I Can… list as a group activity. Every student picks an independent reading or writing activity to work on. As for how the students pick from the list, you can formally assign specific students specific activities, you can allow your students total choice in what they do, or you can do some combination thereof.

Now that you've seen the I Can… list, let's look at how to teach its routines.

Explicit Modeling and Practice: Teaching the Independent Reading Routine

Once they've mastered the independent reading routine, your students should be able to quickly choose a book, go to a reading spot, and read quietly while you're working with other students. They'll do this, however, only if you've trained them to do so and if appropriate books are easily accessible. Warning: Not teaching this routine deeply enough has been a pitfall for many well-meaning teachers who start out full of enthusiasm and end up with a headache and a classroom full of off-task students. So, teach this routine and practice, practice, practice before attempting to initiate guided reading groups. Use these steps to teach the routine:

- Create book bins, using the guidelines discussed next.
- Teach the students where to find the bins.
- Determine an appropriate time for the students to choose books.
- Show exactly what will happen when you're working with an individual student or a group of students. Model what the routines look like.
- Practice the routine. Practice it again—and again! When *every* student can get to the correct spot and begin quietly, extend the time to five minutes, then seven, and then 12. *Muscle memory* is a term frequently used in the arts and sports. Tom Brady practices throwing a football over and over and over again because when it comes time to hurl a Hail Mary pass in the last 30 seconds of a tied game with a 300-pound lineman bearing down on him, he doesn't have time to think before he throws. A similar phenomenon (minus the lineman) must take place during a student's independent reading routine.
- Coach the students as they practice so they know exactly what to do.

- Discontinue the independent reading time immediately if someone begins to walk around, stops reading, begins to chat, or otherwise disrupts the time. Write down how many minutes have passed since the reading time began. The next day, try to stay with the reading for a longer time but always stop as soon as someone disrupts the time.
- When the students can quietly go to their reading places and read for 20 minutes (see Figure 5.8), you're ready to begin guided reading groups and independent reading routines.

A crucial part of the independent reading routine is choosing a book from an individual or assigned book bin. Individual bins are full of books on topics that are of high interest to a specific reader. Each book is on that student's independent reading level. Assigned book bins, each containing books on one specific reading level, are brimming with books that are of general interest to all readers. Another option is to create one large bin full of books on various reading levels. This is the type of bin I use in our third-grade program. The bin contains books of general interest on each of the four levels that my kids are currently reading on. I do tailor it, however, by including both fiction and nonfiction books and by peppering it with high-interest books targeted at specific students who love fishing, puppies, trucks, zombies, and whatever else (see Figure 5.9). In our third-grade classrooms, Jaden loves cats, Mason is nuts about fishing, Emily loves horses, and Richie and Hunter can't read enough about football. As the months go by and the students' reading levels move upward, I swap out lower level books and insert upper level ones.

Figure 5.8. Students Independently Reading

Figure 5.9. Independent Reading Book Bins

I work hard to coordinate with other teachers and my school's librarian to find books that are on topics that specific students prefer and on each student's independent reading level. It's not easy, but it can be done. When you find books that address both student interests and reading levels, you'll see even your most resistant readers sit and read for 10, 15, and even 20 minutes at a pop.

Explicit Modeling and Practice: Complete a Book Slip

Once students are in the habit of reading independently, I add a level of accountability by having them fill out an independent reading book slip. This helps me keep track of who's reading what and how many books have been read. It also gives the students opportunities to practice sentence writing and story analysis. Figure 5.10 shows options for book slips.

I don't require a slip every time a student reads a book, but I do expect to see one or two slips per week for each student. Like all classroom routines, you'll need to model how to do it and then practice

Figure 5.10. Sample Independent Reading Book Slips

General

Name: _____ Date: _____

Book title: _____

What did you like best about this book? _____

_____

_____

Fiction book

Name: _____ Date: _____

Book title: _____

What was the most important thing that happened in this story? Why was it important?

_____

_____

Nonfiction book

Name: _____ Date: _____

Book title: _____

What fact did you find most interesting in this book? _____

_____

_____

it. It's also helpful if you take a few minutes every week (prior to your independent reading sessions and/or guided reading groups) to share with the class book slips that are exemplary. Point out what makes the slip a good or great example and provide specific praise to the student. Once the students know the expectations, they can add to the discussion and comment on what makes a particular slip exemplary. You might say something like this:

> I was looking through your folder of book slips and noticed that Elaine recently read *Buster Catches a Cold* [by Hisako Madakoro]. Elaine did a nice job of

reporting on this book. Her writing is neat, her sentences are complete, and she specifically told me that she enjoyed the illustrations and the part of the story when Buster falls in the puddle. Good work, Elaine!

You might also need to say something like this:

I noticed that Conner, Elaine, Dominick, Hanna, and Pyper have all turned in at least one book slip this week. Other than that, I have no book slips! Don't forget that I want to see at least one independent book slip per week. So, if your name wasn't called, get a book slip into the folder!

Social and Cooperative Learning

Buddy Read. Kids love to get together and talk with one another. Buddy reading provides an educational reason to do so. When students buddy read, they pair up and choose two books (or a big book) from a buddy reading book bin that's assigned to them. In this bin are multiple copies of single titles on specific reading levels.

During buddy reading, one student might be reading a book that's slightly above his or her independent reading level. I pair students who are close to each other's level, but it's not an exact match. It doesn't need to be because the buddy system provides support to the student who struggles the most. Here's an example of what I mean: Tyler, a student reading on DRA level 16, wants to do well but is prone to drifting into la-la land. He's paired with Brianna, who's ready to leave level 18. She's a bit of a mother hen. Her directness (some might call her bossy) and her slightly higher reading level help keep Tyler on task. They both read a book from DRA level 16, which is just right for Tyler and a little on the easy side for Brianna.

Students can buddy read in a variety of configurations. I allow my students to sit on pieces of carpet that are pulled from storage during buddy reading time. *Sit* isn't quite the right word, though, because the kids tend to sprawl and even lay on the carpet as they read (see Figure 5.11). I'm not too particular, though. As long as the students are reading, I allow them to take up almost any position they want. When buddy reading time is over, the students roll up the carpets and put them back into storage.

If you tend toward the more formal, have your students read in chairs. A compromise between the formal hard-backed chair and the informal carpet square would be buddy reading beanbags. Speaking of formal, if noise is an issue for you or your students, there's a specific buddy reading configuration that enables students to hear one another while speaking softly: Have your buddy pairs sit in side-by-side chairs but facing opposite

Figure 5.11. Students Buddy Reading

directions. This allows for the reader's mouth to be in close proximity to the listener's ear.

Read, Record, and Check. In this activity, two students go to the recording center with an independent reading book. While there, they don headphones and read into small digital dictation recorders. Next, they play their recordings back and check their reading for errors. If they made errors, they erase their previous try and work on rereading until they have a recording that demonstrates fluent reading. Then, they listen to another person's recording and read along in the book.

In the grand scheme of things, dictation devices are relatively inexpensive. You'll find numerous voice recorders online and in local stores, and many of them are under $35. Some even come with big, kid-friendly buttons and a display screen.

Review Vocabulary Word Cards. In this I Can... routine, students independently read through their vocabulary word cards (see Chapter 3). When you allow students to do this in buddy pairs, you're harnessing the power of social learning. You're also harnessing physical response, just not in a group.

I typically assign independent practice first. In other words, students practice their vocabulary words before they go on to the preferred activity of working with a buddy. In behavior circles, this is known as employing Premack's principle: Preferred behaviors can be used to reinforce unpreferred behaviors. But I like to think of it as the grandma principle: You can't have cookies until you eat your broccoli!

Whole–Group Physical Response: Repeated Reading With a Toolbox

Repeated reading is a powerful practice that can lead to gains in all areas of fluency: accuracy, rate of reading, expression, and phrasing. It's meant to be a rehearsal routine, and for this reason, students should not use repeated reading tools with a first-time book.

Although accurate and fluent reading can be motivating in and of itself, many students, especially the younger ones, need a few external supports to increase their motivation. Whisper phones, paintbrushes, and witchy-poo fingers fill the bill. The student chooses a book from his or her individual browsing bin and rereads it using one of these tools.

Whisper phones are U-shaped or bracket-shaped tubes that run from a reader's mouth to his or her ear. Held like an old-fashioned phone handset, the tube concentrates the voice and directs the sound into the reader's ear. It's a simple trick that young students love to use (see Figure 5.12).

Figure 5.12. Students Quietly Reading Aloud With Whisper Phones

Figure 5.13. Reading With a Paintbrush

Paintbrushes are just that: paintbrushes. As a student reads, he or she pulls the paintbrush across the page in a smooth motion that mimics smooth reading in long phrases (see Figure 5.13). It's a gimmick with a purpose. Not only is the brush fun to use, but it also gives kinesthetic feedback, helps the student keep track of what line he or she is on, and provides a reason to reread text.

Witchy-poo fingers serve the same purpose as the paintbrushes. Available from any number of novelty stores, the plastic, rubbery fingers with long nails slip over the pointer finger. The student then runs the finger and nail along the bottom of the sentences being read (see Figure 5.14). Like the paintbrushes, witchy-poo fingers are meant to concentrate a reader's attention on smooth and expressive reading in short and long phrases.

I suggest that you create tool bins or one large tool chest to house these materials close to your book bins. Don't fill your container all at once. Introduce the materials one at a time, perhaps one new tool every six weeks. Each time you introduce a tool, model how it's to be used and provide numerous opportunities for guided practice. Once you've guided the students, and once they can use the tools independently, then turn control over to them. I stress to my students that using the tools is a privilege. If they abuse them with silly behavior or behavior that has nothing to do with reading, then they lose their privilege.

Paintbrushes and witchy-poo fingers are good for focusing on smooth reading and longer phrasing. I show the students how to steadily and

Figure 5.14. Students Reading With Witchy-Poo Fingers

smoothly sweep the paintbrush across the bottom of the sentence. This is the opposite of choppy, word-by-word reading. The words should flow in smooth phrases, both long and short.

I use the whisper phones to stress the aspects of reading a little faster and with more expression. I encourage the students to imagine that they are talking to their best friend on the phone. When they talk, they don't want to speak too quickly, but they should speak with a healthy rate of speed and always use appropriate expression.

All of these materials are available from various educational supply sites and catalogs. If you're looking to save money, you can construct sturdy but inexpensive whisper phones with a hacksaw, lengths of PVC pipe, and PVC elbows (see Figure 5.12).

Formative Assessment: Is It Working?

Fountas and Pinnell (2012) have stated that "good assessment is the foundation for effective teaching" (p. 275), and I couldn't agree more. This "good assessment" doesn't need to take up an entire reading block every week, nor does it have to look like students shackled to their desks for hours on end as they read contrived passages and fill in multiple-choice bubbles. Rather, a good assessment can take two minutes here and 10 minutes there, and it can look like teacher notes written on a sheet of paper, a dot on a graph that signifies correct words read in one minute, or a checklist of observed reading behaviors.

One of the best things about guided reading groups is that they allow you to get to know your readers on an individual level. As you run your small groups, you'll begin to notice and remember how individual students approach a text, read through passages, and think about the meaning of a story. To paraphrase Fountas and Pinnell (1996, 2012), when you become a better noticer, you'll be more capable of quickly capturing a student's reading behaviors and then analyzing those behaviors to figure out how to teach each student more effectively.

Capturing reading information allows you to make instructional decisions within your groups as well as reformulate your groups so they're easier to manage and teach. Guided reading groups are meant to be dynamic and changeable, and a steady stream of assessment information allows you to move students into different groups based on reading strengths and needs.

Observation with anecdotal note-taking is a good place to start the formative assessment process because it's a simple way of capturing reading information. When you run a group, keep a pencil and a blank sheet of paper on hand or, better yet, run off a template that provides a box for the date and a heading for each group. Take notes on the reading behaviors you see.

Another way to record observations is to use a computer label and the three-ring binder system that was mentioned in Chapter 4 on grammar. Regardless of the method you use, observing and recording reading behaviors is critical to creating a classroom in which students have the greatest opportunity to make gains. You'll want to note which reading behaviors are taking root and then reinforce them. You'll also want to catch and correct the inappropriate or incorrect use of strategies before the behaviors become bad habits.

On a busy day during a busy week, I'm apt to forget just about everything if I don't write it down, so I work hard to keep some kind of written record of what I see students doing in a guided reading group. At least once a week, as each student in the group reads, I record his or her reading behaviors. You can do this, too. Keep track of the types of errors a reader makes. Make a note if the reader makes errors of omission or substitution and if the substituted words change the meaning of the sentence. Write down which strategies the student uses and make note of the strategies used infrequently or never. Listen to the prosody or lack thereof and note if the student reads with expression, reads in long or short phrases, and pauses briefly at each period. Observe the level of motivation and confidence. Then, plan your instruction so it addresses the most pressing needs of each student.

Many teachers who are skilled in and knowledgeable about guided reading groups use running records as an assessment system. Running records provide lots of information about reading behaviors and can also be used to determine a percentage of accuracy and a rate of reading (correct words per minute). If you can become one of these skilled and knowledgeable teachers, or if you're one already, then, by all means, use running records. There are, of course, other ways to note reading behaviors while simultaneously monitoring progress in both rate and accuracy. Many core reading programs come with a package of assessments. Often, there are fluency passages in these assessment packages, typically ranked by grade level. If the passages are at an appropriate level for your students, conduct an assessment every two or three weeks for the most struggling students and every six to nine weeks for the highest performing ones.

If you use one of these assessment or the oral reading fluency passages in the DIBELS progress-monitoring booklets, try to note what types of errors a student makes (insertions, omissions, substitutions, reversals), the length of their phrasing (long phrases, short phrases, word by word, number of hesitations), whether the student self-corrects a mistake that changes the meaning of the passage, and whether he or she reads with appropriate expression. All of this information, easily gained within the structure of a guided reading group, is invaluable if you want to fit your instruction to the needs of your readers, especially the ones who struggle the most.

Remember, however, that you won't become an assessment expert overnight. Be patient with yourself. When you first begin guided reading groups, you might only be able to jot down a few notes regarding each student's reading behaviors. As you become more comfortable with guided reading, you can add more structured assessments.

Make It So

When teachers give students extended time to read in books on their instructional and independent levels, they'll see growth in those students' reading achievement well beyond what would occur if only a core program's anthology, practice books, and leveled readers were used. This is a personal belief grounded in both reading research and professional experience. Practice makes perfect, whether you're playing a musical instrument, shooting a bow and arrow, or reading a chapter book. Practice also makes permanent, so it's important that strategies be practiced correctly. Guided reading instruction provides the time for practice to be done under the expert eye of the teacher.

I believe that expert teaching coupled with extended reading in instructional-level texts are the two main reasons why 85–95% of the kindergartners in my school achieve a DRA level of 3 or more by the end of the school year. Every kindergarten teacher and reading specialist works to ensure that guided reading is a part of every kindergartner's daily reading experience.

Expert teaching and guided reading enable the struggling readers in our third-grade Title I program to make a great deal of progress, too. Over the last two years, readers in the program have achieved, on average, at least a year's worth of growth in their DRA levels. Many students made a year's worth of growth on their DIBELS scores, and some achieved 1.2, 1.4, and even 1.8 years' worth of growth in their DRA levels. This growth is critical because these students need to make more than one year's growth if they're going to reach important grade-level benchmarks by the end of the year. Grade 3 readers who don't become skilled in word recognition and confident in their comprehension stand a good chance of experiencing the oft-mentioned fourth-grade slump, and these kids might continue to slump for quite a long time. Therefore, if you're working with low-achieving students in first, second, or third grade, it's critical that you design a core reading program that accelerates them to escape velocity. To do this, you'll need a program that goes beyond the basal program.

Can you find the time to seek out and organize books, choose books based on student interest and reading level, plan for multiple reading groups, and still have a life? In fact, yes, you can! The key is to take items off your plate so you have room for something else.

Don't forget these two important points: First, guided reading instruction provides a whole lot of differentiation. When you instruct with guided reading groups and provide additional opportunities for students to read independently from books on their independent reading levels, your students will be swimming in a sea of differentiation. When your principal sees what your class is up to, he or she will have absolutely no reason to ship you off to some "differentiation for all learners" professional development session!

Second, a reading program that emphasizes extended reading and writing as well as the six teaching chops does more with less. Because phonemic awareness, phonics, fluency, vocabulary, and comprehension are infused throughout your lessons, there's simply no need to teach dozens and dozens of isolated skills and concepts to the kids. And because you're regularly using direct and explicit instruction, modeling, and practice (among others), your instruction will be more powerful overall.

I'm reminded of the old Ragu spaghetti sauce commercial in which a grandma's grandchildren come to her with suggestions for what she should put in her spaghetti sauce to make it better: "Oregano," they say. "It's in there," she says. "Plump, red tomatoes," they say. "It's in there!" she quips. It turns out that Grandma's been secretly using jars of Ragu, and all of those wonderful ingredients don't need to be added because they've been there all along. It's much the same when it comes to the specific big ideas and teaching chops (ingredients) within an extended reading and writing program (the spaghetti sauce). Phonics? It's in there! Fluency? It's in there! Mastery learning and formative assessment? They're in there, too!

The funny thing is that as you begin to practice reading instruction on a more sophisticated level, your classroom reading routines will begin to resemble the authentic reading experiences that students and adults have at home. When I read at home, I choose what I want to read. I read books that match my interests. I read books that are just right for my abilities. I sit and read in comfy places. Reading is a joy! Unfortunately, I've heard students as young as first grade say, "I hate reading." A friend told me that she was talking with her son about his reading class, and he said, "Mom, I love to read, but I hate reading time in school!" Providing students with books that they're interested in and are on their level, and extended time to read these books, creates joyful and successful reading experiences in school and helps create students who ask, "Can we read and write all day long?"

CHAPTER 6

New Heights of Extended Writing

• • • • • • • • • • • • • • •

You will need...

• • • • • • • • • • • • • •

- The following materials for each student in your classroom:
  - A double-pocket folder
  - A composition book
  - A thin student dictionary, such as the *The Quick-Word® Handbook for Everyday Writers* (Sitton & Forest, 2010)
  - A Good Writers' Checklist (discussed in this chapter), developed in conjunction with the Common Core's grammar and writing standards and your core reading curriculum
  - A laminated call card (discussed in this chapter), red on one side and green on the other
- A writing rubric that matches the Good Writers' Checklist
- A Writers Think About... poster (discussed in Chapter 2)
- An I Can... list (discussed in Chapter 5)
- A classroom poster and student-friendly graphic organizer that describes the process of paragraph writing, such as hamburger writing (discussed in this chapter) or four square writing

• • • • • • • • • • • •

You will...

• • • • • • • • • • •

- Devote one 30–40-minute period per week to extended writing
- Directly and explicitly teach how to write focused one- and two-paragraph pieces
- Add journal writing, topic writing, and spelling sentences to your I Can... list
- Teach students strategies and routines that enable them to pick topics for writing topics, write focused paragraphs, and revise and edit written pieces
- Implement routines that motivate students to write during independent work time
- Formatively assess the students over time using a writing rubric

've always been a writer, but I didn't come to this realization until earlier this year. It's strange that I never realized this because I've always been one to keep a journal, write a song, or send my Seattle-based sisters a long e-mail. Perhaps I thought I needed formal training (I have none) or full-time employment to be a "real" writer. Writing is something I want to do, and while I'm doing it, I enjoy it! I think that's enough reason to call myself a writer.

I want my students to become writers, too. This means I want them to write regularly, and I want them to *choose* to write. I write of my own volition and for my own purposes, including sharing information, communicating opinions, and scratching the ever-present creative itch, and I'd like my students to write for the same reasons. In the real world, writing has a purpose and an audience. Unfortunately, the basic understanding of what writing is (and why people write) is sometimes lost in schools and classrooms, and writing devolves into exercises in getting ready for a high-stakes assessment or following the dictates of a teacher's manual. These exercises are far removed from real-world writing, in which a student describes a much-loved grandparent, relates a recent family adventure, or creates a story with nothing more than paper, pencil, and imagination.

When I was a learning support teacher with a great deal of control over what I taught and how I taught it, I loved running my writers' workshop program with my fourth and fifth graders. What jazzed me was student writing that was original, funny, or heartfelt. Now that my cooperating teacher and I have arranged our weekly classroom schedule to allow for lots of writing, I'm jazzed once more by my students' writing (see Figure 6.1 for an example). Most of the kids in the class say, "Yay!" or at least smile when I tell them, "Journal writing is on today's I Can... list." Their smiles make me smile, too.

Toni Draksler, my third-grade cooperating teacher, is an eight-year teaching veteran who cut her teeth on our district's core reading program. Just a few years ago, she only had time for one formal writing project every nine weeks, she had no regularly scheduled time for extended writing, and her students rarely wrote about topics they chose. Now, with a new schedule, a lot more writing time, and an instructional program designed to lead students step by step toward mastering the art of writing basic paragraphs, Toni has seen a world of difference in her students' writing:

> I am so impressed with the progress our students are making with their writing. They went from barely being able to write a complete sentence and dreading writing time to writing a complete paragraph or two, enjoying the time they are given to write, and hoping there is enough time to share their writing with the rest of the class. Their transformation has been amazing to witness.

Figure 6.1. A Student's Authentic Writing

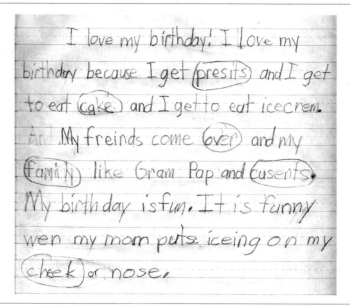

I sincerely believe your core curriculum will be more effective, and your kids will have a lot more fun, if you create extended time for them to write about things they're interested in. Creating writing time is no easy task, but it can be done. Let's begin by looking at why it's important to reconfigure your core reading program to accommodate more student writing.

The Importance of Extended Writing

Students need time to practice the skills that you hope to make permanent. When skills are practiced for extended periods of time, words in sentences flow more easily, sentences in paragraphs come together, and style and voice emerge. Mere time isn't enough, however. Kids need to enter into the flow of writing. To do this, teachers need to give students the freedom to write about topics and events that they know well and find interesting. This freedom provides the motivation to write.

Practicing writing will certainly make students better writers, but does all this writing lead to better reading? Studies have shed light on how exemplary teachers and their instructional processes increase reading and writing achievement. For example, first- and fifth-grade teachers who create high-achieving readers and writers are likely to integrate reading and writing on a regular basis and do so in a thoughtful and thorough manner (Morrow, Tracey, Woo, & Pressley, 1999; Pressley, Yokoi, Rankin, Wharton-McDonald, & Mistretta, 1997). Other studies have shown that students' writing and reading achievement are closely connected because students pull from a reservoir of common knowledge and cognitive processes while reading and writing (Shanahan, 2006).

When you consider both sets of research findings—that writing and reading are connected in student knowledge and cognitive processing and that teachers who produce high-achieving readers and writers combine reading and writing in a thorough fashion and on a regular basis—it makes sense that improving one set of skills would lead to improvements in the other. When Graham and Hebert (2010) conducted a meta-analysis of dozens of studies, they found that certain writing practices do, in fact, lead to greater reading achievement. Their meta-analysis and subsequent report, entitled *Writing to Read: Evidence for How Writing Can Improve Reading*, identified a number of instructional practices that were shown to be effective in improving students' reading achievement. Here are two of their recommendations:

1. Improve reading skills and comprehension by teaching students the writing skills and processes that go into creating text. More specifically, improve comprehension by teaching the process of writing, the text structures for writing, and the skills needed for sentence and paragraph construction; improve reading fluency by teaching spelling and sentence construction skills; and improve reading skills by teaching spelling skills.

2. Improve reading comprehension by increasing how much students write and how often they produce their own texts.

To summarize, if you become a skillful and knowledgeable teacher who integrates reading and writing thoroughly and regularly, teaches students the writing skills and processes that go into creating text, and gives students time to produce their own writings, you'll increase your students' reading achievement as well as their writing achievement.

Core Problems and What to Do About Them

Core programs typically don't provide much time for extended writing, nor do they offer students opportunities to write authentically about real-world interests. Why? Basal programs are clogged with too many worksheets and too much instruction on isolated skills. Practice time is often devoted to filling in blanks or correcting incorrect sentences.

Teaching a child to write by practicing isolated skills is like teaching a teenager to drive a car by having him or her memorize engine schematics and rebuild a fuel injection system. In other words, it doesn't make sense! Driving a car is not predicated on first studying and mastering the intricacies of a car's electrical system, drivetrain, and engine, nor is it accomplished by learning to turn the steering wheel on day 1, learning to use the brake pedal on day 2, and so forth. Rather, a teenager learns to drive by first watching someone model the skill for years on end. Then, after a bit of book learning, he or she gets behind the wheel for some authentic guided practice and has at it! As the teenager practices (with guidance), his or her skills become refined and more accurate. Soon the kid's ready for the open road.

I believe students learn how to write in much the same way. Student writers need to see lots of modeling, thoroughly learn a few basics, and then buckle themselves into their composition books and computers, put their pencils and keyboards into gear, and start writing. You, the teacher, will be there to guide them as they round curves and encounter potholes.

Core reading programs suffer from another writing-related problem: They provide little in the way of motivation. What's missing? In a word, choice. Even the most authentic writing activities in a teacher's manual are still too dictatorial. It's hard to write a paragraph that persuades your friend that pizza is the best food if you don't like pizza in the first place.

Having the freedom to choose writing topics motivates kids to write. Some of them grow to love writing because it allows them to express thoughts and feelings that they may not have expressed before. And writing is a creative act, regardless of whether you write nonfiction or fiction. If students choose to roam the solar system in a spaceship, explore the ocean in a submarine, or describe an evening with Grandma, all they have to do is write about it. For many, the act of creating is a fulfilling one.

Finally, your core writing program probably lacks meaningful differentiation. Differentiation is important because writing is challenging, and some students struggle greatly with the task. Therefore, it's best if you let your students discover their writing comfort level. I call this process self-differentiation.

During topic writing (which I'll discuss in just a bit), every student works on creating a quality paragraph. The end goal is the same for everyone. What's differentiated is the process that each student uses to get to the final goal (different students focus on different skills at different times) and the content (different students pick different topics to write about). For example, a recent writing content was differentiated when Kaitlynn wrote about her dog, but Pyper made up a story about a guy who magically loses all of his hair. Because I'm mostly bald, I didn't have to work too hard to figure out how that story began! Skill work was also differentiated. I didn't have to remind Jordan to write neatly, but I did remind others. Some students concentrated on their spelling, whereas others focused on writing interesting sentences. Regardless of what they write about and no matter what skills they're working on, students work to grow their writing skills and achieve writing standards throughout the year.

To inspire and support writing, give students choice, time to write, and skill practice in small doses.

Create Blocks of Time for Writing

When I went back to public school teaching, I wanted to honor my core value of extended writing. My curriculum director gave me the go-ahead to make this happen, but she also requested that I check with the fourth- and fifth-grade reading teachers about the writing skills that they wanted to see in the students who were coming to them from third grade. Her concern was that if I veered too far from the core reading program's writing sequence, I'd miss teaching the skills that upper-grade teachers thought were essential prerequisites to their programs. The fourth-grade reading teachers said they'd prefer that incoming students be able to write a well-formed five-sentence paragraph, correct in its mechanics (spelling, punctuation, capitalization) and conveying meaning in a focused way, rather than generate lists of adverbs or know the definition of a helping verb. The fifth-grade teachers' expectations were much the same, except that they expected incoming students to be able to write two or three paragraphs.

Writing is a confluence of many skills. Writers need to see the big picture; formulate specific thoughts; put events and ideas in a logical sequence; and apply grammar skills, fine motor coordination, and encoding rules (i.e., spelling). Because student writers need to master many skills, they need to do a lot of writing. In my mind, you can create opportunities for them to write in three ways: First, have students write sentences during grammar, spelling, and guided reading instruction. Second, implement an I Can... list and allow students to write independently during guided reading time. Finally, and most importantly, create a weekly block of time in which you can guide students as they write about issues and events that are important to them.

How much writing time are we talking about? To start, you'll need a contiguous block of at least 35 minutes. If you can find 45 minutes, that would be ideal. "Forty-five minutes!" you might cry. "I don't have five minutes to spare, let alone 45! Regardless, my second graders would never write for that amount of time." If this *is* your cry, I'm here to tell you that yes, you can carve out 25, 35, or even 45 minutes for kids to write, and yes, in time, first, second, and third graders can work up to writing for this length of time. My cooperating kindergarten teacher, Mrs. Kelli Griffith, consistently produces classrooms of kindergartners who love to write (and illustrate) and do so for 25 minutes at least twice a week. Figure 6.2 shows two kindergartners' writing samples from her classroom, both of which were completed during a 25-minute writing block.

You'll also need to create two to four 15–25-minute independent writing opportunities. To free up all of this time, you'll need to rearrange your schedule. This is a big change, but you can do it. Chapter 5 offered options on how to create extended reading and writing time in your schedule. If you're fuzzy about what those options were, go back and review them now because they're important.

Figure 6.2. Two Kindergartners' Writing

Scope: What to Teach in the Writing Block

To hook students on writing, begin by letting them write about topics of their choice. Unless they're internally motivated and love to please adults, most kids aren't interested in writing answers to open-ended questions or constructing contrived paragraphs based on test-related prompts. I'm not saying that kids won't do these types of assignments. I'm simply saying that they aren't preferred.

What do students prefer to write about? I'd say people they know and things they're interested in. Students experience flow in writing when they share information about their best friend, retell a personal event, or describe a favorite hobby or sport. It's all about communication. Kids want to tell their teachers, friends, and classmates about their lives, so I advocate authentic writing activities. Authentic writing hooks kids on the writing process. Once they're hooked, it becomes easier for them to produce quality work on assignments that are less preferred, such as academic tasks and answers to test questions.

Although I advocate letting kids describe and narrate their personal experiences, I realize that school-related writing must extend beyond paragraphs that recall "Thanksgiving at my house" or retell an episode of *SpongeBob SquarePants*. The Common Core's writing standards say many things about writing in kindergarten through fifth grade, and if there's a golden thread running through them, it's that writing has a real-world purpose. The Common Core reminds us of the many reasons for writing and give, in some detail, the types of writing that K–5 students should produce. I've condensed the Common Core's language in Figure 6.3, but I believe I've captured the gist. In each case, the Common

---

Figure 6.3. My Take on the Common Core State Standards on K–5 Writing

Students should be able to write the following:

- Supported opinion pieces that introduce a topic, maintain their focus, use linking words, and provide a concluding statement
- Informative/explanatory pieces that introduce a topic, group information into coherent sections, use facts and details, use precise language, and provide some type of concluding statement
- Narrative pieces, real or imagined, that establish the situation, use a narrator and/or characters, maintain a logical sequence with a conclusion, use details to convey experiences and details, and possibly include dialogue
- Research projects built from investigation, the gathering of information, analysis, and reflection
- Task-specific pieces, such as ones that compare and contrast objects and ideas, retell or summarize a story, or describe and analyze a character

Core says that students' written pieces should be clear and coherent. Additionally, students should use both the writing process and some form of technology to produce and publish their writing.

When it comes to the specific grammar and mechanical skills that make for proficient writing, the Common Core expects teachers to cover a lot of ground. I argue that it's virtually impossible to cover that ground unless you have blocks of time dedicated to teaching and practicing writing. With a weekly writing block of 30–40 minutes plus two or three additional independent writing periods of 15–25 minutes each, you and your students (especially the ones who struggle) have a fighting chance to achieve the Common Core's goals.

Teaching Chops: Guided Writing or Modified Writers' Workshop

In my mind, guided writing is a process in which you teach skills in short bursts of explicit and direct instruction; model the skills; and then allow students to practice them as you circulate around the classroom, pointing out errors, showing what was done correctly, offering encouragement, and guiding students toward the light of good writing. The guided writing process is done with the whole group, and it's done every week (see Figure 6.4).

Figure 6.4. Whole-Group Guided Writing

The remainder of this section explains how I guide my students during a large block of extended writing. I won't explain my process and program through the typical teaching chop categories of whole-group physical response, direct and explicit instruction, and so forth. Rather, I'll discuss extended writing in terms of sequence (broadly at first and then with more detail) and materials.

Sequence

Here's the broad sequence: First, I teach my students how to generate a list of topics that they want to write about. Then, I use a modified writers' workshop model to hook my kids on writing and get them to the point where they consistently write complete sentences in focused paragraphs, five to seven sentences in length. This takes up the first 9–14 weeks. Once the kids are capable writers who are hooked on the idea of writing, I begin to alternate authentic writing topics (i.e., writing from their topics lists) with standard-based topics, such as a persuasive paragraph, a compare-and-contrast paragraph, and a narrative paragraph with quotation marks. This instruction continues until the end of the year.

Rather than have students write mostly on loose sheets of paper, I typically have them write in a writing journal. I'd like them do a lot more writing in word-processing programs, but we currently don't have the technology to do so. Because students do a lot of writing by hand, their paragraphs tend to be a little sloppy. These paragraphs aren't revised, edited, and rewritten to the point where they show no mistakes. That being said, every nine weeks, my third-grade writers also produce at least one fully conceived writing process paragraph, neatly written on lined, white paper, just like the students in many other classrooms.

Materials

To run a guided writing program and teach routines that students can do independently, you'll need a few specific materials. First up is a double-pocket folder for each student. One side contains a composition book, and the other side holds the following (see Figure 6.5):

- A slim student dictionary
- A Good Writers' Checklist (examples shown later in this chapter)
- A double-sided green and red call card (You can use the response card discussed in Chapter 2.)

In addition, you may want to have on hand the Writers Think About... poster discussed in Chapter 2. Finally, you'll need a writing

Figure 6.5. Writing Materials

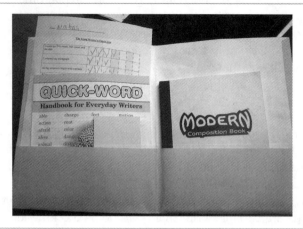

rubric (aligned to the Common Core and the Good Writers' Checklist) for scoring your students' writing, plus a score sheet to keep track of the data you generate. I'll give examples of each of these later in this chapter.

With materials in hand, your students are ready to write!

Topics List in the Composition Book

During the first guided reading block of the year, before I even teach what a sentence is, I discuss writing topics. By the end of my first 40-minute writing lesson, each student will have generated a list entitled "Writing Topics" on the first page of his or her composition book. The topics list is what the students refer to over and over again as they write during guided reading or independent writing time. Some teachers call it an I Can Write About... list. Regardless of what you call it, the page should list 10–20 words or short phrases that describe what a student would like to write about. Figure 6.6 shows beginning lists by two of my recent writers.

To get the kids to generate a topics list, I use task analysis, brainstorming, and think-pair-share. The lesson sounds something like this:

> In this class, we'll all become writers. The first thing a writer does is think about things to write about. These things are called topics. Open your composition book to the very first page. This is a really important page! We're going to title this page "Writing Topics." Write that at the very top. [pauses for students to write]

Figure 6.6. Two Students' Beginning-of-Year Topics Lists

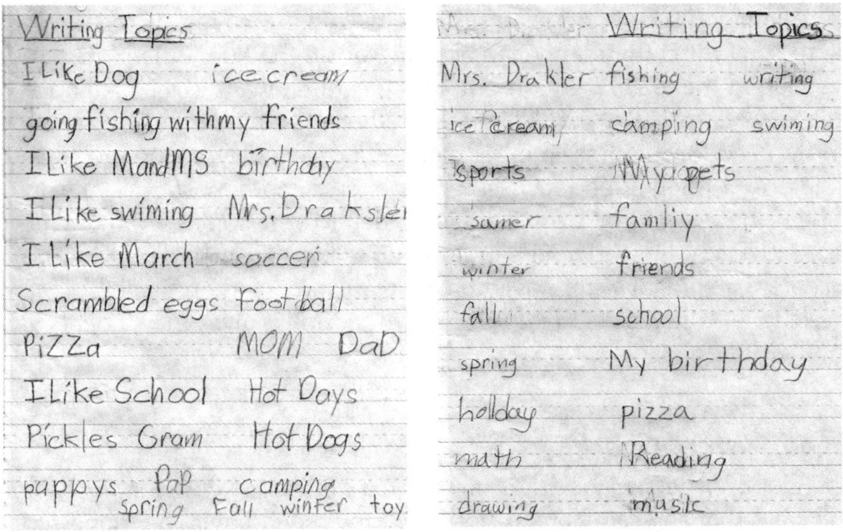

Writing Topics
I Like Dog   ice cream
going fishing with my friends
I Like MandMS birthday
I Like swiming Mrs. Draksler
I Like March soccer
Scrambled eggs football
PiZZa   MOM DaD
I Like School Hot Days
Pickles Gram Hot Dogs
puppys PaP camping
      spring Fall winter toy.

Mrs. Drakler Writing Topics
Mrs. Drakler fishing   writing
ice cream, camping   swiming
sports   My pets
sumer   famliy
winter   friends
fall   school
spring   My birthday
holiday   pizza
math   Reading
drawing   music

Here's my title. [writes "Writing Topics" on the board] Now I need to write some topics. Hmm, what can I write about? Writers often write about things they know or things they love to do. OK, I have some ideas! I'll write down a list of things I love to do. [writes "play music," "ride my bike," and "visit my family" as a list on the board]

Now I want you to think. For the next seven seconds, think of things you love to do. [pauses] OK, now share with the person beside you. [pauses while the students share]

Great! Now I want you to list what you just shared on your topics list. Don't write down a sentence. Just a word or a couple of words will do. Look at how I listed my writing topics. But don't write down my topics! Write down *your* topics. If you don't know how to spell a word, spell it the best you can. [pauses while students write]

OK, now I need some more topics. What else can I write about? I'm going to think about things I know a lot about. First, I'll think. Hmm... Now watch. I'll write down three things I know a lot about. [adds "the TV show *Star Trek*," "cooking," and "teaching" to the list]

You get the idea. Once the process is over, every student should have at least 10 things in his or her topics list. Your most gung-ho students will have 15 or even 20. Don't let them write on the back of the list because at various times in the year, you'll want your students to revisit their lists, go through another brainstorming process, and add topics. You should also encourage your students to add to their topics lists whenever an occasion presents itself.

When you see your students in the morning, they may be chattering about something that happened at home or on the bus. When I first show up in the reading classroom, kids will often want to tell me about their new glasses, the puppies that were born last night, the baby sister who walked for the first time last night, and much more. Oftentimes, I'll interrupt them after a few sentences and say enthusiastically, "I want to hear the rest of that story. Add your idea to your topics list and write about it! Then, I'll read your story and write back to you." This lets me validate the student's story as important while moving on to all the pressing teaching tasks that I need to get to, and it gives the student another writing idea!

Good Writers' Checklist

The Good Writers' Checklist is an ever-expanding list of writing behaviors and skills that serves many purposes. It provides you with a writing scope and sequence (including spelling, grammar, and mechanics) and serves as a tool for teaching and review. For your students, the checklist is a reminder of what they should be doing when they write, revise, and edit their work.

Because I teach writing as an accumulating set of skills, I use three different versions of the checklist, each presented at different points in the year (see Figure 6.7). The first is introduced after students have mastered writing complete sentences and are ready to begin writing paragraphs. The second is introduced about 12 or 16 weeks into the school year. This version includes a spelling correction strategy and reflects an expectation for more sentences in each paragraph. The third is introduced around the end of the third nine weeks. At this point, the capitalization and punctuation prompts on this checklist include a broader sense of when to capitalize (e.g., proper nouns) and punctuate (e.g., in dialogue).

I'm constantly tweaking the Good Writers' Checklist so it matches the skills and needs of my students. You can do the same. For instance, this past year, many of my writers kept forgetting to date their writing, which caused me to page madly through their journals as I tried to figure out which piece of writing was from what date. I revised the checklist to include a prompt for a date, I gave everyone a new copy, and with a serious face and a stern tone of voice, I gave a three-minute minilesson on "labeling every piece of writing with today's date!"

Earlier, we discussed how reading and writing are different sides of the same coin. You can use the checklist to encourage your students to

Figure 6.7. Three Versions of the Good Writers' Checklist

Name: _____

The Good Writers' Checklist: First Nine Weeks

	Date							
My writing is sloppy (1), OK (2), neat (3), or very neat (4)!								
I indented my paragraph.								
Except for my first sentence, I started at the beginning of the line.								
I wrote to the end of the line.								
All of my sentences begin with a capital letter.								
All of my sentences end with punctuation.								
Every sentence is complete.								

Name: _____

The Good Writers' Checklist: Second Nine Weeks

	Date							
My writing is sloppy (1), OK (2), neat (3), or very neat (4)!								
I indented my paragraph.								
Except for my first sentence, I started at the beginning of the line.								
I wrote to the end of the line.								
I wrote six or more sentences.								
Every sentence begins with a capital letter.								
Every sentence ends with punctuation.								
Every sentence is complete.								
No sentences begin with *And, But,* or *Because.*								
I circled words that I thought were misspelled, and I tried to correct them.								

(continued)

Figure 6.7. Three Versions of the Good Writers' Checklist (*continued*)

Name: _____

The Good Writers' Checklist: Third and Fourth Nine Weeks							
Date							
My writing is sloppy (1), OK (2), neat (3), or very neat (4)!							
I put a date on my writing.							
I indented my paragraph.							
Except for the first sentence, I started at the beginning of the line.							
I wrote to the end of the line.							
I wrote seven or more sentences in one or more paragraphs.							
I used capital letters correctly (beginning, proper nouns, the pronoun *I*).							
I used punctuation correctly (end, commas, quotation marks).							
Every sentence is complete.							
No sentences begin with *And, But,* or *Because.*							
I circled words that I thought were misspelled, and I tried to correct them.							

read like a writer. Soon you'll see them noticing writing techniques in the books they're reading. Sometimes students will incorporate these techniques into their writing, and they'll grow curious about why adult writers break the rules, such as not beginning sentences with *and, but,* or *because.* Curiosity about writing styles and sentence structure is an excellent entry point for a talk about advanced writing techniques. I've taken to saying something like this: "People who become very good writers know that it's OK to write this way. Because you're just now learning how to write, we're not going to use that technique."

Right now I'm seeing my points about very good writers take root in a guided reading group of six third graders. This particular group is reading *Balto and the Great Race* by Elizabeth Cody Kimmel (1999). The book is on the most advanced level that these students have ever read, and the kids are seeing complex sentence structures that they've never seen before. Right at the start, the students encountered this passage: "Who was Balto? Why is he remembered and talked about to this very day? And what could a dog from Alaska have done to deserve a statue in New York City?" (p. 2). As soon as they saw the last sentence, Larry, Pyper, and Nico exclaimed simultaneously, "Hey, she's breaking the rules! She started a sentence with *and.*" Almost as quickly, Nico added, "I guess she's a really good writer." "Yeah," said Pyper, "she sure is!"

Writers Think About... Poster

This poster, which was discussed at length in Chapter 2, reminds the teacher to weave grammar instruction into the writing lessons. It also reminds the students that good writers think about sentence structure, mechanics, and word choice every time they write. Although you may sometimes teach writing and grammar skills in isolation to practice a particular skill, you should always strive to connect the two. Regularly review both the Writers Think About... poster and the Good Writers' Checklist and make sure you explicitly connect the poster, the checklist, and student writing. I connect the dots between the students' writing and the Good Writers' Checklist every three or four weeks. Otherwise, my students begin to slide into a "stream of consciousness" style of writing. Actually, even when I explicitly teach and model, some of the students still slide. As we all know, that's typical in teaching.

Sometimes a student's bad writing habits are my fault. In my rush to hook the kids on writing, I let them get away with too much sloppiness and creativity. I pay for this leniency later when I have to break bad writing habits. Even as I write this book, I'm struggling to reign in two of my more enthusiastic writers who, in their desire to create a story and communicate it to the class, are devolving into writers of rambling sentences crammed with misspelled words, incorrect grammar, and sloppy printing. I'm now in the process of reeling them back in, making them stop after every five sentences so they can cross-check their writing against their Good Writers' Checklist.

Minilesson Routine

I start my guided writing block with a minilesson. If I only have 30 minutes for writing, it's a 10-minute lesson, but if I have 40 minutes, I might do a 15-minute lesson. In this lesson, I quickly review a previous concept or skill, such as verb tense or the use of adjectives. If the students haven't mastered that skill, I teach it again with a new spin. If they *have* mastered it, I teach a new skill or concept with modeling and direct instruction. In the case of reteaching, I might repeat a particular minilesson three or four times. Gradually, I extend the focus by bringing in a new skill. Even when I'm reteaching, I try to be clear about the instructional goal of the lesson, and I always model, model, model.

Topics for minilessons can come right out of the teacher's manual. Keep yourself focused on the most essential skills by consulting with other teachers and the Common Core State Standards. Minilessons can also come from the Good Writers' Checklist. For example, midway through the third nine weeks, my formative assessment may show that many students are failing to check and correct the spelling of their words. Others may have handwriting that's sliding into chicken scratch. When these problems crop up, I address them with minilesson reminders and a rundown of the Good Writers' Checklist.

Finally, I develop minilessons out of student writing, and I use student stories as positive models. Sometimes there's not enough time at the end of the writing block for kids to share their writing. If this is the case, at the beginning of the next lesson, I might briefly point out what some writers did really well, and I might read an excerpt from one or two pieces of student writing.

For example, my third-grade students recently completed compare-and-contrast assignments. In one, they compared cookie crisps with fruit snacks. In another, they compared two sea creatures of their choice, such as a starfish and a sea sponge. When the assignment was done, I pulled Dominick's and Hannah's writing to illustrate aspects of the assignment that they did really well (see Figure 6.8). After I checked with the kids to make sure it was OK for me to use their writing, I posted large sheets of paper on which I had written their paragraphs.

Dominick had written spot-on introductory sentences in both assignments, indented both paragraphs, and used interesting and

Figure 6.8. Two Third Graders' Compare-and-Contrast Writing

> Startish and shalls are alik because thay are sea crechers and thay live in salt water and thay are both hard and riged.
> Starfish and shalls are difrent because the shall does not have arms. It has a fhone shape and no suckshin caps. Starfish Have Arms, Star shape, it dose have suckshin caps.

> Cookie Chisps and Fruit Shacks are alike in somen ways. Cookie Crisps and Fruit shaks are doth sweet and bumdy.
> Cookie crisps and Fruit Shacks are diferent in some ways. cookie crisps is diffrent frum fruit Shacks. The cookie is Wete and chocklet. The cookie is crekelrunchy. On the uther hand the fruit is vahy suwer and punch foue. The color is orangeis redish.

descriptive vocabulary terms, such as *rigid* and *suction cups* (albeit spelled "suckshin"). Hannah wrote well-constructed introductory sentences, created short sentences in the second paragraph, and used compare-and-contrast terms such as *both* and *on the other hand*. In addition, Hannah circled the words that she thought were misspelled, looked them up in her student dictionary, and tried to correct them, all on her own.

Of course, both of these students have lots and lots of room for improvement. Spelling continues to be a big issue, as does capitalization and indenting. But if you could compare their September writing with their February writing, you'd see how much progress they've made. Dominick was especially pleased with his writing. He pulled me aside at the end of class, after I'd taken down the easel paper: "Mr. Weakland, can I have that big paper with my writing on it?" he asked quietly. "Sure," I said, handing him the long tube of rolled paper with a rubber band around it, "just don't use it as a sword on the bus." "No way," he exclaimed, smiling, "I want to show my pap my writing!"

Strategies for Spelling

During our dedicated spelling time, I teach struggling readers and writers to zap out the phonemes in a word and then blend them back together. Zapping means that each time a student says a phoneme, the student taps his or her bicep with a finger. The word *out* gets two taps, first from the pointer finger for the phoneme /ow/ and next from the middle finger for the phoneme /t/. After the student has zapped out the phonemes, he or she slides the fingers down the arm, from bicep to forearm, while blending the phonemes back into the word.

Zapping, which I'll discuss further in Chapter 7, is a strategy that students in my class use to spell a word they don't know. The most frequently asked question at the beginning of the year is, "Mr. Weakland, how do you spell ___?" My answer is always another question, such as, "Did you zap it out?" "Did you write down the sounds you hear?" "What letter or word chunk says that sound?" or "Did you think of another word that sounds like that word?"

Zapping out a word gets the kids close to the correct spelling, especially as the year goes on and the students master more syllable types, word families, and spelling rules. I encourage my students to zap out the phonemes, write letters that match those phonemes, and then circle that word. At the end of their writing, the students go back to their circled words and look at them. Perhaps on second examination, they'll realize that they can spell the word based on a previously learned syllable type or word chunk. If they're still stuck, they try to look the word up in a dictionary. As I monitor the class, I rotate among the students and guide them as they zap and use their student dictionaries. In Figure 6.8, you saw the "circle the word" strategy in Hannah's writing sample. Figure 6.9 is another example of a student using that strategy.

Figure 6.9. A Student's Writing With Circled Words

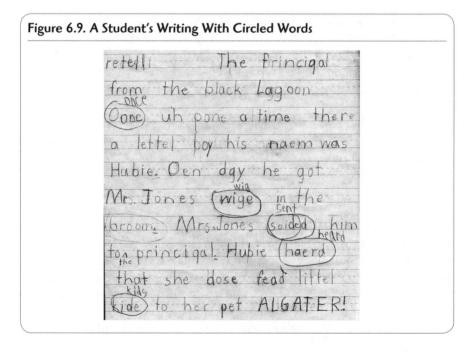

Call Cards

Call cards help you monitor a busy classroom full of attention-seeking writers, so teach your students how to use them early in the year. Over the years, using a call card during writing time has reduced the noise in my classroom, kept kids focused and in their seats, and saved me from any number of migraines and heart palpitations. The double-sided green and red card (which doubles as a response card, as discussed in Chapter 2) simply signals one of two states, either "I'm good to go," or "I'm stuck and need help."

Before the students begin to write, have them place their call cards on the corner of their desks, green side up. As they write, they'll begin to generate questions and encounter problems. When that happens, rather than allowing them to sit and dramatically wave their hands in the air, teach your students to flip the cards to red. But before they flip their cards, they should have used the problem-solving strategies that you've taught, modeled, and practiced with them. If they've tried to solve their problem with a strategy but still can't solve it, then it's red card time.

Students who use strategies and call cards are the answer to a common classroom problem, namely, how does one manage a classroom of 25 kids, all of whom have questions about writing? Table 6.1 lists some common writing roadblocks and solutions that you can teach the students to use prior to flipping their call cards.

Each of these teacher responses can be the subject of a minilesson and can be incorporated into your day-to-day instructional language. Students learn what you teach well, so if there's something in Table 6.1 that your kids can't do, teach them to do it. Model explicitly and provide guided practice, too. Regular doses of each will serve you well.

Once your students become more adept at solving their problems with strategies, their call card questions will typically involve things that you haven't taught yet, such as when to use a comma or if it's OK to write a one-word sentence like "Wow!" Or maybe a student really wants to show off a piece of writing that's progressing particularly well. At this point, it's OK for the student to flip his or her card to red. Some teachers have their students turn their cards over when they need to use the bathroom or get a drink of water. I prefer to teach kids the routine of responsible self-breaks, but this is your decision. The downside to self-breaks is that some button pushers and rule stretchers will abuse their freedom.

When a student's call card is on red, it's important that the student knows what to do while waiting for his or her question or concern to be addressed. Students' wait time activities include the following:

- Correct circled words by looking them up in the dictionary.

- Quietly reread a piece of writing to make sure it all makes sense.

Table 6.1. Common Writing Roadblocks and Solutions

When a Student Says...	You Say...
"I don't know what to write!"	• "Look at your topics list. Pick one. Start writing." • "Look around the room. Pick something in the room. Start writing." • "Think about your life. Focus on something you did recently. Start writing." • "Think of a story that you read recently. Write your own version of that story. Start writing."
"How do you spell ___?"	• "Did you zap it out?" • "What sounds do you hear? Write down the sounds that you hear." • "Do the best that you can do. Write down the sounds at the beginning and the end of the word and circle the word." • "When you are done writing, correct the circled words by finding them in the dictionary." • "Ask a friend or the person next to you."
"Am I done? Is this good enough?"	• "Did you say everything that you needed to say?" • "Is your writing interesting? If your friend picked up your writing, would your friend want to read it?" • "Did you use your Good Writers' Checklist?" • "Did you revise and edit your writing to make it as good as it can be?" • "Did you check it by reading to the wall?" • "Did you read it to a buddy?"
"I'm done."	• "Did you read it to the wall?" • "Did you read it to a buddy?" • "Did you revise and edit?" • "I don't see any evidence that you used your Good Writers' Checklist. Did you use it?" • "Look at the I Can... list. Pick something else. Start reading and writing!"

• Continue on with the rest of the writing until the teacher can get to you.

Just like any other routine, you'll need to teach your students how to use their call cards and what to do during the wait time. Then, you'll have to have the class practice until the routines become a habit.

One final word on call cards: During the last four years of my stint as a special education teacher, I taught special-needs students in a full inclusion program. This is when I first began to use call cards. Some teachers, who also ran writers' workshops in their inclusion classrooms, came up with creative variations on the flat, double-sided call card. I especially remember the stacking cup and the feather in the cap.

In the first example, the students had two small stacking cups sitting on the corner of their desks. When a student was good to go, he or she stacked the red cup inside the green one so the green was showing on the outside. When a student needed help, he or she reversed the order so the red was showing.

The "feather in the cap" version was more elaborate and fun. Prior to writing time, the students would don thinking caps, a battered collection of fedoras that were housed on a shelf above the classroom's coat hooks. Within each student's writing folder, housed with the composition book and various writing tools, was a large feather. If a student needed help, he or she signaled by plucking the feather from the folder and tucking it into the hatband, just like Yankee Doodle!

Graphic Organizers

Graphic organizers increase the effectiveness of your teaching and lead to greater student learning (Marzano et al., 2001). However, I don't introduce them until my students have mastered the art of the three-sentence paragraph. This may sound counterintuitive, like asking a builder to construct a home without a blueprint, but when it comes to elementary school writing, my first goal is to motivate kids to write, not to have them produce a well-planned and perfectly constructed five-sentence paragraph. My philosophy is that the perfected paragraph will come more easily if the students are already inclined to write, so I suggest you hold off on the introduction of graphic organizers until the end of the first nine weeks. There's a danger that your students will pick up some bad habits or learn incorrect paragraph construction, but your tightly focused Good Writers' Checklist (with its cumulatively introduced sequence of skills) will help keep the kids on track.

Once the students are happily writing away in the second nine weeks, I introduce formal paragraph construction with the hamburger graphic. My version is presented in Figure 6.10a. Our fourth- and fifth-grade teachers use the same type of graphic, but variations can be found online, mostly as blackline masters (see Figure 6.10b), and many of them are free.

I teach the graphic this way: The top bun is the topic sentence or opening, the meat patty is the detail sentences, and the bottom bun is the conclusion or a final detail sentence. Later, tasty extras such as adjectives, descriptive verbs, interesting word choices, and series commas are added. These details turn the simple hamburger into a complex cheeseburger

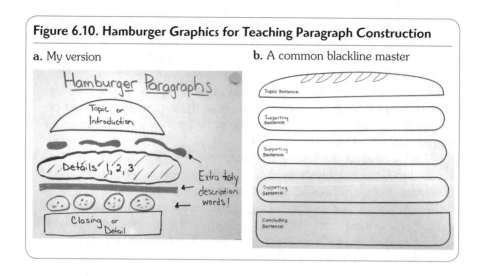

Figure 6.10. Hamburger Graphics for Teaching Paragraph Construction

a. My version

b. A common blackline master

(with pickles and ketchup) or, depending on your gastronomic inclinations, a tomato, lettuce, and hummus burger.

Although the hamburger organizer is a valuable tool, my students use it only once or twice every nine weeks. The use of a graphic organizer is time consuming, and I prefer that my students write a higher number of informal paragraphs than a lower number of formal paragraphs every nine weeks. To be clear, I'm not saying don't use a graphic organizer. I'm just saying you don't need to make your students use it every time they write a paragraph.

The four square graphic organizer is another tool that helps students write well-developed paragraphs. Developed and championed by Gould and Gould (1999), four square writing is a teaching method and a graphic organizer all rolled into one. I've seen it help many struggling writers, and I've known teachers who enjoy using it. However, I also know many teachers who don't like to use it because they find that its formulaic approach leads to formulaic paragraphs.

Other than the hamburger, the only other graphic organizer that I use for expository (nonfictional/informational) writing is the Venn diagram. We use this organizer, of course, to help us produce a compare-and-contrast paragraph, and I introduce it at the beginning or in the middle of the third nine weeks.

Note that the graphic organizers I've mentioned—four square, hamburger, and Venn diagram—do a great job of teaching students the expository writing formula of one topic sentence, one to three detail sentences, and one concluding sentence. An organizer that can be used for narrative (story) writing is a different animal, though. These organizers (sometimes called story maps) help students produce writing that has a logical sequence of events (beginning, middle, and end), a problem and solution, and details about characters and settings. It's beyond the scope of this book to discuss the many varieties of story maps that exist. Suffice it to say that it's good practice to teach at least one version of a narrative graphic organizer. Once you settle on a good one, teach your students the differences between writing from a story map and writing from an expository graphic organizer.

Revising and Editing

It's important for students to know that writers everywhere are engaged in a quest to make their writing as good as it can be. This quest is known as the writing process, and it involves planning, revising, editing, and final publication.

I teach the writing process informally for the first 12 weeks of third grade. During this time, I expect my students to do some type of planning before they write, but I don't require anything more than an oral and/or written brainstorm, some extended think time, and a think-pair-share session. Likewise, when it comes to revising, early in the year, I encourage the students to make changes so their writing is interesting to the reader, but I don't demand formal rewrites that include specific types of revisions. Editing is a slightly different story, though. The Good Writers' Checklist demands that students go back and check their work for correct grammar, spelling, and mechanics.

Only when the kids are hooked on writing and able to crank out a solid paragraph in 30–40 minutes do I raise the expectations and require them to use a graphic organizer, engage in revisions, or formally publish a paragraph that's rewritten from a sloppier copy. If you teach grade 4 or 5, you'll need to put more emphasis on graphic organizers, revising, and perfected final copies, but I caution that too much emphasis on process and not enough emphasis on writing can make writing such a chore that it turns kids off.

Revising and editing is a natural place to incorporate social learning. During informal revisions and editing, you can have authors buddy up and read their writings to each other. Reading with a buddy allows both writers to make sure their writing is readable, understandable, and grammatically and mechanically correct. Like any routine, proper buddy behavior, such as close listening and helpful comments, must be taught, modeled, and practiced. Buddy reading also allows for sharing. It's exciting for kids to share their ideas, tell about events in their lives, and show off a funny, well-written, and interesting piece of writing.

Presenting to the Class

Just like adults, kids want to communicate and share their ideas, opinions, and stories. Buddy sharing has already been discussed. Presenting to and sharing with the entire class are also important. Before students read and present to a large group, though, it's important that you establish a welcoming, respectful, and safe environment for the kids to present in. Presenting in front of peers can be a very big deal, and the presenter has to know that everyone will pay respectful attention and that no one will snicker if the reader makes a mistake or is halting at times.

After a safe and respectful environment is established, model what a quality oral presentation looks and sounds like. I typically list three qualities on the board and then model examples of each one. The qualities I want my students to focus on are stance, voice, and fluency. The presenter's stance should be upright and relaxed with a minimal amount of movement and no leaning, the presenter's voice should be clear and fairly loud so everyone can hear, and the presenter's fluency should include a good rate of speed, few hesitations, longer phrases with minimal word-by-word reading, and appropriate expression. If possible, the presenter should briefly pause every now and then and make eye contact with the audience.

Before presenting to the class, writers should practice reading their writing out loud. This gives soon-to-be presenters a chance to practice multiple times before they present to the group. Presenters can practice by reading their writing to the wall and then to a buddy. Reading to the wall looks like punishment—the room is full of students standing and facing various walls—but it's really about speaking to a reflective surface. Have the kids stand close to a wall or door (not a window), just five or six inches away, and softly read their writing. The wall bounces the sound waves back, so the kids don't need to read very loudly. For this activity, I typically use a timer set for two to four minutes. The students are to read their writing over and over again until the timer beeps. While reading, they practice fluency, including expression, and looking up from their writing.

Before students present their writing, take a little time to model what presenters should *not* do. Modeling nonexamples (or bad examples, in the vernacular) is fun because it gives you a chance to mumble, read like a robot, pace madly up and down the floor while yelling, and demonstrate any number of ridiculous behaviors that good presenters would never do. Modeling nonexamples also gives your students a chance to point out everything that you're doing wrong. What kid doesn't like to critique the teacher?

Presenting and sharing with the class is the perfect opportunity to work in a few of the Common Core's speaking and listening standards. When you allow for a few audience questions about the writing (e.g., "Why did you pick that topic?") and give the audience a chance to identify a fact they heard in the reading, you've covered three of the six speaking and listening standards for grades 2–5.

Because time is always in short supply, I use student name cards to randomly pick a student presenter. When that student finishes, he or she picks another name card at random. Sometimes, if we have time, presenters read their writing two times in a row. First, the presenter reads his or her writing while the class listens for enjoyment. Meanwhile, I listen critically because when the presenter is done, I praise two things done well and offer one suggestion for improvement.

After I give two praises and one suggestion for improvement (remember task analysis and mastery learning), the presenter reads again. This time, the audience listens carefully and looks critically for stance, voice, and fluency. When the presenter is done, I solicit comments from the audience on what the reader did well or improved on from the first reading. After a few students have weighed in with positive comments, we offer up a round of applause. The presenter then picks another name card, and we move on to the next reader.

Sometimes, especially in kindergarten or when I'm working with a class of struggling readers, I read examples of student writing rather than have the students present. I can make any story sound interesting and exciting, and I can save some time, too. Of course, I always ask the students' permission before reading their work aloud, and I sometimes call a student up to stand beside me as I read.

Teaching Chops: Independent Writing

It takes time to get students to the point where they can write independently for 15, 20, or 25 minutes at a time. Use your guided writing lessons to get students to a place where they feel comfortable writing on their own. Through your explicit teaching and repeated practice, your students will build muscle memory for writing, just like they did for reading. Once that muscle memory is in place, turn your students loose to write on their own.

Before we look at the details of what kids can do during independent writing, let's delve into three practices that you'll want to incorporate into any guided writing lesson: explicit modeling, whole-group physical response, and task analysis and mastery learning.

Explicit Modeling

As always, model everything that you want your students to do. Don't assume that they know what a complete sentence, a focused paragraph, or a completed graphic organizer looks like. Before you have your students write a sentence, model how *you* write a sentence, and explicitly talk through your thinking process. Explicitly show your students how to complete the Venn diagram or hamburger graphic organizer, mindfully talk your way through the process, and do it prior to each student assignment.

We know from Graham and Hebert's (2010) meta-analysis that students' reading skills and comprehension are improved when you teach the process of writing *and* paragraph and sentence construction skills, so teach and model and then model some more! This might seem like overkill, but you and I know that some students need repeated practice to master even a basic skill.

As a final note, pointing out and discussing well-written text can be a form of modeling, so try to get in a little bit of both. Look for appropriate text in the books that your students are reading as well as well-written student writing samples.

Whole-Group Physical Response

When students write as a group, you're free to move about the room, observe writing behaviors, and analyze writing strengths and weaknesses. So, make sure to take advantage of these opportunities to monitor the class, check on mechanics and grammar, encourage proper sentence construction, correct errors, and provide feedback as soon as possible so wrong behaviors aren't learned.

Task Analysis and Mastery Learning

Mastering the technical aspects of writing (the science of writing, if you will) takes time. Mastering the art of writing, where voice, word selection, cadence, and style become apparent, takes even more. Because time is limited, it's essential that you teach with a focused writing sequence in mind and that you aim to teach certain skills and concepts to mastery. To do this, introduce them one at a time and with a certain amount of direct and explicit instruction. Each of these instructional practices increases the chances that your students will permanently learn the information.

Additionally, find as much time as possible for students to practice what you've taught. Your core reading program's end-of-the-week assessment can provide an additional writing opportunity. Each story test in my school's program typically includes at least a couple of well-constructed writing prompts. Students can practice their writing skills (as well as show their understanding of the story selection) when they respond to writing prompts, such as "Compare Earth to one other planet. How is it alike and different?" "Describe the animal home that you find most interesting," and "Which idea in the selection did you find most interesting? Tell why."

I try to look over each story test in advance to make sure that the test prompts match the writing skills and concepts that the students have learned or are learning. If the prompt doesn't line up with my scope and sequence of writing skills, then I insert a writing prompt that does, or I rewrite one of the multiple-choice questions as a writing prompt. When completing the writing portion of the test, students should have their Good Writers' Checklist on hand so they know what rules to follow during their responses.

Consider the end-of-the-story assessment to be as much of an instructional tool as an assessment tool. My cooperating teacher and I go so far as to use our writing rubric to grade the written responses on these tests. Doing this expands your end-of-the-story assessment into a formative writing assessment.

Independent Writing: The I Can... List

Once you've hooked your students on writing, and they've mastered complete paragraphs and can sit and write independently for a solid 15 or 20 minutes, it's time to begin independent writing activities. The independent writing activities on the I Can... list should be presented cumulatively over time. They should also be presented in conjunction with independent reading activities. Figure 6.11 gives examples of writing activities that can be added to the I Can... list. The first chart lists the activities and routines that my third graders have (hopefully) mastered by the beginning of the second nine weeks. The second list is for the third and/or fourth nine weeks. It's longer because the students have been introduced to more activities and routines. As you progress through your teaching career, I'm sure you'll find activities that work best with the students in your school, in your grade level, and in your classroom. Add your own activities and have fun.

There are numerous ways to manage the I Can... list, ranging from giving your kids the freedom to choose whatever they want to assigning each activity during each independent work session. My path is in the middle. I typically give the kids a choice of three activities. For example, I might say, "Today your choices are independent reading,

> ### Figure 6.11. I Can... Lists With Writing
>
> | _First nine weeks_ | _Second nine weeks_ |
> |---|---|
> | I can... | I can... |
> | • Read independently | • Read independently and complete a book slip |
> | • Buddy read | • Buddy read |
> | • Repeat reading with my toolbox | • Repeat reading with my toolbox |
> | • Write about a topic | • Read, record, and check |
> | | • Review my vocabulary cards |
> | | • Write about a topic |
> | | • Write in my dialogue journal |
> | | • Write spelling sentences |

dialogue journals, and rereading with your toolbox." The students are free to choose to spend all or part of their time on any one of the three activities. Giving limited choice allows me to control (and keep track of) what activities the students are engaged in while still giving them freedom to choose.

If you choose the middle path, visually show what choices are available. Toni and I have our I Can... list posted on part of our whiteboard. To show what the choices are, I simply draw arrows pointing to three activities. Sometimes I write an assignment on the whiteboard, such as completion of a previous writing assignment, that must be done before the kids can move on to the three choices marked with arrows on the I Can... list. Other options for providing visual reminders include a sticky-note arrow beside each of the three choices or a clip-on arrow. If you're using a pocket chart for your I Can... list, you can remove the activities that aren't available, cover them with a blank paper strip, or insert tiny green lights or red stop signs.

This brings me to a very important point: You must teach, remind, and continually stress to your students, especially during the beginning of the year, that they should always be doing something from the I Can... list during independent work time. If they choose to read a book independently and finish it, then they must pick another book and start reading. Your job as a classroom manager is to teach the classroom routines and then constantly remind the students to "get to work!" If students write to you as part of a dialogue journal and finish that writing, then they must begin to write something else. Under no circumstances should any student approach your guided reading group and ask, "What do I do now?" Every student in your class should know the answer to that question: "Choose something from the I Can... list and get to work."

Here's one final point about kids and independent work routines: Keep your eyes open for students who flit from one activity to another without ever finishing a piece of writing or reading. You may need to teach your students these two rules for independent work time: (1) Vary your activities and (2) finish the work you started.

Regarding rule 1, I peruse the students' composition books and look for dates. If I haven't seen some type of solid writing from any given student in a couple of weeks, I give the student a stern reminder to choose writing. If another week goes by and I still don't see writing, then I assign writing as an activity. Now the student no longer has a choice.

As for rule 2, I understand that every now and then, a student may pick the wrong book and want to bail out, or may hit a roadblock with topic writing. These instances, however, should be the exception and not the norm. I stress to my students that I give them the freedom to make choices, but with that freedom comes responsibility. If they're incapable of being responsible and can't abide by the rules, then they lose their freedom, and I make the choices for them.

The following segments give a bit more detail regarding each of my three big independent writing activities.

Independent Topic Writing

Once your students have mastered how to write about a topic during extending writing time, it's time to add it as a choice on the I Can... list. Make the writing folders available and let the kids write about their favorite topics while you teach one of the guided reading groups.

You'll need to routinely check these independently generated writings. When students write on their own, they often forget that good writers think before they write, reread to make sure the writing makes sense, correct their spelling, and so on. Every now and then, gather up their composition books, note what writing skills are being used, and give a minilesson that reminds the class of what good writers always do, no matter the setting. During these minilessons, pull out exemplary student work, praise those students for a job well done, and point out what makes the writing excellent. On the flip side, remind those who need it that everyone must follow the Good Writers' Checklist during independent writing so words are neatly formed, sentences make sense, and so forth.

The ratio of monitoring to independence is up to you. My philosophy is that it's more important to use independent writing as a tool to build motivation than as a tool to teach writing exactitude. To this end, I encourage kids to write neatly, use correct grammar, and spell to the best of their ability during topic writing, but I don't grade these writings or ever mark them with a correction pen. You may choose to do things differently, however.

Take the time to discuss the importance of grammar and mechanics in independent writing but also spend some time talking about subject matter. When students share their writing with the class, they give the audience ideas on more topics to write about. It also promotes personal connections between the students and the teacher. You can validate student topics, such as a day out with a grandparent or playing video games, by making personal connections to them, such as, "I can really relate to your writing because when I was a kid, I used to love to visit my grandfather," and "I tried playing video games when I was at my nephew's yesterday. Boy, was I lousy!"

Topic writing goes hand in hand with the independent reading that kids do. When kids read lots of books, they see lots of good writing. My third graders independently begin to write original stories around the middle of the year (see Figure 6.12 for an example). Perhaps it's because they've had almost half a year of independent reading under their belts by this point. Recently, I had three girls in my class who were very interested in writing stories about outer space and aliens, talking dogs, and teachers

Figure 6.12. A Third Grader's Story for a Topic Writing Assignment

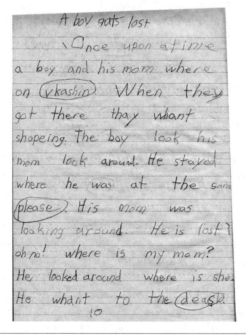

who fly around the room. I'm all for this type of writing because it often provides the perfect opportunity to work in a minilesson on punctuating dialogue; constructing a beginning, middle, and end to a story; and using interesting words to engage the reader.

Dialogue Journal

This activity, which can take the form of a letter or a simple, unstructured conversation, is a give-and-take between teacher and writer (see Figure 6.13). During independent writing time, some students write to me to tell me what's on their mind. I collect their writing at the end of the period, read over it when I have a few minutes (e.g., during breakfast duty), and then respond in writing.

Figure 6.13. Samples of Students' Dialogue Journal Writing

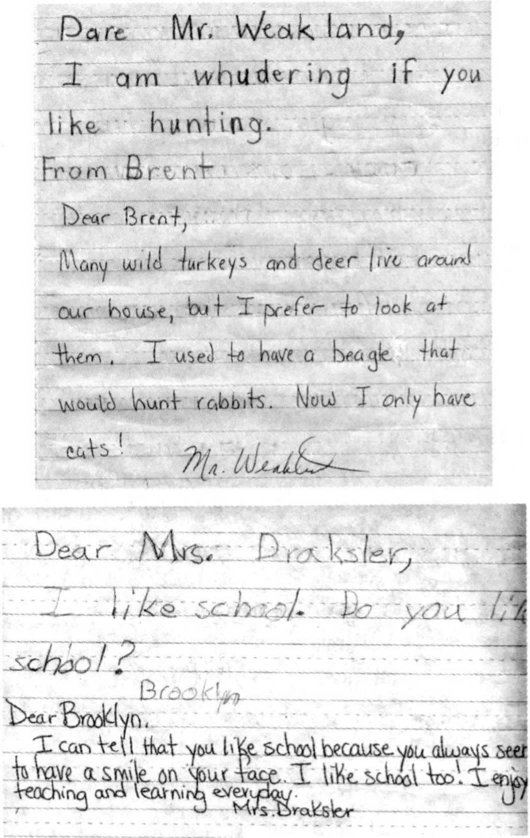

Dare Mr. Weakland,
I am whudering if you like hunting.
From Brent

Dear Brent,
Many wild turkeys and deer live around our house, but I prefer to look at them. I used to have a beagle that would hunt rabbits. Now I only have cats! Mr. Weakl

Dear Mrs. Draksler,
I like school. Do you like school?
Brooklyn

Dear Brooklyn,
I can tell that you like school because you always seem to have a smile on your face. I like school too! I enjoy teaching and learning everyday.
Mrs. Draksler

Some kids absolutely love this activity. I used to think that it was the girls who enjoyed it the most, but this year I have a number of boys who can't wait to write to me and have me write back. Regardless of whether the student begins the writing with, "Dear Mr. Weakland," I typically write back, "Dear Nick," or "Dear Tianna." Then, I simply respond to the writing, commenting on an interesting topic, a funny story, or answering a question that the student may have asked. One bonus to this activity is that when you respond with a hefty number of sentences, you create another opportunity for your students to read connected text!

As the year goes on, I try to work in the two praises and a push. When a student turns in a heartfelt dialogue about visiting a family member in the hospital, I might praise the student's attention to writing detail and his or her caring attitude. I also work in a statement like, "I enjoyed reading your writing. Don't forget to end your sentences with punctuation!" Just as in topic writing, freedom may beget bad writing habits, and you may find it necessary to remind about, review, and reteach the Good Writers' Checklist.

One of the unfortunate downsides of modern-day school life, especially in this era of high-stakes testing, is that the days can be an endless exercise in grinding out instruction. There seems to be little, if any, time to talk with students, tell a few stories, or hear about the joys and sorrows that students are experiencing. Dialogue journals tap into the needs that we all have to communicate our feelings, to share our stories, and to make a connection with others. The students who write to me seem to enjoy the opportunity to communicate, and the feeling is mutual. I get to know my students through their writing, and I can share some of my life when I respond to them.

Spelling Sentences

I introduce this activity early in the year, along with topic writing. The purpose of the activity is twofold: First, students practice writing complete and interesting sentences. They do this in lieu of "fill in the blank" worksheets. Second, the activity provides a chance to discuss the meanings of words. Of course, correct spelling is also stressed.

Writing an interesting sentence involves choosing descriptive verbs, adding adjectives, and constructing more complex sentences. I also challenge the students to write spelling sentences that incorporate more than one spelling word in a sentence. Austin, a quiet boy who's a real worker bee, turned this sentence in: "The insisting chipmunk ate a sandwich then did a handstand." Wow! Austin's four-spelling-word sentence earned him a bonus point and a round of applause from the kids in the class. By the way, the week's spelling focus was multisyllable, closed-syllable words, which we'll talk more about in Chapter 7.

At the beginning of the year, I assign six sentences every week during independent work time. By the second nine weeks, I assign the sentences every other week, and by the third nine weeks, the activity is by choice only. Some students voluntarily choose this activity, especially the ones who prefer cut-and-dried activities over more complex activities like topic writing.

Formative Assessment

If your students write on a regular basis, formative assessment is easy. Simply collect writing samples, observe and record which skills are present and which are absent, and plan your future instruction accordingly. Of course, you'll need an assessment instrument that provides focus and allows you to generate meaningful data. I suggest a writing rubric.

A well-constructed writing rubric functions as the backbone of a writing assessment system. Constructing one is easier said than done, however. You'll want to craft a rubric that's easy to understand and use, as objective and quantifiable as possible, and expansive enough to address all that you teach but not so wide ranging that it takes 15 minutes to grade one piece of writing. Also, the rubric should be aligned to the Common Core State Standards, your school's curriculum, and most importantly, your classroom practice. I can't stress this enough: Your assessment rubric, your writing curriculum, your Good Writers' Checklist, and the Common Core should all contain the same information. Each of these documents is merely a different way of presenting the same essential writing skills and concepts that you want your students to master.

For those of you who want to design your own rubric, I offer mine as an example (see Figure 6.14). I break it into four areas: mechanics, grammar, writing skills, and applied spelling skills. Some might argue that spelling is really a subset of mechanics, and I wouldn't disagree. I break out spelling into a separate category, though, because I want to keep track of it and have a firm grip on whether my students, especially the more needy ones, are applying the phonic rules I'm teaching them in their writing. By the way, these four categories match our district report card. Your school or district report card is yet another factor to take into account during rubric creation.

Some of you may teach writing with the six traits of writing in mind. If this is the case, the categories of your rubric should reflect the six traits:

Figure 6.14. My Third-Grade Paragraph Writing Rubric

Proficiency benchmarks: First nine weeks = 12. Second nine weeks = 14 or 15. Third nine weeks = 16+.

Points / Skill	5 = A	4 = P (proficient)	3 = B (basic)	2 = BB (below basic)	1 = BB (below basic)
Mechanics	• Indent • Writes to end of lines • Mostly neat writing (form and space) • Correct use of capitals	• Missing one	• Missing two	• Missing three	• Missing all four
Grammar	• Correct grammar: Complete sentences, subject–verb agreement, tense endings • Correct periods and no run-on sentences	• Missing one	• Missing both	• More than 50% of sentences have incorrect grammar or missing three	
Writing skills	• Accurate completion of assignment: Compare/contrast, summarize, etc. • Varied sentence structure • Interesting word choice • Seven or more sentences • On topic the entire time • Introductory and closing sentences (if applicable)	• Missing one	• Missing two	• Missing three	• Missing four
Applied spelling skills	• Spells all words correctly	• Misspells one or two words and attempts to correct spelling	• Misspells three to six words or does not attempt to correct spelling	• Misspells seven or more words	

ideas/content, organization, voice, word choice, sentence fluency, and conventions. I think you'll be able to see them in one form or another in my rubric, which is very basic compared with a typical six-traits rubric. That's because my philosophy is to teach the essentials and expand outward. I put my instructional focus on the basics: correct construction of basic sentences, tight focus on one topic throughout the paragraph, correct use of mechanics and grammar, and accurate completion of the assigned task. This is not to say that some of my students don't write with a bit of voice, use interesting and advanced vocabulary, and demonstrate some pacing and flow in their writing. Some of them do, and I encourage and nurture it.

I score an informal paragraph every two weeks or so and one formal paragraph every nine weeks. This gives me three or four writing scores per nine weeks, enough for me to monitor each student's progress toward mastering skills. The rubric totals 20 points, and each skill area gets 5. I note the scores in each area on a tracking sheet (see Figure 6.15) and then highlight 4s in yellow and 5s in green. Over time, I should see two things: (1) The scoring sheet, which takes on the aspect of a graph because of the highlighting, should blossom from white to yellow to green; and (2) the total score should climb from an 11 or 12 in the first nine weeks, to a 14 or 15 in the second nine weeks, and to a 17 or 18 in the third and fourth nine weeks. Thus, I'm able to see increasing, decreasing, or flatline trends in both the general 20-point score and in each of the 5-point categories.

In my third-grade cotaught classroom, the students finished a compare-and-contrast assignment around Valentine's Day. Almost all the kids scored between a 13 on the low end and a 16 on the high end. Scores of 13 and 14 were disappointing. Analyzing these scores more closely, I found that most students scored a 5 in the category of writing skills. This means they completed the particulars of the assignment, used varied sentences, kept their focus, and wrote seven or more sentences. However, many were not applying spelling strategies, some were still writing run-on sentences, a few had unacceptably sloppy printing, and a couple weren't bothering to use their Good Writers' Checklist to make sure their paragraphs were indented. That last one really drives me nuts!

The good news, however, was that about half of the students scored a 16 or higher, right where I'd expect them to be in mid-February. Digging a little deeper, I saw that three of the 16s could have been a 17 or even an 18 if more words were spelled correctly. Because these students were writing a lot of sentences and using more sophisticated words, their chances of misspelling a word were increased. Thus, their ability to write more sentences with more interesting words was leading to a depressed

Figure 6.15. My Third-Grade Paragraph Writing Rubric Score Sheet (surnames deleted)

Quarter: _____

Key: G = grammar. M = mechanics. S = applied spelling skills. W = writing skills.

Date																																			
Assignment																																			
Skill	M	G	W	S	M	G	W	S	M	G	W	S	M	G	W	S	M	G	W	S	M	G	W	S	M	G	W	S	M	G	W	S	M	G	W	S
Kaitlynn																																				
Pyper																																				
Natali																																				
Hannah																																				
Nico																																				
Austin																																				
Connor																																				
Ethan																																				
Trent																																				
Jordan																																				
Larry																																				
Elaine																																				
Amara																																				
Winn																																				
Dominick																																				
David																																				

spelling score. This just goes to show that one should never judge a student strictly by a score!

The best news was that with a minimal amount of teacher guidance, David and Jordan both scored 19 out of 20—exceptional scores for this time of year. Both of these students finished the assignment with great accuracy, wrote complete sentences that made sense grammatically, went back to correct capital and lowercase letters that were initially incorrect, and corrected misspelled words (or didn't misspell them in the first place). Kudos to them!

The beauty of a rubric that remains constant throughout the year is that it enables you to see progress toward the general benchmark number (a 16 and above for the third nine weeks) and the specific benchmarks (a score of 5 in at least one of the four specific categories by the third nine weeks). I tell my students that everyone should be scoring a 5 in the mechanics category by the third nine weeks. All they have to do is remember to follow the simple rules of indenting, punctuating, writing neatly, and capitalizing in the right places. I also tell them that failing to indent, capitalize, or properly punctuate is like me handing out dollar bills and them turning around and throwing the money in the garbage. That's crazy!

Make It So

Extended writing is an opportunity to teach writing skills, increase reading achievement, and have students practice communication and self-expression. During extended writing time, students practice writing to prompts and writing for enjoyment, expression, and communication. Does extended writing time always result in well-written paragraphs of authentic writing? In a word, no. Typically, one or two of my students actively resist my attempts to guide them into the life of a student writer. During extended writing time, they suddenly need to take numerous bathroom breaks, or they develop terrible headaches, sore throats, and bouts of educational amnesia. When they do finally turn in some writing, it often fails to follow the guidelines outlined in the Good Writers' Checklist.

As you know, teaching can be a struggle! All one can do is teach, provide opportunities for practice and success, and hope that the dogs will eventually begin to hunt. Most do. For every student who turns in writing that disappoints me, there are 10 who excitedly embrace writing and exceed my expectations for achievement. I firmly believe that if you create time for kids to write, and if you teach writing well, many of your students will look forward to it and enjoy it. And I bet that you'll get a real kick out of reading what they've written.

CHAPTER 7

Strengthen Your Spelling

You will need...

- Your teacher's manual with its lists of spelling words
- Additional word lists pulled from secondary sources, such as *Recipe for Reading: Intervention Strategies for Struggling Readers* by Frances Bloom and Nina Traub (2000), *Phonics From A to Z: A Practical Guide* by Wiley Blevins (2006), and a grade-level book in the Making Words series by Patricia M. Cunningham and Dorothy P. Hall (e.g., 2001)
- Tables of common graphemes and phonograms (included in this chapter)
- Word work materials, such as magnetic tiles and boards, whiteboards and dry-erase markers, spelling words for word sorts, and so forth
- A reading/writing journal for dictation exercises
- Student writing folders with a Good Writers' Checklist and a student dictionary included in each

You will...

- Teach students *how* to spell rather than *what* to spell
- Assess your students at the beginning of the year using spelling inventories
- Teach fewer phonograms to struggling spellers but teach to mastery
- Use kinesthetic techniques to tap out the sounds of a word, clap out the syllables, and blend the sounds back into words
- Refrain from using most spelling worksheets and practice book pages
- Teach letter–sound relationships by using direct and explicit instruction and word work activities
- Formatively assess your students over time

Reading and spelling are two sides of the same coin (Ehri, 2000). Research tells us that spelling and reading are built on a shared foundation of knowledge. This foundation includes the relationships between letters and sounds. When you read, you decode letter symbols into sounds to form words; when you spell, you encode the sounds of language into symbols. "Spelling and reading build and rely on the same mental representation of a word. Knowing the spelling of a word makes the representation of it sturdy and accessible for fluent reading" (Snow et al., 2005, p. 86). I love that quote's use of the word *sturdy* because when it comes to building a solid and enduring house of reading, students must experience their words as sturdy bricks, not brittle twigs or flimsy pieces of straw. Words become sturdy for students when we teach letter–sound relationships to the point of mastery. When students master these relationships, the result is better reading, as well as better writing and spelling (Ehri, 2000).

There are strong connections between spelling and writing, too. Fluent writers employ spelling strategies automatically and have a large repository of words that they know how to spell. Conversely, poor writers write more slowly, in part because they struggle over the spellings of words. Poor writers may also limit their writing vocabulary to words that they know how to spell (e.g., *nice, good*), and they may lose their focus as they attempt to spell unknown words (Graham & Harris, 2000). These students are like Jamar, the little boy whose mother asked him after school one day, "What did you do in school today?" "We wrote about our favorite animal," replied Jamar. "Oh," replied Mom, "did you write about a meerkat?" "No," said Jamar. "A giraffe?" asked Mom. "No," said Jamar. "A lemur?" "No," said Jamar. "Well, why not?" asked Mom, "You love all of those animals!" "Well," said Jamar, "I didn't know how to spell any of those words, so I wrote, 'I do not like animals.'"

My preference is to think holistically about phonics, spelling, reading, and writing. Each area is like a facet on a diamond: It shines more brightly when light reflects from neighboring facets. This chapter will help you polish your core spelling and phonics program so your reading and writing programs will, in turn, shine more brightly. We'll start with a broad perspective: How can teachers move away from a spelling program that teaches students *what* to spell and move toward a spelling program that teaches students *how* to spell? To enable this transition, we'll look at ways to transform your spelling program, currently a weekly set of lists meant to be memorized, into a logical and organized system of spelling, which you can use to teach, and your students can use to learn, encoding strategies for writing and word-decoding strategies for reading.

As the changes you make to your core spelling program become instructional habits, you'll discover that you're simultaneously addressing many of the Common Core's standards, positioning yourself to differentiate your spelling instruction even further (when the time is right) and even having fun as you embrace a few new classroom traditions.

Most importantly, you'll find that your lowest achieving students will have gradually improved their ability to fluently read and write unknown words. For a reading teacher, what's better than that?

The Importance of Spelling

To more fully understand the importance of spelling within the context of a complete reading program, it may be helpful to first talk about what happens when a student applies phonics and other reading strategies to decode a word. When a good reader encounters an unknown word, such as *strict* or *employment*, he or she uses a number of strategies to figure out just what that word is (Adams, 1990; Cunningham & Allington, 1998; Snow, Burns, & Griffin, 1998). Typically, the student stops at the unknown word and reads through it, looking at each letter left to right. While looking at the unknown word, the reader begins to search his or her memory for words with a similar phonic pattern. Once found, the letter–sound association of the known phonic pattern may help the student read the unknown word. If the unknown word is multisyllabic, he or she may chunk it into parts or decode it one grapheme at a time. After this period of observation, association, and decoding, the reader produces a pronunciation. The student then checks it for meaning by wondering, Is this a word I recognize? If it is, the reader may go back to the beginning of the sentence and reread it, or simply move on, now that he or she knows what the word is and understands how it contributes to the meaning of the text. If the reader's pronunciation doesn't match a word stored in his or her memory banks, the reader may try another pronunciation.

Good readers who know that words should make sense within the context of what they're reading seem to toggle back and forth quickly between decoding and sense making. I remember listening to my sister Melissa read a book to me when she was young. She had chosen the story of Rapunzel, but she kept pronouncing the heroine's name "Rap-u-NUN-zel." In the grand scheme of reading, that's no big deal. Her pronunciation didn't change the meaning of the story, and Melissa was able to continue reading nonplussed. But when she came to the word *determined* and read it as "detter-minded," as in "Rap-u-NUN-zel was detter-minded to escape from the tower," she stopped and looked at me in puzzlement. "I don't know what that means!" she exclaimed. Because I was a simple-minded and loving big brother rather than an educated and hard-nosed teacher, I didn't say, "Well, what word has some of the same sounds as that word but makes sense in the story?" or "Let's try chunking that word into different syllable types, like open, *R*-controlled, and closed!" I simply gave Melissa the word. "That word is *determined*," I said. "Oh," she said, "thanks!" And she continued on.

To read words like *Rapunzel* and *determined* by sight, a reader must have the ability to fluently map letters and letter combinations to sounds (Ehri & Snowling, 2004). In other words, readers must have strong decoding skills. When readers have weak decoding skills, they may employ other strategies to deal with unknown words. Unfortunately, poor readers employ strategies that are terribly ineffective. As a Title I teacher, I listen to a lot of students read. I typically find that in many grades, about 30–50% of the kids who've been identified as low achieving haven't mastered the fluent mapping of letters and letter combinations to sounds. In other words, they lack the ability to decode grade-level words. What do these low-achieving readers do when they come to a word that they can't decode? Sometimes they skip over it. At other times, they sit passively and wait for the teacher to give them the word. But most often, they employ the "glance and guess" reading strategy.

I'll describe this strategy to you, but I bet you've seen it in action. When a poor reader encounters a word not instantly recognized, he or she doesn't carefully read through the word, trying to associate sounds with graphemes or patterns. Instead, the reader simply looks at the first letter of the unknown word and substitutes another word with the same beginning sound. If the substituted word preserves the meaning of the sentence, then the reader may continue to try to preserve meaning (if not within the greater passage, then at least within the sentence itself) by substituting, omitting, and/or inserting additional words each time another unknown word is encountered. Thus, a sentence such as "My best friend sat at the table with his mother and stepfather" becomes "My best friend stood all the time with his mother and stepfather." If the reader never learned that sentences should always make sense, or if the reader is simply tired of struggling through sentences that he or she can't read, then the reader might read the sentence as "My big friend sat at the turtle with his mom and sister."

When I dig a little deeper and administer a phonics inventory and a spelling inventory, I typically find that most, but not all, students who habitually use the "glance and guess" strategy haven't mastered the most basic phonic patterns of the English language. Results from my diagnostic assessments and error analysis usually show that these readers have mastered the letter–sound correspondence of most consonants and consonant blends as well as some consonant digraphs (such as *sh*), but they haven't mastered even basic vowel patterns, such as C–V–C words or high-frequency vowel digraphs. Thus, when I ask one of these readers to read the word *intake*, the student is just as likely to say, "intack," or, "inside," as she is to say, "intake." Similarly, when I look at how the lowest achieving students spell unknown words when they write, it's obvious that they're simply taking a guess and not employing strategies that get them close to the actual spelling. When asked to spell the word *stripe*, they're likely to spell it "srip," "streip," or "stap."

Because they haven't mastered basic phonics, low-achieving students seem to rely on picture cues, syntax, context, and their background knowledge to sustain their progress through a reading passage. While writing, they seem to hear and identify a few key consonant sounds and then guess the rest. This reliance on picture cues, background knowledge, and guessing terribly inhibits their reading and writing progress.

How is it that after years of reading instruction, some older readers still lack the ability to decode and encode basic words? To answer that complex question, we'll need to look more closely at the organization and scope of a core reading program's spelling component.

Scope:
Spelling Components and Program Philosophies

Although spelling is tied intimately to reading, it's best taught as a stand-alone subject (Gentry & Graham, 2010). This begs the questions, What content should be included in a spelling program, and how should it be taught? Informed opinions are many and varied. Although there may be a lack of consensus regarding what exact methodology to use, there's strong consensus that teaching phonics and spelling improves the reading skills of both young readers and older struggling readers and that spelling and phonics should be taught in a systematic fashion (Gentry & Graham, 2010; NICHD, 2000a).

The spelling component of a core reading program typically comes with a scope and sequence chart that parallels the phonics scope and sequence. In other words, the grapheme or phonogram presented in the third week's phonics lessons is the same grapheme or phonogram presented in the third week's spelling lesson. All in all, the scope and sequence is very systematic, just as research says it should be.

There are other positives to core reading programs. First, they do a great deal of work for the harried teacher, providing ready-made lists of words, spelling activities that go with the lists, phonic activities that align with the spelling, and workbook pages that can be given as in-class practice or homework. All of these materials save teachers time and energy. In addition, core reading programs teach spelling words within the context of patterns and word families (e.g., -am, -old, -ight), categories of syllable types (e.g., V–C–e, vowel teams), and spelling rules (e.g., change the *y* to an *i* and add *-es*). They also make use of a strong decoding sequence, starting off with short-vowel (C–V–C) and long-vowel (V–C–e) words in first grade, moving to more complex vowel teams in second grade, and continuing with more vowel teams in third grade (Dewitz & Jones, 2013). This sequence of skills, which is present in almost all basal reading programs, continues in third and fourth grades as various affixes and grammar-based rules are added to the mix.

With their lists of words based on patterns and their well-defined scope and sequence through the grade levels, basal spelling programs are off to a good start. But as instruction progresses from week to week, the many positives of a core program begin to show a problematic side. Let's take a look at what the problems are.

An Inflexible Sequence

If you move faithfully (or, to use the educational buzzword, with fidelity) through the spelling scope and sequence of your core reading program, you may soon find yourself between a rock and a hard place when you discover that some of your students haven't mastered the important step of matching short-vowel sounds to specific letters. What should you do when students don't truly know what letter is associated with the short /a/ sound (as in *strap*, *lad*, and *flash*), but the spelling sequence dictates that you move to the short /i/ sound next week? Some teachers may continue teaching the sequence because they sincerely trust in the efficacy of their core reading program. Others may know it's a bad idea to introduce a new letter sound when many students haven't mastered the previous one, but these teachers move on because someone somewhere told them not to deviate from the program.

It's my belief that presenting an inflexible spelling and phonics scope and sequence is a huge failing of core reading programs. Why? At some point, students must crack the code, looking at every letter or pattern in decodable words and matching phonemes to phonograms (and vice versa) with a high degree of accuracy. If students never learn the letter–sound associations that they need for reading and spelling, there's a good chance that their reading will contain numerous errors and that their spelling of unknown words will be nothing more than randomly picked letters cobbled together into the semblance of words.

Pushing students into new phonic patterns when they haven't mastered old ones leads to a lot of guessing, a lot of fudging, and many bad habits that are very resistant to unlearning. Whether pushing students through a spelling/phonic sequence comes from a district's blind obedience to the basal or from an individual teacher's lack of knowledge about how reading develops in students (see value 3), the result is the same: struggling readers who pronounce the word *flesh* as "flash" and struggling spellers who spell the word *flame* as "flam."

It makes sense to me that when students fail to master short-vowel sounds but are pushed into long-vowel sounds (e.g., in V–C–*e* words, words with vowel teams), they become confused. This confusion leads to guessing about vowel sound spellings. Researchers such as Invernizzi and Hayes (2004) support my hunch when they suggest that students must master short-vowel patterns (or closed syllables) before they can successfully navigate long-vowel patterns.

I recently worked with two girls who were habitual users of the "glance and guess" strategy. An untrained observer who saw these students read DIBELS progress-monitoring passages might have said, "Wow, those are two good readers! They sound fluent, and most of what they're saying makes sense." However, both girls were highly inaccurate readers. While reading a timed passage, one girl made almost 30 errors in a minute yet still scored 58 words correct!

The same was true of a boy I recently worked with. Our district had no information on his reading achievement because he matriculated midyear, and our guidance counselor asked me to assess him. I sat down with the boy, pulled a midlevel book from my DRA kit, and began my assessment. After only one paragraph, it was obvious that this level was way over his head. Moving down to a level 12, I asked him to read once more. He rolled merrily through the first two pages, making only two errors. From there on out, though, it was substitution city. All told, he made 39 substitution, omission, and insertion errors. His errors included skipping phrases, reading "pink and beautiful" for "purple butterfly," and inserting words so the story would make sense.

Later, I gave each of these three students informal spelling and phonic inventories. I found that none of them had mastery of basic syllable types: closed (or short vowel), V–C–*e*, *R*-controlled, and so on. Whether spelling or reading a controlled list of words, all three students were able to achieve only 20–25% accuracy on the word lists.

When readers come to teachers with thoroughly learned but highly inefficient strategies, it takes months of dogged persistence on the part of the teacher to break these habits and replace them with effective strategies, such as read through the word, remember another word with the same pattern, and cross-check for meaning. However, there is no other way around it: Ineffective strategies *must* be replaced with effective ones. Students must master basic phonic patterns, and the sooner the better. Therefore, you shouldn't allow the core reading program to dictate the pace of your phonics instruction. I cannot stress this enough: When struggling readers and spellers lack the basics of encoding and decoding, we must take them back to the beginning of the phonics sequence and teach short-vowel sounds to mastery.

I wholeheartedly agreed with Dewitz and Jones (2013) when they said, "We believe that it is the teacher's responsibility to continue to work on a phonics skill, using differentiated small-group instruction until data suggest that students are ready to move on" (p. 396). To do this, you'll need to provide more opportunities for students to practice and master phonic patterns in many settings. This means you'll need to program for more word work activities, which will be discussed and described in just a bit.

Scope Is Too Broad

One way to think about spelling is to consider the five spelling stages described by Bear, Invernizzi, Templeton, and Johnston (2008). These stages can help organize the details of a spelling scope so we can see the spelling forest through all the trees. The stages are as follows:

1. Emergent (3–5 years old)
2. Letter name (5–7 years old)
3. Within word pattern (7–9 years old)
4. Syllables and affixes (9–11 years old)
5. Derivational relations (11–14 years old)

Without getting into too much detail, the stages are developmental rather than grade specific, although, as you can see, students generally experience them in age bands. In this broad arc of development, the spelling focus of a student changes from sound based, to pattern based, to meaning based.

In the letter name stage, students understand the alphabetic principle and can match phonemes to letters. The specific focus is on short-vowel sounds, consonant blends, and consonant digraphs. Spelling development really takes off in the within word pattern stage, in which a student uses more complex consonant patterns, *R*-controlled vowels, long-vowel spelling patterns, and so forth.

I mention stages 2 and 3 in particular because I believe many of the older struggling readers I encounter are stuck between these stages. Furthermore, I believe the milewide scope of a basal's spelling program is doing little to help them get unstuck. In fact, it may be contributing to their being stuck in the first place!

There are only so many ways to spell a short-vowel sound. For example, according to Moats's (2005b) informative and enlightening LETRS spelling book, the short /a/ sound in *cat* is spelled with the letter *A* 97% of the time, whereas the short /o/ sound is spelled with the letter *O* 94% of the time. So, when students encounter the unknown word *slat* while reading or attempt to spell the word *hotshot*, they have a good chance of accurately reading and spelling these words if they've mastered the short /a/ and short /o/ sounds. Other sounds, however, are more complex. Sometimes, as in the case of the long /i/ sound, upward of six different spellings are possible. Unfortunately, some core reading programs unleash all of these spellings at once.

Here is a list from a basal program published in 2009. The focus of the list is the long /i/ sound, and the time frame for teaching the list is beginning third grade (unit I). Because the spelling patterns on the following week's list change completely, I assume the core program's expectation is that students need only one week to master all the long /i/ spellings.

bright	dye	flight	mild	sky
buy	fight	fry	pie	ties
child	find	might	right	tight

You'll notice that there are seven ways to spell the /i/ sound in this list, including the "once in a blue moon" spellings of -*uy* and -*ye*. If our purpose is to teach practical spelling patterns that students should apply when they write, why teach these low-incidence patterns? After all, is the word *dye* really that useful to a third grader? And how many words other than *bye* and *dye* are spelled with the -*ye* phonogram and likely to be used by most third graders when they write?

This spelling list is especially unhelpful when viewed in light of phonogram frequency for vowel sounds in the English language. What are the three most commonly used spellings for the long /i/ sound? Once again, I'll refer to information from Moats (2005b) and LETRS. The three most common spellings for the long /i/ sound are *i_e* (as in *time* and *pipe*), open-syllable *i* (as in *silent* and *triangle*), and open-syllable *y* (as in *my* and *flying*). Together, these three spellings account for 88% of long /i/ spellings in all words, so this is where to focus your teaching. Leave *rye* and *pie* for another day!

Memorize and Move On

The weekly routine of a typical core reading spelling program consists of the following four steps:

1. Students receive a list of spelling words.
2. Students practice the spelling patterns in school (or at home) via worksheets.

3. Students memorize the list.

4. Students take a summative test.

The routine is repeated weekly, over and over again, through the end of the year. When it comes to this basal program routine, it's important to ask the question, Are we really testing a student's ability to spell, or are we simply testing a student's ability to memorize a list of words, possibly with the help of concerned and attentive parents, and spell that list at the end of the week? A broader question is, What is the purpose of the weekly spelling list?

The traditional spelling routine presented in most core reading programs seems to be a "memorize and move on" routine. The main purpose seems to be that students will give a weekly demonstration of the spelling of memorized words. I offer the following as evidence to support my claim. This example comes from a third-grade core reading program's spelling list. Its focus is three-letter consonant and consonant–digraph blends. Here's the list:

scraped	screens	spread	strength	three
scratch	scrubs	spree	strong	throne
screams	spray	streams	thread	throw

It's important to know that students were exposed in previous years to short-vowel patterns, the V–C–e pattern, and the vowel teams of *ee*, *ea*, and *ay*. Let's consider the word *throw*. Because we understand how task analysis and mastery learning work, we know it's best to expose struggling students to only one unknown piece of information at a time, in this case, the week's spelling patterns of *thr-*, *spr-*, *scr-*, and so on. So, we must assume that students have previously learned and mastered the -ow spelling pattern during one week in first grade when they were first introduced to it (via two words on their list) and during an additional week in second grade in which they encountered the pattern once again. If the -ow pattern hasn't been mastered, then the students have two spelling patterns to learn for *throw*: the consonant–digraph blend and the vowel digraph -ow. This spelling scope and sequence is systematic, but it's not systematic enough.

Additionally, the words *strong* and *strength* contain spelling patterns (-ength, -ong) that the students have never been taught before, in any grade level. Because the kids haven't been taught these patterns, there's no possible way for them to spell these words other than to memorize them or, even less likely, remember them from words that they've encountered while reading in the past. In the end, the students with the ability to hold these briefly encountered words in long-term memory will benefit because they'll be able to recall the spellings while writing. Many other students, however, won't be able to generalize these weekly spelling patterns to their writing.

I'd bet that you have students who routinely score 100% on weekly spelling tests but can't spell to save their lives when they write a paragraph. I've known more than a few over the years. If I used the traditional spelling routine of my core reading program—a routine in which students memorize long /i/ patterns in words such as *why, buy, child*, and *fight* and then move on to long /o/ patterns the following week and long /u/ patterns the week after that—I doubt that after three weeks of spelling instruction, even 20% of my class would be able to write with any degree of accuracy a sentence such as "Why do you fight me for a kite when you can buy one?"

Teaching Chops: A Plan for Spelling Success

I believe the purpose of spelling instruction is to enable fluent writing and reading. How does a teacher bring spelling and phonics instruction back to a model that teaches students to independently use strategies to spell and decode words? What routine might replace the "memorize and move on" routine? And what student-used strategies help students spell as well as decode? Here are answers in the form of a four-part action plan:

1. Begin by finding out what spelling and decoding skills your students have.

2. Focus the weekly spelling list on high-frequency phonograms and teach these select phonograms to mastery. Differentiate for students with more decoding/spelling abilities.

3. Construct for yourself a logical and organized system of spelling and teach it to the students. This system must be more than a phonics scope and sequence; it must be a way of teaching spelling and word attack strategies so students can spell and read unknown words.

4. Teach with your logical and organized system in mind. First, model and repeatedly practice strategies through the use of word work and writing activities, not worksheets. Second, explicitly connect spelling to writing, and phonics to reading. As students write, reinforce the use of strategies to correctly spell words and, as students read, reinforce the use of strategies to identify unknown words. Finally, use formative assessment to monitor spelling progress.

Now that we have an action plan, let's look more deeply into each part.

Find Out What Skills They Have

At the beginning of the year, use diagnostic assessments to determine what spelling and phonic patterns your students have mastered and to find spelling and decoding deficits. Spelling inventories are helpful diagnostic tools, and they're easy to administer because you give them to the whole group, just like a spelling test. After the students spell words such as *fan*, *rope*, *shine*, and *snowing* to the best of their ability, you note their correct responses and errors on a score sheet, which is categorized by initial consonants, short vowels, vowel teams, and so forth. The book *Words Their Way: Word Study for Phonics, Vocabulary, and Spelling Instruction* (Bear et al., 2008) has a user-friendly spelling inventory associated with it; other inventories are easily found with a quick search online.

A word of caution: When students are used to the "memorize and move on" model, they experience a certain amount of anxiety when a teacher asks them to spell unknown and unpracticed words. Help your students overcome this anxiety by explaining that it's OK to make mistakes. Tell them that mistakes are an important part of how we learn. You can also say that you're a doctor and you're giving them a spelling X-ray with the goal of finding out what spelling skills are inside of them.

A phonics inventory works in reverse. Rather than encoding sounds into letters, students read words presented by the teacher. I like to use the CORE Phonics Survey, which is published by Scholastic. It has both a phonics component and a spelling component, so you can catch two fish with one net. It's a K–8 assessment that includes both real words and pseudowords. Like a good spelling inventory, the CORE Phonics Survey categorizes words read and spelled as short-vowel C–V–C words, short-vowel words with consonant blends, long-vowel spellings (including V–C–e and vowel teams), R-controlled vowels, and so on. One downside is that because the inventory must be given one on one, it takes 10–15 minutes per student. However, you won't be giving it to all of your students. Focus on those who are struggling or most likely to struggle.

Finally, you can corroborate assessment evidence with samples of student writing (see Chapter 6). Simply categorize the spelling errors that students make while writing, and compare them with the information you've gathered from your spelling and phonic inventories. Alternatively, you can use writing samples as a screening tool; students who have misspelled many words might be the students that you target for a spelling inventory.

Focus on a Few Phonograms

Because vowel sounds are especially problematic for some students, carefully choose which vowel patterns to focus on. Use the data you gathered from your spelling and phonic inventories to guide you. Before you begin picking phonograms, however, I suggest you sit with your basal's spelling scope and sequence for some time and really get to know what spelling patterns are taught. Our school's Title I team created a document that clearly lists the sounds and spellings taught in grades 1–3 (see Figure 7.1). This chart really gives me the broad picture of our

Figure 7.1. Primary Grades' Phonic Scope and Sequence

Grade 1	Grade 2	Grade 3
/ă/	Short vowels	ay, ai
/ĭ/	/ī/: i_e	oa, ow, old, oal
R blends	/ō/: o_e	igh, ind, ild, y, ie, uy, ye
nd, st, nt, nk	/ū/: u_e	ea, ee, ie
/ŏ/	/ā/: a_e	ch, tch
/ĕ/	/ī/: igh, y, ie	th, ch, sh
sh, th	/ō/: oa, ow, oe	thr, spr, scr, str
/ŭ/	/ē/: ee, ea, y	wr, gn, kn
bl, cl, fl	ch, sh, th, wh	ar, or
/ā/: a_e	ch, tch	air, are, ear
sl, sn, sp	ph	er, ur, ir, or, ear
ch, tch, wh	spr, str	oo, u_e, ue, ew
/ī/: i_e	ar, or	oi, oy
sc, spr, str	er, ir, ur	aw, augh, all, aul, ough
/ō/: o_e	oo, ou, ui, ew, oe, ue	ou, ow
/ū/: u_e	au (e.g., Paul), aw	Soft C and G
/ē/: ee	ow, ou	Homophones
/ē/: ea	oi, oy	Plurals: s, es, i + es
/ō/: o_e, oa	Schwa	Compound words
/ī/: -y	gn, kn, wr, mb	s, ed, ing
ar	Hard/soft C and G	Change y to i and add es or ed
or	ge, dge, lge, nge, rge	V–C–C–V = two syllables, both closed
ur	ar	V–C–V = two syllables, first one open and second one closed
ou	air, are	le, el
oo (e.g., book)	eer, ere, ear	un-, pre-, re-, dis-
oo (e.g., food)	or, ore, oar	Final er, ar, and or
oi	ire, ure	-ful, -less, -ly

primary grades' spelling program. Perhaps you and a few like-minded teachers will want to create a similar chart for your core reading program, or maybe you already have!

Once you're familiar with your core program's spelling patterns, you'll want to compare them with other documents that examine the scope of the sounds and spelling patterns of English. You'll also want to take a look at your grammar program. Spelling rules, such as adding -es for plural nouns that end in -x, -ch, and -sh, are often presented in grammar lessons. Finally, you'll want to go back to those initial spelling assessments and remind yourself of the strengths and needs of your students. Comparing all this information may take some time, but it will be time well spent. Once you find points of intersection and overlap, you can decide which phonograms to teach and the best sequence in which to teach them. By focusing on select spelling patterns and teaching them to mastery, you'll greatly increase the chances of your students mastering the foundations of decoding and encoding.

Selecting spelling patterns and teaching them to mastery are variations on task analysis and mastery learning. At times, you'll need to teach two unknowns (i.e., two spelling patterns in any given lesson), but I suggest no more than two, especially if you're working with struggling readers. Therefore, don't give a spelling list with seven ways to spell the long /i/ sound. Give two and get rid of the other spellings, bringing in new words that provide more practice on the pattern or patterns that you're teaching.

Here are three charts that may be helpful. Table 7.1 is a chart adapted from Moats's (2005b) LETRS program. I love this little chart! By showing which phonograms occur most frequently in our English language, it helps me quickly focus my instruction on the patterns that will most likely be used by young spellers on a day-to-day basis. For example, if the /er/ sound is spelled "er" 77% of the time, why would I want to initially teach a list that also includes the -ir, -or, and -ear patterns?

Table 7.2 lists the six syllable types. I first learned of the six syllable types during my learning support days, and I encountered it again as an educational consultant. The idea that every read or written syllable can be categorized as one of six basic categories captivated me to the point where I now use the six syllable types as the organizing principle for my weekly third-grade spelling and phonics instruction. I've found it to be a simple way to organize the many letter–sound relationships that students encounter across the K–5 grade levels, plus it's a powerful way to show students that words are made up of patterns.

Finally, Table 7.3 lists the 37 most common phonograms (spelling patterns) as identified by Wylie and Durrell in 1970. I've known more

Table 7.1. Frequency of Graphemes for Vowel Phonemes in English

Specific vowel sounds in the majority of words (approximately 75% or more) are spelled using only two or three specific graphemes!

Phoneme	Grapheme (word example)	% of Use*	Phoneme	Grapheme (word example)	% of Use*
/ē/	y (happy)	41	/ū/	oo (moon)	38
	e (me)	40		u (truth)	21
	ee (see)	6		o (who)	8
	ea (eat)	6		u_e (tube)	7.5
				ou (through)	6.4
/ĭ/	i (sit)	92	/yū/	u (human)	69
	i_e (give)	6		u_e (use)	21
	y (gym)	2		ew (few)	3
/ā/	a (baby)	45	/oi/	oi (oil)	62
	a_e (make)	35		oy (boy)	32
	ai (rain)	9			
	ay (play)	6			
/ĕ/	e (bed)	91	/ou/	ou (out)	56
	ea (breath)	4		ow (cow)	29
				ou_e (house)	13
/ă/	a (cat)	97	/er/	er (her)	77
	a_e (have)	3		or (odor)	12
				ar (cellar)	8
/ī/	i_e (time)	37	/ar/	ar (cart)	89
	i| (pi)	37		are (are)	5
	y (cry)	14		ear (heart)	3
	igh (right)	6			
/ŏ/	o (fox)	94	/or/	or (sport)	97
	a (swap)	5		ore (core)	3
/ŭ/	u (cup)	86	/er/	er (experience)	32
	o (cover)	8		ear (fear)	25
				eer (deer)	18
				e_e (here)	14
				ier (tier)	7
/aw/	o (lost)	41	/ar/	ar (parable)	29
	a (call)	22		are (bare)	23
	au (pause)	19		air (fair)	21
	aw (saw)	10		ere (there)	15
				ear (bear)	6
/ō/	o (open)	73	/ə/	o (other)	24
	o_e (vote)	14		u (circus)	20
	oa (boat)	5		a (about)	19
	ow (snow)	5		i (panic)	18
/o͝o/	u (put)	61		e (elect)	11
	oo (took)	35		ou (famous)	5
	o (woman)	5			
/əl/	le (table)	95			

(Hanna, Hanna, Hodges, & Rudorf, 1966; Fry, 2004)
*Not all graphemes are included; thus, totals do not equal 100%.
Note. The table and the notes above are from *LETRS Module 3: Spellography for Teachers: How English Spelling Works* (2nd ed., p. 32), by L.C. Moats, 2005, Boston, MA: Sopris West. Copyright © 2005 by Sopris West Educational Service. Reprinted with permission.

Table 7.2. The Six Syllable Types

Syllable Type	Explanation	Examples	Exceptions
1. Closed	• The syllable has a single vowel followed by one or more consonants. • The vowel sound is typically a pure short sound or a nasalized short sound.	*athletic, best, cat, ham, moss, ostrich, puppet, robin, shrink, strap, thanking*	*-ild* as in *wild, -ind* as in *find, -ost* as in *most*
2. Open	• The syllable ends with a single vowel that is not closed in by a consonant. • The vowel sound is typically long.	*baby, flu, go, hero, lady, potato, shy*	Schwa
Examples of open and closed combinations		*adjacent, frozen, pretend, protect, robot, topaz, volcano*	*Alaska*
3. Vowel–consonant–silent e (V–C–e)	• The syllable ends with a vowel, consonant, and silent *e*. • The vowel sound is typically long.	*hike, mine, plate, pride, stone*	*give, live, love*
Examples of open, closed, and V–C–e combinations		*compensate, microwave, patronize, rebate, rotate, textile, valentine*	
4. Vowel teams	• The syllable contains two adjacent vowels. • The first category type is the long vowel, or "two vowels go walking" type, in which the first vowel gives a long sound. • The second category type is the variant or vowel diphthong type.	*blue, boat, cloud, few, green, law, moon, oil, plain, play, slow, steam, toy*	
Examples of open, long-vowel digraph, and vowel-variant combinations		*cloudy, delay, replay*	

(continued)

Table 7.2. The Six Syllable Types (*continued*)

Syllable Type	Explanation	Examples	Exceptions
5. *R*-controlled	• The syllable contains a vowel plus an *r*. • The vowel sound is not long, short, or a variant and is sometimes known as the "bossy *r*" syllable.	barnyard, corn, corner, harm, order, term, turn, word	
Examples of five syllable types in combinations		cornflake, fertile, harmless, powder, saucer, surgery	
6. Final stable	• Syllables found in multisyllabic words • Include a number of different sets, including *-le*, *-al*, and *-el*; *-sion* and *-tion*; and *-ture* and *-sure*	adventure, composure, dazzle, duffel, global, intrusion, mantel, maple, pollution, regal	

Table 7.3. The 37 Most Common Phonograms

Children can use these 37 common phonograms or spelling patterns to read and write hundreds of words.

ack	ale	ap	aw	est	ight	ing	ock	ore	ug
ail	ame	ash	ay	ice	ill	ink	oke	ot	ump
ain	an	at	eat	ick	in	ip	op	uck	unk
ake	ank	ate	ell	ide	ine	it			

Note. The phonograms are from "Teaching Vowels Through Phonograms," by R.E. Wylie and D.D. Durrell, 1970, *Elementary English*, 47(6), pp. 787–788. Copyright © 1970 by the National Council of Teachers of English.

than a few teachers who use this chart as the basis for their first-grade spelling program.

It's critical for students to master the foundations of decoding and encoding. If you're a third- or fourth-grade teacher who has just given a spelling and/or phonics inventory, you may find that some of your students haven't yet mastered even the most basic C–V–C spellings. If this is the case, you must go back and reteach, and if you can't do it, somebody else must! Problems with breadth and pacing of a spelling scope and sequence are relatively easy to rectify, but it takes the courage of one's conviction (and permission from administration) to break free of the basal spelling sequence. When teaching struggling readers in kindergarten, the teachers I work with make sure that *all* of the lowest achieving students get into an intervention group in which they can master C–V–C words. If you feel like you don't have the time or the resources to do this, then press your administrators to figure out ways to get an effective intervention program in place.

Construct a Logical and Organized System

A logical and organized spelling and phonics system can be constructed in any number of ways. My construction, gathered from a number of different programs and researchers/writers, including Moats, the Wilson Reading System, and concepts found in writers' workshop, consists of four basic parts:

1. Basic letter–sound relationships
   a. Some sounds of language (or speech sounds) are represented with single letters.
   b. Other speech sounds are represented by letter combinations (up to four letters).
   c. To spell or decode a word, it's helpful to apply one's knowledge of phonic patterns.
2. Advanced letter–sound relationships
   a. The position of a sound in a word can determine its spelling or pronunciation.
   b. You can't spell or decode based only on sounds because a word's meaning may determine its spelling and pronunciation.
   c. Parts of speech determine spellings and pronunciations when reading.
3. Meaning should always be considered and applied when decoding text.
4. Students can use a process to spell unknown words.

I teach different parts of this construction depending on the grade level and achievement level of the students I'm working with. I use parts 1 and 3 with my kindergartners, but I use all four (some more than others) with my third graders. Each area contracts or expands in complexity depending on the grade level. For example, the spelling patterns of *-ture*, *-sure*, and *-augh* patterns (part 1b) might not be taught until fourth grade, and more complex, Latin-based root words (part 2b), such as *fide* (faith, trust), might not be taught until fifth grade.

Teach With Your Logical and Organized System in Mind

In the next section, I present five strategies that students can use to spell and read unknown words. After students have practiced these strategies to mastery, they'll have a toolbox full of spelling and reading tools at their disposal. To teach these strategies, use your teaching chops. That is, teach each strategy directly and explicitly, provide explicit modeling and guided practice in the use of the strategies, and formatively assess the students to see if they're using them on a regular basis.

Each strategy lends itself to teaching activities, which I'll present in a bit. When combined, the strategies and activities cover a lot of the same ground that the Common Core State Standards cover. In a general sense, the phonics instruction you give and the decoding strategies you teach will help your students achieve the Common Core's range of reading and level of complexity standards that exist across grade levels and types of text. In addition, as your students apply spelling strategies when writing, they'll be working toward standards that ask them to produce and publish written pieces, be they informational, narrative, or persuasive.

Second, and more specifically, your decoding and encoding instruction will enable students to reach the Common Core's all-important foundational skill standards found under the headings of phonological awareness, phonics and word recognition, and fluency. Additionally, students will accomplish the conventions of standard English standard, which asks them to generally demonstrate a command of spelling when writing and specifically spell grade-appropriate words correctly, consulting references as the need arises.

Teach students how to spell, not what to spell; use word work activities and writing as vehicles for practicing spelling.

It's beyond the scope of this book to spell out (pun intended) the standards in detail, but you get the idea. One of the beauties of embracing the "teach them how to spell, not what to spell" philosophy is that your instruction will touch on a multitude of standards, not just the one that says, "spell grade-appropriate words correctly."

Teaching Chops: Strategies for Spelling Success

Zap It Out!

Students must be phonemically aware to spell. Spellers first hear the word aloud or in their heads (audiation) and then translate or encode the sounds (phonemes) into letters (graphemes). At first, this encoding may involve matching one letter in a word to one sound, as in the words bat, *flop*, and *invest*. Because spellers must accurately hear the individual sounds of words and recognize sound chunks, spelling requires that students be the masters of phonemic awareness activities, such as segmenting words into separate sounds and blending separate sounds into words.

If some of your students struggle with spelling, it would behoove you to provide phonemic awareness instruction on skills such as segmenting and blending. Reporting on its meta-analysis of research studies, the National Reading Panel (NICHD, 2000b) said,

> Teaching phonemic awareness helps many different students learn to read, including preschoolers, kindergartners, and 1st graders who are just starting to learn to read. This includes beginners who are low in PA [phonemic awareness] and are thus at risk for developing reading problems in the future. This includes older disabled readers who have already developed reading problems. (p. 2-41)

Speaking from personal experience, explicit phonemic awareness instruction greatly helps kindergartners read and write, but it also helps struggling third and fifth graders, too, especially when it comes time for them to spell unknown words.

I teach students to spell unknown words by segmenting their sounds. We call it zapping out the word. This technique works wonders with my kindergarten students (all kindergarten teachers in my school teach this technique), but zapping also helps my third graders zero in on the sounds of the words they're trying to spell. We zap words with two to five phonemes, such as *it* and *on*, *lake* and *inch*, *tilt* and *slate*, and *sprain* and *plant*. Refer back to the "Strategies for Spelling" section of Chapter 6 for a recap of how to zap it out.

It's important that you teach your students to blend sounds back into words because you want students to think in terms of words, not sounds. So, be explicit in your teaching: Words are made of sounds, and sounds blend together to make words.

Zapping works with multisyllable words, too, but you have to do it for each syllable and not the entire word. I teach my third graders to quietly clap out the syllables of a word and then zap out the sounds of each syllable by tapping (in order) their pointer, index, ring, and pinky finger against their thumb. Later, they can use this strategy covertly by clapping their hand lightly on their thigh for the syllables and tapping the phonemes of each syllable with fingers on a thumb. For example, the word *research* would get two claps for two syllables. The first syllable would get two taps for /r/ and the long /e/, and the second syllable would get three taps for the sounds /s/, /er/, and /ch/. Each tap denotes a phoneme that must be encoded into writing. In the end, younger students will experience a kinesthetic way of representing the sounds of language, and older students will have a support that's mostly invisible to their classmates.

The zapping strategy is more than a spelling strategy. Students can use it as a decoding strategy when they encounter words that they can't read. I offer one note of caution, though: Always teach students to think about the meaning of the word, even as they're attempting to decode it. I'll talk more on this later, but for now let's say that you don't want your readers to rely solely on "sounding out" strategies.

Regardless of whether your students are younger or older, it's important that you and the kids *say* the word prior to zapping it out. You'll need to model and practice the correct pronunciation of the word because the only way students will be able spell it correctly is if they hear and then say it correctly. Lazy listening and sloppy speaking play a part in incorrect word pronunciation, but dialect and accent play a part, too. Here in the hills of western Pennsylvania, folks tend to shorten long vowels, swallow consonants, and mangle digraphs and blends. Thus, *I'll* and *crayon* become "Aw'll" and "cron," the word *mitten* is pronounced "MIH-en," and *street* and *tree* become "shtreet" and "chree."

Here's an example of a little routine that I run for 10 minutes *every* Monday when I introduce the week's spelling list. The routine is direct, explicit, and fast paced. I teach this example after the *ou* and *ow* vowel teams are introduced in January. All the words mentioned come from the basal spelling list, and the /er/ sound in *tower* was previously taught during lessons on *R*-controlled syllables.

Teacher: This lesson is all about vowel teams. In this lesson, there are two ways to spell the /ow/ sound: "ou" and "ow." What are the two ways to spell the /ow/ sound?

Students: "Ou" and "ow."

Teacher: Our first word is *shout*. Say it.

Students: Shout!

Teacher: Zap it.

Students: /sh/ /ow/ /t/. Shout! [They tap their biceps with a finger for each sound, and then they slide their fingers to their forearm and blend the sounds into a word.]

Teacher: Write it. [pauses while the students look at the word list and then write the word] The next word is *cloud*. Say it.

Students: Cloud!

Teacher: Zap it.

Students: /k/ /l/ /ow/ /d/. Cloud!

Teacher:	Write it. [pauses while the students look at the word list and then write the word] The next word is *tower*. Say it.
Students:	Tower!
Teacher:	That's two syllables! Let's clap it first.
Students:	Tow [clap] er [clap].
Teacher:	Good. Zap the first syllable.
Students:	/t/ /ow/.
Teacher:	Zap the second syllable.
Students:	/er/.
Teacher:	Write it. Remember, the /er/ sound has two letters, and one is a vowel. Every syllable has to have at least one vowel in it. [The students write.]

Apply Patterns

Once students have applied letters to sounds, they need to go a step further and ask themselves, Does this word rhyme with or look like another word I know? This question prompts the speller to check his or her spelling by comparing the pattern to like-sounding words that he or she already knows.

In a one-syllable word, the vowel and the letters that follow it are known by a variety of names, including phonograms and word families. Linguists call the initial consonant of a word the onset and everything that follows it the rime. Regardless of what they're called, spelling patterns, such as -*ack*, -*ick*, and -*op*, help students make sense of a seemingly nonsensical language. I say seemingly nonsensical because believe it or not, English is fairly decodable, predictable, and sensible. As we saw earlier in Table 7.1, vowel sounds in the majority of words are spelled using only two or three specific graphemes. This specificity and predictability enables students to use known patterns to spell unknown words.

To promote spelling mastery among the students who struggle the most, weed out the words on your spelling lists that are spelled with infrequently used graphemes. If you'd like to hold onto words that make use of infrequent spellings, offer them as challenge or bonus words. But when it comes time to review, stick to the most frequently used graphemes.

Here's a little routine that you can teach your students for spelling an unknown word:

1. Say the word aloud.
2. Ask yourself, Do I hear any word patterns/families in the word I just said?

3. Write the letters that correspond to the letter pattern or word family.

4. Check the word: Do the letters match the sounds? Do you know of another word that rhymes with this one? Can you use the rhyming word to cross-check this word? Does your word look like it's spelled correctly?

Think About the Positions of Sounds

Once students are phonemically aware and regularly tune into the sounds of words, teach them that the position of a sound helps spellers correctly spell a word. For example, when the /oi/ sound in a syllable is closed in (or followed) by a consonant, as in *coin, toil,* or *foisting,* the spelling of the sound is "oi." However, when the /oi/ sound is hanging at the end of a word (or base word) and isn't closed in by a consonant, as in *toy, boy,* or *cloying,* the spelling of the sound is "oy." The same holds true for the long /a/ sound spelled "ai" and "ay." Think of the words *plain* and *braided* compared with the words *stray* and *praying.*

Many spellings have to do with sound position. The /k/ sound is often spelled with a C when it occurs at the beginning of a word (e.g., *cat, crazy, cantaloupe*), but use *ck* when the sound immediately follows a short-vowel sound in a one-syllable word (e.g., *black, snuck, crock*). Additionally, when you hear the /s/, /f/, or /l/ sound at the end of a short-vowel (or closed) syllable, the ending letter must be doubled, as in *dress, fluff,* and *pill.*

The point is that spelling rules may be less frustrating to you and your students than you think. When you consider broad principles of spelling, you begin to see how the majority of words are in fact predictable in their spellings. As Moats (2005a) says, "These principles provide a framework for understanding those seemingly endless lists of rules that have given English spelling its bad reputation" (p. 20).

Think About the Meaning of the Word or Word Part

Spelling by segmenting words into individual phonemes, spelling sounds based on their positions in a word, spelling according to patterns— every spelling strategy that we've discussed so far is predicated on hearing sounds and word chunks in words. We should never forget meaning, however. Just as words have sound parts (phonemes) and letter parts (graphemes), they also have meaning parts (morphemes). Teach morphemes to students, and they'll learn to spell words based on meaning.

Affixes are word parts that hold meaning: *un-* means not, as in *unkind* and *unknowable*, and *uni-* means one, as in *unicycle* and *unicorn*. Students learn to spell these meaning-based word parts early on. Paying attention to the meanings of base words and root words is an even more powerful strategy, especially if the sound of the morpheme changes between words. If students understand that *know* is spelled "know" (and not "no") and if they realize that the word *knowledge* has a meaning related to the word *know*, they can use that information to correctly spell the word *knowledge*, even though its initial vowel sound is different from the one in *know*. The same holds true for words such as *pray* and *prayer*, and *wild* and *wilderness*.

Because reading and spelling are two sides of the same coin, readers can use morphemes in reverse. That is, they can use spelling to construct meaning. For example, *astro-* and *aster-* have their roots in *astron*, the Greek word for star. Knowing the morphemes *astro-* and *aster-* helps readers understand the meaning of *aster* (the flower), *asterisk*, *astronomy*, and even *disaster*. As a small aside, I love the story behind the word meaning for *disaster*, which I discovered while researching my children's book *The Lonely Existence of Asteroids and Comets* (Weakland, 2012). A word that literally means bad star, *disaster* has its roots in the ancient belief that comets were the harbingers of bad news. When a comet appeared in the sky, war, tsunami, pestilence, or some other disaster was sure to follow.

Get Close, Circle the Word, and Look It Up

In Chapter 5, we touched on the term *metacognition*. Good readers think about their thinking as they read, are aware of when they make a mistake or don't understand the text, and use strategies to fix up their mistakes and better understand the text. Metacognition can also be brought to bear on spelling. Good spellers know their spelling strengths and weaknesses, are aware of when they don't know how to spell a word, and use a variety of strategies (not just "ask the teacher") to spell a word correctly. Writers need to be aware that some of their words may not be spelled correctly when they write. Awareness is only the first step, however. Spellers need to actively fix their roadblocks.

Teach the "circle the word" spelling strategy, and you'll put the spelling onus on your students. This is a good thing! This strategy, first mentioned in Chapter 6, has three parts:

1. Students zap out the words and/or use their spelling pattern knowledge to spell the words as best they can. Words that are difficult to spell should be circled right away.

2. After their paragraphs are complete, students go back and reread their writing. As they reread, they circle other words that they think are misspelled.

3. Once their words are circled, the students look them up in their dictionaries to the best of their abilities. During this step, they can ask a friend and then the teacher whether the dictionary word is indeed the word that they're trying to spell.

At first, your students may be resistant to this strategy, especially if they've had teachers who simply spell a word for them. But don't lose heart. Keep modeling the strategy and keep your expectations high. You should expect students to regularly circle words and then use the dictionary as a reference to spell the circled words correctly. Table 7.4

Table 7.4. Teacher Comments for Students' Spelling Questions

When a Student Says...	The Teacher Can Say...
"How do you spell ___?"	• "What sounds do you hear in ___? Did you write down those sounds?" • "Did you zap out ___ and use your spelling patterns?" • "Hmm, what do you think?"
"Is this word spelled correctly?"	• "No, it isn't spelled correctly, but you have some of its sounds spelled correctly." • "It's close to correct. Did you cross-check your spelling with the dictionary?" • "Did you ask a friend?" • "Wow, that word is spelled correctly! How did you figure out how to spell it?"
"I don't have any misspelled words in my paragraph(s)."	• "It's best to double-check your most difficult words with a dictionary or spell checker just to make sure. Which words *may* not be correct? I want you to find three words that may not be correct and cross-check them with the dictionary." • "You said the same thing before, but when I checked your writing, I found four misspelled words. I want you to find four words in your writing that are difficult to spell, circle them, and then cross-check them with the dictionary."
"My word isn't in the dictionary."	• "Your initial spelling is close but not close enough. Your word is spelled with ___. Look for this ___ word part in the dictionary." • "You're right, it isn't in the dictionary! Your word is spelled ___. Write this spelling down in your dictionary and use it the next time you use this word."

gives suggestions for teacher responses to common student questions and statements regarding spelling.

Teaching Chops: Activities for Spelling Success

Getting rid of worksheets has been a constant throughout this book, so why stop now? I encourage you to replace your spelling worksheets and workbooks with word work activities that explicitly teach students to see word patterns, provide engaging ways to practice encoding and decoding, and teach foundational skills to mastery. To that end, a number of word work activities are given in this section, and they're all relatively easy to implement.

If you explicitly model and practice the activity, formatively keep track of which students master the skill and which do not. If you do the activity with a large group, you'll be using three teaching chops at once: task analysis and mastery learning, formative assessment, and whole-group physical response. Teach the activities initially in a direct and explicit way, and you'll have added a fourth teaching chop: direct and explicit instruction.

Look, Touch, Say

I learned this quick and engaging routine during a LETRS training session. It's a nifty way to review syllable types or spelling patterns while promoting mastery learning. Whichever patterns or phonograms you use, each one should have been previously taught. Sets of premade phonograms, written on magnetic tiles, on loose tiles, or as stand-alone letter combinations, can be found as materials in kits and programs from companies such as Step By Step Learning, Touchphonics, and Wilson Language Training. If you want to make your own phonograms, simply construct a table in a word-processing document, type in the phonograms in a large font, print the phonograms on card stock, cut them with a paper cutter, and store them in ziplock bags, much like the vocabulary words mentioned in Chapter 3.

Start the "look, touch, say" activity by having your kids spread out the patterns on their desks. At the beginning of the year, students might have four patterns on their desks, but if you do this activity in February, the kids might have a dozen. Make the number appropriate for the age of your students. If you teach fifth grade, 12–15 is fine. If you teach first grade, I wouldn't go above seven. As always, use data to inform your instruction. Pick the patterns that your students have yet to master.

Pick a pattern, such as -ight or -unk, and say it aloud to the class. At this point, the students should only be looking or scanning for the phonogram. No touching yet! After two to five seconds, depending on the age and ability of your students and the number of cards on their desks, say, "Touch." The students should now touch the phonogram. Monitor the responses and guide and correct errors as needed. Then, say, "Say." At this point, the students should read the phonogram aloud. After praising their attentiveness, go to the next pattern. The beginning of a three-minute "look, touch, say" session might sound something like this:

Teacher: -ight. [The students look, and some touch the phonogram.]
Remember, don't touch the pattern until I say touch.
Touch. [Most of the students touch the phonogram -ight, but two touch -it. The teacher moves to those two students and points to -ight.] This is -ight. Point to -ight. [The two students correct their error.] Say.

Students: -ight!

Teacher: Very good. Ryan and Keisha are right with me and are really paying attention. Listen for the next pattern: -ake. Look. [pauses while the students look] Touch. [They all touch the correct phonogram.] Say.

Students: -ake!

Teacher: Good job! You followed the directions perfectly that time.

A variation of this activity is to use the words from your weekly spelling list. For example, using a list of words with the stable syllable pattern -tion, you might ask students to look for the word solution and then touch the word solution. If you're thinking in terms of patterns, you could use the same routine but say, "Look for a word with the -tion pattern." The touched words may be different from one another. For example, one student might point to pollution, whereas another might point to nation. When you say, "Say," the students will respond with the word that they picked.

You can also think in terms of syllable types rather than patterns. Say, "I'm thinking of words with open syllables. Look." After the students look over their spelling list, say, "Touch." Your students should then touch a word with that pattern. Once again, the words can be different from one another. For example, one student might point to pollution (po- and lu-), whereas another might point to nation (na-).

Turn a Word

This activity, which is appropriate for kindergartners, first graders, and struggling readers/spellers, is especially useful for reviewing inner vowel sounds. I learned of it from a friend who found it online. I don't know what the activity was called originally, but I call it Turn a Word because it involves turning one word into another word, one letter at a time. As students turn one word into another, they listen for differences in the sounds of the words, associate the correct letters with the sounds and write those letters, and identify the patterns that exist between similarly spelled words.

I suggest you have your students write on paper or a whiteboard. Paper (or a computer tablet) is especially good if your list of words is longer than five or seven words. Don't let the students erase the previous word. You want them to look back and see the relationships between the words.

When my friend modeled this activity for teachers at reading workshops, she often began with a reading of Mem Fox's book *Hattie and the Fox*. Then, she'd tell the class that they were going to magically change a hen into a fox.

Before you jump into reading and spelling the words, model how to break off the beginning, middle, or end letter of a word and replace it with a new letter to make a new word. Start with the word *hen*. Say the word and have the kids repeat it back to you. It's important that students pronounce the word correctly and hear all the sounds in the word. You may even want to have the students "grab hold of the word like a rubber band" and "stretch it out so you can hear the sounds in the word." You can model this with a big rubber band, stretching it out as you say the sounds. Highlighting inner vowel sounds is especially important because these sounds are hardest for students to hear, reproduce, and associate with letters.

Once you've said and maybe even stretched the word, tell the students to zap out the sounds of the word and then write the word. Next, write the word *hen* on the board and have the students check their spelling. Then, follow this little routine:

> Let's change the hen into a pen! Change one letter in *hen* and write *pen* under the word *hen*. [The teacher pauses while the students write. Then, the teacher writes *pen* on the board under *hen* and models segmenting the sound of each letter and then blending the sounds into a word.] Now change the pen into a pet! Write the word *pet* under the word *pen*.

The teacher pauses while the students write. Then, the teacher writes *pet* on the board under *pen* and models segmenting the sound of each letter and then blending the sounds into a word. Next, the teacher repeats the process for *pet* → *pit* → *sit* → *six* → *fix* → *fox*. Voila! The hen has been changed into a fox!

You'll find other Turn a Word sequences online, but I enjoy making up my own, including longer sequences that arrive at the same place (hen → ten → tin → sin → sun → fun → fan → fat → sat → mat → max → mix → six → fix → fox) or sillier sequences, such as turning cats into dogs (cats → bats → bits → hits → hats → hags → hugs → hogs → dogs) or poor little pigs into ribs (pigs → pugs → rugs → rubs → ribs)! For older kids, use Patricia Cunningham and Hall's Making Words lessons, which follow the same basic process but draw on a much wider selection of patterns and phonograms.

Making Words

Making Words, an activity pioneered by Cunningham and Cunningham (1992), is a process in which the teacher and the students manipulate a limited number of letters (on cards or tiles) to make a series of words that evolve from short and simple ones to longer, more complex ones. As the students manipulate the letters, they create various spelling patterns and see the relationships between them. The activity is engaging because it's hands-on and culminates in the discovery of a mystery word.

The goal of the activity is twofold. First, students discover letter–sound relationships and learn that adding or changing even one letter of a word can change the entire word (e.g., stop becomes step, stain becomes strain). Likewise, changing the sequence of a set of letters can change one word into an entirely different word (e.g., stop becomes pots, alert becomes alter). Second, by drawing attention to how words are formed, students learn to look for patterns in words. As the teacher spells words on the smartboard, whiteboard, or overhead projector, the students do the activity at their desks. After each word, the teacher can briefly discuss the pattern that's being employed, the phoneme–grapheme correspondence, and even the meaning of the word.

I won't go into too much detail on how to run the activity because the Making Words series has been around for decades now, and it's easy to find lessons and how-to guides online and purchase Making Words books from any number of sources. Be aware that you should read and understand the lesson prior to teaching it because you need to provide knowledgeable guidance if your students get stuck. Also, be aware that because each student needs to have a handful of free-floating letter tiles, classroom management can be an issue during this lesson. However, if you spend time on teaching the routine beforehand and develop a system for selecting the letters, you shouldn't have problems with management.

One management solution is to purchase a small plastic bin and a drawer unit meant for storing screws and nails for each student in your class. You'll need a unit with 26 or more drawers because the intent is to stock the drawers with letters. Before a lesson, pull out the appropriate drawers and give one responsible student the job of putting the required letters into each student's letter bin. This job can be done the day before the lesson during "get ready to go home" time. This preparation gives each student the exact letters needed for each particular lesson and keeps you from losing instructional time. For letters, you can use nonmagnetic tiles or the paper letters that come with the various Making Word books. I prefer magnetic tiles and small magnetic whiteboards (I use magnetic journals) because the letters are less likely to get jostled around or spill onto the floor.

Segment to Spell

Matching letters and letter combinations to the speech sounds they represent is a process that all spellers and readers must master. Teachers can support young spellers and struggling spellers in this matching process by providing them with a spelling grid or a series of Elkonin boxes. Students then fill in the grid spaces one phoneme at a time. For all practical purposes, Elkonin boxes and spelling grids are one and the same; each box represents one phoneme.

Elkonin boxes and spelling grids can be purchased as whiteboards or magnetic boards. You can easily make grids by printing them on card stock and then laminating them. To do the "segment to spell" activity, you'll need letter tiles and spelling grids of varying lengths. Let the students know up front how many boxes they'll need to fill in. Then, follow this procedure:

- Say the target word and have the students repeat the word.
- With the students, stretch the word and/or zap it.
- The students are free to segment the word again as they fill in each box on the grid with the appropriate phoneme, either by writing in the letter or letters of the sound or placing the appropriate tile. Each box may contain only one phoneme, but the phoneme may be spelled with more than one letter.
- Say, "Check your word. Read the sounds and then blend them back together into the word."
- Write the spelling in your grid, modeling how to say the sounds and write the phonemes.
- The students correct the word if it's spelled incorrectly.

Figure 7.2 shows three boxes with varying numbers of discrete sounds.

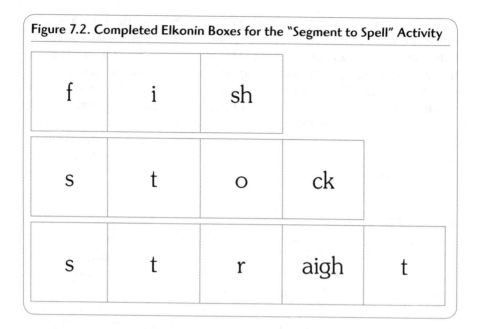

Figure 7.2. Completed Elkonin Boxes for the "Segment to Spell" Activity

f	i	sh	

s	t	o	ck

s	t	r	aigh	t

Practice Test With Instant Error Correction

Like the "look, touch, say" routine, a practice test with instant error correction is a great way to promote mastery learning. It's also a chance for you to engage in formative assessment and whole-group physical response. The key to this activity is to change your mind-set from test and summative to learning activity and formative.

In a practice test, you needn't give all the spelling words from the weekly list. If you have a 15-word list, give only seven or eight words. After you give each word, immediately give the correct spelling. Do *not* give the whole test and then go back and do the corrections. Why? Errors should be immediately addressed, explained, and corrected so incorrect learning doesn't have time to sink in!

As you write the correct spelling, model your thought process by saying it out loud. Time spent on discussing vowel spellings is especially worthwhile. If a student has spelled the word incorrectly, have him or her spell the word correctly right then and there. Rather than erasing, I prefer that students simply cross out a misspelled word and then write the correct spelling right next to or directly below the incorrect spelling. This allows students to see where they've made mistakes. Praise the kids when spellings are correct. When the spellings are incorrect, tell the students that they should pay special attention to the patterns in the words when they study.

Take this activity a step further with highlighters. During the test, have your students highlight the part of the correctly spelled word that was difficult for them (which is often the vowel pattern). This gives them a visual reminder of what they need to study.

Instant error correction is a powerful tool. Conversely, incorrect learning, whether it happens with a child or an adult, is akin to a powerful weed. Learned misinformation quickly becomes so entrenched that it takes a tremendous amount of digging and tugging to remove it from the fertile lawn of the mind.

Recently, I was working with David, one of my kindergarten readers. We were reading the pattern book *Where Are the Babies?* by Beverley Randell (1996). I picked this book because each spread introduces a new animal to the sentence pattern. Some of the animals, such as the kingfisher and the hedgehog, were unfamiliar to the students, so the kids had to attend to the beginning letter sound of each animal rather than just use the sentence patterns and picture cues. Each page had the following pattern: "Here is Mother ___. Where are her babies? Here are her babies!"

The first time David got to the word *her*, he read it as "my." So, instead of saying, "Where are her babies? Here are her babies!" he said, "Where are my babies? Here are my babies!" I stopped him and said, "David, look at this word. It begins with the letter *H*. Get your mouth ready to say the sound of that letter. Let's say the sound." He said the /h/ sound, and I told him the word was *her*. "What is that word?" I asked. "*Her*," he said. We reread the sentences together, David pointed to each word, and he correctly read the sentences as "Where are her babies? Here are her babies!"

We turned the page, and David started reading: "Here is Mother Fox. Where are my babies?" I stopped him again and said, "Look at the first letter of this word. It's an *H*. *H* says /h/. The word is *her*. Get your mouth ready for the /h/ sound and say the word *her*." David went back and reread the sentence correctly.

On the next page, David slowed down as he approached the word *her*. "Where are...," he said and then stopped and looked at me quizzically. "Look at the first letter of the word," I said, "and think about the deer being a mother. What word says /h/ and makes sense in the sentence?" David smiled and said confidently, "Where are my babies!"

Behold the power of incorrect learning! It took me the majority of a 15-minute lesson to get David to unlearn a mistake that he had made in the space of five seconds. If we can set up our lessons in ways that minimize incorrect learning, we'll make our jobs a little easier for ourselves, and we'll create more success for our students.

Sentence Dictation

I picked this activity up from my Wilson Reading training. In the activity, students write a sentence that's completely decodable based on what they've previously learned in spelling. I used to do it once a week as a challenge activity, but now I incorporate the activity into my students' weekly spelling test as a bonus point. If they spell the entire sentence correctly and include correct capitalization and punctuation, they get 1 bonus point that can be used to offset a misspelled word. Next year, I'm planning on doing this activity for 10 minutes as part of my classroom's regular spelling instruction.

The trick is to come up with a sentence that's created from spelling patterns that your students have learned to mastery. So, if you teach kindergarten or first grade and are confident that your students have mastered the sight words *I, to, the, my,* and *you* (or if you use a word wall of high-frequency words, and these words are on the wall) and all the short-vowel sound spellings (C–V–C words), then you can give your class a sentence like one of these:

- Ted can nap on the bed.
- Sam had a bad rash on his lip and leg.

If you teach fourth grade and know that your students have mastered open, closed, and V–C–e syllables, then you can give a sentence like one of these:

- My dad went to demand a refund.
- Bob plans to retire and devote his time to the project.
- He must deduct that item from his bill.

The dictation book from the Wilson Reading System is a great source for decodable sentences, especially if you follow the scope and sequence of the Wilson program. Step By Step Learning also has decodable sentences, many of them silly, that are based on a tightly controlled spelling sequence. Another resource is *Recipe for Reading* (Bloom & Traub, 2000), which contains sentences with controlled spelling. You can make your own sentences, however. Just make sure that the words in your sentences are made up of mastered spelling patterns.

Finally, I suggest that you say the sentence once and that the students say it twice. I use the direct instruction, saying, "I do, we do, you do," to help me remember to do this. Thus, I say the sentence once to the class, they repeat the sentence once with me, and then they say it together as a class without my support. I call this "I say, we say, you say, you write!" Repeating the sentence numerous times helps ensure that the kids remember the sequence of words and pronounce each of the words correctly.

Make It So

When spelling is taught as a strategy for encoding words rather than as a memorization task, students are free to carry the strategy everywhere and use it anywhere. To paraphrase the old Chinese proverb, spell a word for a kid, and the kid is successful for a moment; teach a kid how to spell, and the kid is successful for a lifetime.

The sentiment is similar for phonics: Tell a kid a word, and the kid is successful for a moment. Teach a kid to decode, and the kid is successful for a lifetime. So, dig in and begin making your core reading program's spelling and phonics components more effective and engaging. Your students may not thank you, but when you see the results, your heart will be happier!

Beyond the Basal

W e've looked at the four values from a broad perspective and then unpacked each one in some detail. We've laid out the pros and cons of core reading programs and closely examined basal components, from grammar and comprehension to vocabulary and spelling. We've also discussed an abundance of activities, instructional techniques, and resources that will enable you to supercharge your basal reading program. What's left to talk about? I'd like to wrap up this book with a restatement of why it's important to reimagine core reading programs, move briefly to thoughts on the future of your specific program, and end with some encouraging words about you, the teacher.

A Double-Edged Sword

The focus of this book is how to make core reading programs more effective, especially for those students who struggle the most. As we've learned, the ubiquitous basal is a double-edged sword. On the one hand, it's easily obtained, it does a decent job of covering the basics of reading and writing, and it provides program continuity between buildings. Many aspects of these programs, such as the explicit teaching of spelling and phonic patterns and the use of phonemic awareness activities with young students, are supported by educational research. Additionally, a basal program delivers ready-made teaching sequences for grammar, spelling, and phonics; worksheets and practice book pages that match grammar, spelling, and decoding skills; dozens of comprehension strategies; writing prompts; an anthology of stories; and even leveled books written on multiple reading levels. Stressed by heavy workloads and burdened by the demands of high-stakes tests and needy students, teachers are relieved that they don't have to find or create all of this stuff on their own.

On the other hand, core reading programs have numerous and serious flaws. In general, they aren't flexible enough, powerful enough, or motivating enough to enable all students to reach important reading goals (Dewitz, Leahy, Jones, & Sullivan, 2010). More specifically, core reading programs often fail to directly and explicitly demonstrate the most engaging and effective instructional practices to teachers. Students have little choice about what they read or what they write about, and thus an important motivational tool is lost. Not enough time is given to having students practice reading and writing on their instructional and independent reading levels. Most programs introduce too many comprehension strategies and don't provide teachers with ways to teach these strategies to the point of mastery (Dewitz et al., 2009). What's more, basal programs can create an environment in which reading teachers become less effective over time instead of more effective (Baumann & Heubach, 1996). Thus, a core reading program shouldn't be used as your complete reading program (Dewitz et al., 2010).

The Ultimate Goal of Super Core

If you've arrived at this point in the book, then you've already accomplished something significant. You've read the words, and you understand the call to action. You've considered the steps that I've laid out for creating greater reading success within a core reading program, and perhaps you've already done something to make it so. Maybe you've rearranged your schedule to create time for guided reading once a week, or perhaps you've committed yourself to teaching 12 comprehension strategies to the point of mastery. Regardless of what you've done specifically, if you've implemented even one idea in this book and committed yourself to doing that one thing really well over an extended period of time, then you're on your way to creating a more effective and engaging reading program.

In the future, you may implement more and more ideas, a few next year and a few more after that. Before too long you may find that you've left much of your manual behind, rid yourself of most "drill and kill" worksheets, and rocketed off to a more student-centered classroom in which most students engage in reading and writing because they love to read and write. But is this all there is? Let's say for the sake of argument that you'll fully implement all the ideas presented in this book in the next three years. Does anything come after that?

The answer is no. This book is the be-all and end-all, and other than transforming yourself into an enlightened being of pure energy and light, there really will be nothing else to accomplish.

Just kidding, of course. When it comes to the big ideas of reading and writing, there's always more to learn, and new information comes to light every year. As for teaching chops, one can never practice enough. It's possible to spend months and even years on developing your independent reading routines, guided reading groups, and formative assessments. At some point, you may have the opportunity to tie all of this together outside of the boundaries established by a publisher-created program. Perhaps you'll have the chance to lead a classroom independent of the basal and exercise your knowledge and teaching chops as you run a writers' workshop, a readers' workshop, or a Four Blocks, guided reading, or Daily Five program, none of which are dependent on a core reading program.

Of course, you may not want to move to a reading program that has no manual, anthology, or worksheets. As we've learned, basal programs aren't all bad. So, maybe you'll hold on to your core program, even as you work to change it. Or perhaps your district's school board or your administrator won't allow you to leave the basal totally behind—a reality that's very possible. But if you can't move beyond it, at least you can make your situation better, and I hope I've given you enough research and well-reasoned arguments that you can go before your administrator or school board and say, "We have a problem, but I know how to fix it." With any luck, the powers that be will exclaim, "Please, make it so!"

At some point in my consulting career, I watched a video that featured a professor from Columbia University's Teachers College. She told her audience, and I'm paraphrasing here, that her goal was to prepare her student teachers to step into a classroom ready to teach reading using only some paper, some pencils, and a bunch of books. I loved hearing that line because it spoke to my core belief: To teach reading, you need knowledge and know-how much more than you need materials.

The Expert Teacher and the Noble Profession

The four values that I've explained—extended reading, extended writing, the big ideas of reading and writing, and teaching chops—are the foundation blocks of my particular vision for this book. There are, of course, many other ways to build a framework or model or to organize a book or program. Regardless of what framework someone creates or what book someone writes, educational structures will never exist unless hardworking, caring, intelligent, and very capable teachers are there to bring ideas to life.

Perhaps in the future, when technology and neuroscience come together to create the perfectly optimized online education course or computerized teaching machine, the current model of flesh-and-blood teachers teaching flesh-and-blood students will fall by the wayside. Perhaps screens, videos, and hyperlinks will become the prevailing delivery system of information and wisdom. As someone who loves to be a part of a classroom that's alive with the energy of students, and as a believer in the power of the human spirit to uncover and convey subtle truths, I have a hard time imagining classrooms not led by teachers, but I acknowledge that I can't predict the future and that the world is a rapidly changing place.

For now, however, teachers matter the most, even more than specific instructional practices and approaches or reading programs and materials (Allington & Johnston, 2001; Chetty et al., 2011; Darling-Hammond, 1999; Taylor, Pearson, Clark, & Walpole, 2000). Thus, expertise is critically important, especially when you consider that the ultimate reading fate of a student rests not in the pages of a teacher's manual or the books in a browsing bin, but mostly in the hands of you, the teacher. When it comes to imparting information—that is, getting kids to learn something—the teacher is where it's at.

To be a teacher is to be self-sacrificing, moral, and generous. We do our jobs for little or no recognition, and the work is often difficult. Our students try our patience, test our charity, and sap our energy. Our buildings can be crowded and decrepit, our students' parents can run the gamut from demanding to uninterested, and our careers can be micromanaged by school boards, voters, and politicians. But we put up with a lot for both pragmatic and idealistic reasons. Teaching gives us a solid paycheck and a schedule that's very accommodating for the most part. The work can be intellectually stimulating and challenging. We love working with young people, and we know that the future of our world, now more than ever, depends on these students. These students, in turn, depend on us.

Because students depend on us, we must be more than idealistic. We must have a grasp of the broad history of reading research, and we must thoroughly understand the big ideas of reading and writing. Additionally, we must know how those big ideas interact as reading ability and writing ability develop in a student. If these abilities don't develop and if achievement doesn't occur, we must know how to step in and do something different to get the learning across. We must be knowledgeable about effective instructional techniques, and we must be fluent and artful in our exercising of those techniques. We must be masterful in our blending of this knowledge and technique. In short, we must aspire to become expert teachers. And as we become experts who, for whatever reasons, use a core reading program, we must step up and attempt to make educationally sound changes to those programs whenever possible so they're as effective as they can be.

All of this will be neither quick nor easy, but don't let this dissuade you. Start out small if you have to, but move ahead. Make a commitment to do something more effective than what you did last month or last year. Keep pushing for change and keep practicing.

Because I'm a musician, I'm into the concepts of process and practice. I don't approach teaching as a job in which I go through the motions, like an old-time fire stoker shoveling anthracite into the boiler until my day is finally done at 3:40 p.m. Rather, I practice my teaching chops (and I try to do it mindfully), and I reflect on my performance, my choice of materials, and my assessments. I take some quick mental notes on what can be better, and then I show up for the gig the next day and begin again. I'm in pursuit of perfection, knowing full well that I'll never get there!

If you've gathered from this book that I'm a lean, mean, super effective teaching machine who regularly converts struggling readers into reading champions, you're wrong. There are days when the kids are lethargic, distractible, moody, or some combination thereof, and there are days when I feel the same. I do my best, but my teaching turns out to be sloppy and my assessments less than exact. On some days, after much preparation and practicing, things still don't go as planned. The kids haven't learned what I want them to, their academic and behavioral achievement is progressing slowly, and I leave school at the end of the day tired and discouraged. Such is life.

On other days, I'm at my best, and so are the kids. My teaching is rolling down the track at a brisk pace, strong and unhindered, and the kids are writing and reading and practicing like crazy. All of my hard work seems to be paying off. Finally, I'm achieving that wonderful sense of flow, and so are the kids.

My hope is that this book will help you get into that state of flow, too, as well as advance your teaching expertise, give you new things to practice, and encourage you to keep pushing toward more effective teaching. Be kind to yourself and be gentle, but keep moving forward because great teaching, and the student learning that comes with it, are goals worth pursuing.

REFERENCES

Adams, M.J. (1990). *Beginning to read: Thinking and learning about print.* Cambridge, MA: MIT Press.

Adlof, S.M., Perfetti, C.A., & Catts, H.W. (2011). Developmental changes in reading comprehension: Implications for assessment and instruction. In S.J. Samuels & A.E. Farstrup (Eds.), *What research has to say about reading instruction* (4th ed., pp. 186–214). Newark, DE: International Reading Association.

Allington, R.L. (1977). If they don't read much, how they ever gonna get good? *Journal of Adolescent & Adult Literacy, 21*(1), 57–61.

Allington, R.L. (1983). The reading instruction provided readers of differing reading abilities. *The Elementary School Journal, 83*(5), 548–559.

Allington, R.L. (2001). *What really matters for struggling readers: Designing research-based programs.* New York, NY: Longman.

Allington, R.L. (2002). What I've learned about effective reading instruction from a decade of studying exemplary elementary classroom teachers. *Phi Delta Kappan, 83*(10), 740–747.

Allington, R.L. (2006). Fluency: Still waiting after all these years. In S.J. Samuels & A.E. Farstrup (Eds.), *What research has to say about fluency instruction,* (pp. 94–105). Newark, DE: International Reading Association.

Allington, R.L. (2009). If they don't read much…30 years later. In E.H. Hiebert (Ed.), *Reading more, reading better* (pp. 30–54). New York, NY: Guilford.

Allington, R.L. (2011). What at-risk readers need. *Educational Leadership, 68*(6), 40–45.

Allington, R.L., & Johnston, P.H. (2001). What do we know about effective fourth-grade teachers and their classrooms? In C.M. Roller (Ed.), *Learning to teach reading: Setting the research agenda* (pp. 150–165). Newark, DE: International Reading Association.

Archer, A.L., & Hughes, C.A. (2011). *Explicit instruction: Effective and efficient teaching.* New York, NY: Guilford.

Baumann, J.F., & Heubach, K.M. (1996). Do basal readers deskill teachers? A national survey of educators' use and opinions of basals. *The Elementary School Journal, 96*(5), 511–526. doi:10.1086/461842

Bear, D.R., Invernizzi, M., Templeton, S., & Johnston, F. (2008). *Words their way: Word study for phonics, vocabulary, and spelling instruction* (4th ed.). Upper Saddle River, NJ: Pearson.

Beck, I.L., McKeown, M.G., & Kucan, L. (2002). *Bringing words to life: Robust vocabulary instruction.* New York, NY: Guilford.

Blevins, W. (2006). *Phonics from A to Z: A practical guide* (2nd ed.). New York, NY: Scholastic.

Bloom, F., & Traub, N. (2000). *Recipe for reading: Intervention strategies for struggling readers* (3rd ed.). Cambridge, MA: Educators Publishing Service.

Boushey, G., & Moser, J. (2006). *The Daily Five: Fostering literacy independence in the elementary grades.* Portland, ME: Stenhouse.

Brenner, D., & Hiebert, E.H. (2010). If I follow the teachers' editions, isn't that enough? Analyzing reading volume in six core reading programs. *The Elementary School Journal, 110*(3), 347–363. doi:10.1086/648982

Brenner, D., Hiebert, E.H., & Tompkins, R. (2009). How much and what are third graders reading? Reading in core programs. In E.H. Hiebert (Ed.), *Reading more, reading better* (pp. 118–140). New York, NY: Guillford.

Calkins, L.M. (1994). *The art of teaching writing*. Portsmouth, NH: Heinemann.

Chard, D. (2011, September 23). The three elements of effective school reform. *The Dallas Morning News*. Retrieved from www.dallasnews.com/opinion/sunday-commentary/20110923-david-chard-the-three-elements-of-effective-school-reform.ece?action=reregister

Chetty, R., Friedman, J.N., & Rockoff, J.E. (2011). *The long-term impacts of teachers: Teacher value-added and student outcomes in adulthood* (NBER Working Paper No. 17699). Cambridge, MA: National Bureau of Economic Research. Retrieved from www.nber.org/papers/w17699

Csikszentmihalyi, M. (1993). *The evolving self: A psychology for the third millennium*. New York, NY: HarperCollins.

Cunningham, P.M., & Allington, R.L. (1998). *Classrooms that work: They can all read and write* (2nd ed.). New York, NY: Longman.

Cunningham, P.M., & Cunningham, J.W. (1992). Making words: Enhancing the invented spelling–decoding connection. *The Reading Teacher, 46*(2), 106–115.

Cunningham, P.M., & Hall, D.P. (2001). *Making words: Lessons for home or school, grade 3*. Greensboro, NC: Carson-Dellosa.

Dalton, B. (2013). Engaging children in close reading: Multimodal commentaries and illustration remix. *The Reading Teacher, 66*(8), 642–649.

Darling-Hammond, L. (1999). *Teacher quality and student achievement: A review of state policy evidence*. Seattle: Center for the Study of Teaching and Policy, University of Washington.

Dewitz, P., & Jones, J. (2013). Using basal readers: From dutiful fidelity to intelligent decision making. *The Reading Teacher, 66*(5), 391–400. doi:10.1002/TRTR.01134

Dewitz, P., Jones, J., & Leahy, S. (2009). Comprehension strategy instruction in core reading programs. *Reading Research Quarterly, 44*(2), 102–126. doi:10.1598/RRQ.44.2.1

Dewitz, P., Leahy, S.B., Jones, J., & Sullivan, P.M. (2010). *The essential guide to selecting and using core reading programs*. Newark, DE: International Reading Association.

Dewitz, P., & Sullivan, P.M. (2010, June 3). *Selecting and using core reading programs* [Webinar]. Newark, DE: International Reading Association. Retrieved September 26, 2013, from www.reading.org/downloads/publications/core_reading_webinar.pdf

Diller, D. (2003). *Literacy work stations: Making centers work*. Portland, ME: Stenhouse.

Duke, N.K., & Pearson, P.D. (2002). Effective practices for developing reading comprehension. In A.E. Farstrup & S.J. Samuels (Eds.), *What research has to say about reading instruction* (3rd ed., pp. 205–242). Newark, DE: International Reading Association.

Duke, N.K., Pearson, P.D., Strachan, S.L., & Billman, A.K. (2011). Essential elements of fostering and teaching reading comprehension. In S.J. Samuels & A.E. Farstrup (Eds.), *What research has to say about reading instruction* (4th ed., pp. 51–93). Newark, DE: International Reading Association.

Ehri, L.C. (2000). Learning to read and learning to spell: Two sides of a coin. *Topics in Language Disorders, 20*(3), 19–36. doi:10.1097/00011363-200020030-00005

Ehri, L.C., & Snowling, M.J. (2004). Developmental variation in word recognition. In C.A. Stone, E.R. Silliman, B.J. Ehren, & K. Apel (Eds.), *Handbook of language and literacy: Development and disorders* (pp. 433–460). New York, NY: Guilford.

Fountas, I.C., & Pinnell, G.S. (1996). *Guided reading: Good first teaching for all children.* Portsmouth, NH: Heinemann.

Fountas, I.C., & Pinnell, G.S. (2009). *Leveled books K–8: Matching texts to readers for effective teaching.* Portsmouth, NH: Heinemann.

Fountas, I.C., & Pinnell, G.S. (2012). Guided reading: The romance and the reality. *The Reading Teacher, 66*(4), 268–284. doi:10.1002/TRTR.01123

Gambrell, L.B., Marinak, B.A., Brooker, H.R., & McCrea-Andrews, H.J. (2011). The importance of independent reading. In S.J. Samuels & A.E. Farstrup (Eds.), *What research has to say about reading instruction* (4th ed., pp. 143–158). Newark, DE: International Reading Association.

Gentry, J.R., & Graham, S. (2010). *Creating better readers and writers: The importance of direct, systematic spelling and handwriting instruction in improving academic performance.* Columbus, OH: Saperstein.

Gladwell, M. (2008). *Outliers: The story of success.* New York, NY: Little, Brown.

Gould, J.S., & Gould, E.J. (1999). *Four square writing methods for grades 4–6: A unique approach to teaching basic writing skills.* Dayton, OH: Teaching & Learning.

Graham, S., & Harris, K.R. (2000). The role of self-regulation and transcription skills in writing and writing development. *Educational Psychologist, 35*(1), 3–12. doi:10.1207/S15326985EP3501_2

Graham, S., & Hebert, M. (2010). *Writing to read: Evidence for how writing can improve reading.* Washington, DC: Alliance for Excellent Education.

Graves, D.H. (1994). *A fresh look at writing.* Portsmouth, NH: Heinemann.

Graves, M.F., & Watts-Taffe, S.M. (2002). The place of word consciousness in a research-based vocabulary program. In A.E. Farstrup & S.J. Samuels (Eds.), *What research has to say about reading instruction* (3rd ed., pp. 140–165). Newark, DE: International Reading Association. doi:10.1598/0872071774.7

Guthrie, J.T. (2002). Preparing students for high-stakes test taking in reading. In A.E. Farstrup & S.J. Samuels (Eds.), *What research has to say about reading instruction* (3rd ed., pp. 370–391). Newark, DE: International Reading Association. doi:10.1598/0872071774.16

Harvey, S., & Goudvis, A. (2007). *Strategies that work: Teaching comprehension for understanding and engagement* (2nd ed.). Portland, ME: Stenhouse.

Hunter, M. (1994). *Mastery teaching: Increasing instructional effectiveness in elementary, secondary schools, colleges and universities.* Thousand Oaks, CA: Corwin.

International Reading Association. (2012). *Literacy implementation guidance for the ELA Common Core State Standards.* Newark, DE: Author.

Invernizzi, M., & Hayes, L. (2004). Developmental-spelling research: A systematic imperative. *Reading Research Quarterly, 39*(2), 216–228. doi:10.1598/RRQ.39.2.4

Ivey, G., & Fisher, D. (2006). *Creating literacy-rich schools for adolescents.* Alexandria, VA: Association for Supervision and Curriculum Development.

Keene, E.O., & Zimmermann, S. (2007). *Mosaic of thought: The power of comprehension strategy instruction* (2nd ed.). Portsmouth, NH: Heinemann.

Kelley, M.J., & Clausen-Grace, N. (2013). *Comprehension shouldn't be silent: From strategy instruction to student independence* (2nd ed.). Newark, DE: International Reading Association.

Kissel, B., Wood, K., Stover, K., & Heintschel, K. (2013). *Digital discussions: Using Web 2.0 tools to communicate, collaborate, and create* [IRA E-ssentials series]. Newark, DE: International Reading Association. doi:10.1598/e-ssentials.8002

Kuhn, M.R., & Schwanenflugel, P.J. (2009). Time, engagement, and support: Lessons from a 4-year fluency intervention. In E.H. Hiebert (Ed.), *Reading more, reading better* (pp. 141–160). New York, NY: Guilford.

Kuhn, M.R., Schwanenflugel, P.J., & Meisinger, E.B. (2010). Aligning theory and assessment of reading fluency: Automaticity, prosody, and definitions of fluency. *Reading Research Quarterly, 45*(2), 230–251. doi:10.1598/RRQ.45.2.4

Lai, E. (2011). *Metacognition: A literature review* (pp. 4–24). Upper Saddle River, NJ: Pearson. Retrieved September 17, 2013, from www.pearsonassessments .com/hai/images/tmrs/metacognition_Literature_Review_Final.pdf

Leinhardt, G., Zigmond, N., & Cooley, W.W. (1981). Reading instruction and its effects. *American Educational Research Journal, 18*(3), 343–361. doi:10.3102/00028312018003343

Marzano, R.J., Pickering, D.J., & Pollock, J.E. (2001). *Classroom instruction that works: Research-based strategies for increasing student achievement.* Alexandria, VA: Association for Supervision and Curriculum Development.

Merrow, J. (2012, May 14). Boosting reading skills: Will 'Common Core' experiment pay off? *PBS NewsHour.* Retrieved September 26, 2013, from www.pbs.org/ newshour/bb/education/jan-june12/commoncore_05-14.html

Miller, D. (2013). Reading with meaning: Teaching comprehension in the primary grades. Portland, ME: Stenhouse.

Miller, S. (2005, October 10). *50 ways to use Twitter in the classroom.* Retrieved October 3, 2013, from www.universityreviewsonline.com/2005/10/50-ways-to-use-twitter-in-the-classroom.html

Moats, L.C. (2005a). How spelling supports reading: And why it is more regular and predictable than you may think. *American Educator, 29*(4), 12, 14–22, 42–43.

Moats, L.C. (2005b). *LETRS module 3: Spellography for teachers: How English spelling works* (2nd ed.). Boston, MA: Sopris West.

Morrow, L.M., Tracey, D.H., Woo, D.G., & Pressley, M. (1999). Characteristics of exemplary first-grade literacy instruction. *The Reading Teacher, 52*(5), 462–476.

Nation, K. (2008). Learning to read words. *The Quarterly Journal of Experimental Psychology, 61*(8), 1121–1133. doi:10.1080/17470210802034603

National Endowment for the Arts. (2007). *To read or not to read: A question of national consequence* (Research Report No. 47). Washington, DC: Author.

National Governors Association Center for Best Practices & Council of Chief State School Officers. (2010). *Common Core State Standards for English language arts and literacy in history/social studies, science, and technical subjects.* Washington, DC: Authors.

National Institute of Child Health and Human Development. (2000a). *Report of the National Reading Panel. Teaching children to read: An evidence-based assessment of the scientific research literature on reading and its implications for reading instruction* (NIH Publication No. 00-4769). Washington, DC: U.S. Government Printing Office.

National Institute of Child Health and Human Development. (2000b). *Report of the National Reading Panel. Teaching children to read: An evidence-based assessment of the scientific research literature on reading and implications for reading instruction: Reports of the subgroups* (NIH Publication No. 00-4754). Washington, DC: U.S. Government Printing Office.

Oczkus, L.D. (2010). *Reciprocal teaching at work: Powerful strategies and lessons for improving reading comprehension* (2nd ed.). Newark, DE: International Reading Association.

Palincsar, A.S., & Brown, A.L. (1984). Reciprocal teaching of comprehension-fostering and comprehension-monitoring activities. *Cognition and Instruction, 1*(2), 117–175. doi:10.1207/s1532690xci0102_1

Paris, S., & Parecki, A. (1993). *Metacognitive aspects of adult literacy* (NCAL Technical Report TR93-09). Philadelphia: National Center on Adult Literacy, University of Pennsylvania.

Paris, S.G., & Winograd, P. (1990). Promoting metacognition and motivation of exceptional children. *Remedial and Special Education, 11*(6), 7–15. doi:10.1177/074193259001100604

Pearson, P.D., & Gallagher, M.C. (1983). The instruction of reading comprehension. *Contemporary Educational Psychology, 8*(3), 317–344. doi:10.1016/0361-476X(83)90019-X

Pressley, M. (2006). *Reading instruction that works: The case for balanced teaching* (3rd ed.). New York, NY: Guilford.

Pressley, M., Yokoi, L., Rankin, J., Wharton-McDonald, R., & Mistretta, J. (1997). A survey of the instructional practices of grade 5 teachers nominated as effective in promoting literacy. *Scientific Studies of Reading, 1*(2), 145–160.

Raphael, T.E., & Au, K.H. (2005). QAR: Enhancing comprehension and test taking across grades and content areas. *The Reading Teacher, 59*(3), 206–221. doi:10.1598/RT.59.3.1

Reutzel, D.R., & Daines, D. (1987). The text-relatedness of reading lessons in seven basal reading series. *Reading Research and Instruction, 27*(1), 26–35. doi:10.1080/19388078709557923

Richardson, J. (2009). *The next step in guided reading: Focused assessments and targeted lessons for helping every student become a better reader.* New York, NY: Scholastic.

Rosenshine, B. (2012). Principles of instruction: Research-based strategies that all teachers should know. *American Educator, 36*(1), 12–19.

Schoenbach, R., Greenleaf, C., Cziko, C., & Hurwitz, L. (1999). *Reading for understanding: A guide to improving reading in middle and high school classrooms.* San Francisco, CA: Jossey-Bass & WestEd.

Shanahan, T. (2006). Relations among oral language, reading, and writing development. In C.A. MacArthur, S. Graham, & J. Fitzgerald (Eds.), *Handbook of writing research* (pp. 171–183). New York, NY: Guilford.

Sitton, R.A., & Forest, R.G. (Eds.). (2010). *The Quick-word® handbook for everyday writers.* North Billerica, MA: Curriculum Associates.

Snow, C.E., Burns, M.S., & Griffin, P. (Eds.). (1998). *Preventing reading difficulties in young children.* Washington, DC: National Academy Press.

Snow, C.E., Griffin, P., & Burns, M.S. (2005). *Knowledge to support the teaching of reading: Preparing teachers for a changing world*. San Francisco, CA: Jossey-Bass.

Stahl, S.A., & Shiel, T.G. (1999). Teaching meaning vocabulary: Productive approaches for poor readers. In *Read all about it! Readings to inform the profession* (pp. 291–321). Sacramento: California State Board of Education. (Reprinted from *Reading & Writing Quarterly*, 1992, *8*(2), 223–241)

Stanovich, K.E. (1986). Matthew effects in reading: Some consequences of individual differences in the acquisition of literacy. *Reading Research Quarterly, 21*(4), 360–407.

Taberski, S. (2010). *Comprehension from the ground up: Simplified, sensible instruction for the K–3 reading workshop*. Portsmouth, NH: Heinemann.

Taylor, B.M., Pearson, P.D., Clark, K., & Walpole, S. (2000). Effective schools and accomplished teachers: Lessons about primary-grade reading instruction in low-income schools. *The Elementary School Journal, 101*(2), 121–165. doi:10.1086/499662

Topping, K.J., Samuels, J., & Paul, T. (2007). Does practice make perfect? Independent reading quantity, quality and student achievement. *Learning and Instruction, 17*(3), 253–264. doi:10.1016/j.learninstruc.2007.02.002

Treptow, M.A. (2006). *Reading at students' frustrational, instructional, and independent levels: Effects on comprehension and time on-task*. Minneapolis: University of Minnesota Center for Reading Research.

Vygotsky, L.S. (1978). *Mind in society: The development of higher psychological processes* (M. Cole, V. John-Steiner, S. Scribner, & E. Souberman, Eds. & Trans.). Cambridge, MA: Harvard University Press.

Webb, S. (2007). The effects of repetition on vocabulary knowledge. *Applied Linguistics, 28*(1), 46–65. doi:10.1093/applin/aml048

Wylie, R.E., & Durrell, D.D. (1970). Teaching vowels through phonograms. *Elementary English, 47*(6), 787–791.

Wyne, M.D., & Stuck, G.B. (1979). Time-on-task and reading performance in underachieving children. *Journal of Reading Behavior, 11*(2), 119–128.

CHILDREN'S LITERATURE CITED

Aliki. (1972). *Fossils tell of long ago*. New York, NY: Crowell.

Kimmell, E.C. (1999). *Balto and the great race*. New York, NY: Random House.

Randell, B. (1996). *Where are the babies?* Crystal Lake, IL: Rigby.

Weakland, M. (2011). *The delicious chocolate donut: And other off-kilter poems*. Hollsopple, PA: Happy Hummer.

Weakland, M. (2012). *The lonely existence of asteroids and comets*. North Mankato, MN: Capstone.

INDEX

Note. Page numbers followed by *f* or *t* indicate figures or tables, respectively.